Ridi

24/10/95

DEAR SIDNEY,

I HOPE YOU ENJOY

THE BOOK.

BEST WISHES TO YOU!

Other books you may enjoy from this publisher:
Zen & the Art of Post-Modern Canada, by Stephen Schecter
The Last Cod Fish, by Pol Chantraine
No Mud on the Back Seat, by Gerald Clark
The Jesuit and the Dragon, by Howard Solverson
A Canadian Myth, by William Johnson
Economics in Crisis, by Louis-Philippe Rochon
Dead-End Democracy? by Yves Leclerc
The Bernonville Affair, by Yves Lavertu
Moral Panic, by John Fekete
The Traitor & The Jew, by Esther Delisle
The Making of a Spy, by Gordon Lunan
By a Jury of His Peers, by Henry Steinberg

Canadian Cataloguing in Publication Data

Libman, Robert, 1960-

Riding the rapids : the white-water rise and fall of Quebec's Anglo Protest
Includes index.
Autobiography.
ISBN 1-895854-44-X

1. Libman, Robert, 1960- . 2. Equality Party. 3. Quebec (Province) - Politics and government - 1985-1994. 4. Politicians - Quebec (Province) - Biography. I. Title.

FC2925.1.L52A3 1995   971.4'04'092   C95-941366-9
F1053.25.L52A3 1995

To receive our current catalogue
and be kept on our mailing list for announcements of new titles,
please send your name and address to:
Robert Davies Publishing,
P.O. Box 702, Outremont, Qc Canada H2V 4N6

Robert Libman

RIDING THE RAPIDS

*The white-water rise and fall of
Quebec's Anglo Protest*

Robert Davies Publishing

MONTREAL—TORONTO—PARIS

ISBN 1-895854-44-X

This book may be ordered in Canada from

General Distribution Services
1-800-387-0141 / 1-800-387- 0172 FAX 1-416-445-5967;

in the U.S.A.,
from Associated Publishers Group,
1501 County Hospital Road, Nashville, TN 37218

dial toll-free 1-800-327-5113;

or call the publisher,
toll-free throughout North America:

1-800-481-2440, FAX (514)481-9973.

The publisher takes this opportunity to thank the
Canada Council and the Ministère de la Culture du Québec
for their continuing support of publishing.

Dedicated to a wonderful little guy,
my 5 year old son Kevin,
whose good nature and sweet face
never fail to lift my spirits.

Table of Contents

ACKNOWLEDGEMENTS **9**

CHAPTER ONE
Origins *11*

CHAPTER TWO
Bucking the Odds *26*

CHAPTER THREE
Chasing Stars *48*

CHAPTER FOUR
Courting the Vote *59*

CHAPTER FIVE
Coping With Success *79*

CHAPTER SIX
Behind the Scenes at the National Assembly *94*

CHAPTER SEVEN
Party Problems *111*

CHAPTER EIGHT
Feeling the Heat *118*

CHAPTER NINE
Holding the Fort for Canada *131*

CHAPTER TEN
Hydro-Quebec Power Storm 145

CHAPTER ELEVEN
Up To Here With Holden 156

CHAPTER TWELVE
The Constitutional Divide 167

CHAPTER THIRTEEN
Letting Go of the Leadership 178

CHAPTER FOURTEEN
Signs of Progress 184

CHAPTER FIFTEEN
Leaving the Party 191

CHAPTER SIXTEEN
The Price You Pay 204

CHAPTER SEVENTEEN
Looking Forward 211

ACKNOWLEDGEMENTS

When one does a stint as a real politician, being a sitting member of a major house of parliament, there are so many people with whom you naturally come into contact. My adventure of the last seven years brought me to meet, befriend, mingle and associate with thousands of people. It forced me to oppose, speak to, argue and debate with many. It allowed me to be harassed by, shake hands with, be nice to, be phony with, and tolerate an incredibly large number of people. From flaky to brilliant, from supportive to antagonistic, it is this vast array of human beings that shaped the political path that I walked. Despite the fact that my political journey of the past seven years was such a roller coaster, nothing beats the thrill of it all nor erases the imprint left by such a diverse cast of characters.

Being out of active politics, I rarely see the people that so shaped my life for the past seven years. I would therefore like to thank everyone who contributed in their small way to providing me with such a unique experience. Particular thanks to the many supporters for believing in me. Especially those who worked on my campaigns. To list them would put me in danger of forgetting someone. I would also like to thank my constituents in D'Arcy McGee, especially the over 10,000 who voted for me as an independent this time around.

Special thanks to my mother, Goldie Libman, and Joanne Shapiro for spending hours and hours at the computer, deciphering my small notes and corrections. I would also like to thank Chris Mostovac for reviewing the book before it went to print and making very important suggestions.

And finally, thanks for editing the text to Hubert Bauch, one of the best political journalists in the business.

ROBERT LIBMAN
August 1995

CHAPTER ONE
Origins

A journey of a thousand miles must begin with a single step.
—Lao-Tzu

It was late July 1989, an unusually hot summer in Montreal, in more ways than one. A provincial election call was right around the corner. It was just before noon and I was standing in the entranceway to the Cage Aux Sports restaurant on Guy Street with Doug Robinson, a notary, who for the past few months had been my closest political advisor. For decades Robinson had been an organizer for the Quebec Liberal Party. He was president of its St. Louis riding association back when St. Louis always sent Harry Blank to the National Assembly, no matter who formed the government in Quebec City. A classic product of the smoke-filled-room school of political enterprise, the gruff-voiced Robinson was your typical, hard-nosed, short tempered back-room mechanic, who was now helping me lead a brand new political party into its first election.

Robinson, like many other English speaking Quebecers, including a fair number of Liberal supporters, had joined our party after quitting the governing Liberal Party the year before when Premier Robert Bourassa invoked the notwithstanding clause of the Canadian Constitution to pass Bill 178, which continued the ban on English on commercial signs in Quebec, despite a Supreme Court ruling. This decision by the premier had so incensed English speaking Quebecers, that they were giving the new party that I had recently co-founded, the Equality Party, a serious look as the election neared.

It seemed like every day for the past several months I'd been holding court in different restaurants, taking extra long lunch hours from Tolchinsky and Goodz Architects, where I had been employed for the past three years. However, this particular meeting offered a little added cachet. Growing up as a Montreal sports fanatic and former Alouettes football fan, one of my heroes was place-kicker George Springate. When I was a Boy Scout in the 1970's, Springate was invited to speak to our troop in Chomedey, and we were properly awed at meeting a former professional football player. He was also introduced as an MNA, and when I got home I asked my father what an MNA was.

He was now the public relations and promotions director of the *Montreal Daily News,* and Doug and I were waiting for him to join us for lunch. The reason we were meeting, ironically, was because I wanted him to make a comeback as an MNA by running as our candidate in Westmount. He had been prominently involved in holding up the English side in the language confrontation 15 years ago, co-ordinating the 600,000 signature petition against Bill 22—which then-Premier Robert Bourassa subsequently tossed into the trash can. In a line that would become legend, Springate called Bourassa "the most hated man in Quebec" not long before Bourassa lost the 1976 election to the PQ. I'd spoken to him over the phone a few days earlier, and was still unsure whether he'd actually show up. But then suddenly the bright light from the open doorway that lit most of the darkened restaurant was momentarily blotted out by a formidable figure crossing the threshold.

George Springate turned out to be down to earth and very friendly. He was talkative and extremely outgoing. You'd have thought he was still in his political heyday from the way he glided through the restaurant, chatting up the waitress and other patrons, as though every last one was a longtime friend. When he settled down at the table he spoke at length about his days in the National Assembly and provided much interesting insight and anecdotal backstage details about the Liberal Party in the 1970's, and its lack of consideration for its anglophone members. You really got the sense from him that this man relished the opportunity for a political battle. This was why I was surprised to eventually hear his reasoning for refusing our request, once I popped the question.

Though he believed in our cause, he felt the war had been fought. The language battles were now lost and behind us, he told me. Nonetheless, as we were trying to get the waitress' attention for the bill, he sincerely wished us well, saying he hoped we would teach Bourassa a lesson for Bill 178.

Springate was only one in a long line of prominent anglos who turned me down that summer in my dogged and often discouraging quest for credible candidates for an upstart, unproven political movement born out of the growing alienation of the anglo community from the governing Liberal party. All were outwardly sympathetic to our cause and angry at the Liberals, yet they figured that we had no chance to win any seats. Conviction can only go so far, as I came to learn. It is pragmatism and the degree of personal risk involved that ultimately guide politically experienced and/or professionally established people when it comes down to deciding whether or not to take an electoral plunge.

This was undoubtedly what guided Joan Dougherty when I met her at a Snowdon Pizzeria next to my office a month earlier. She had been the Liberal MNA for the West Island riding of Jacques Cartier since 1981. Having voted against Bill 178 in the National Assembly, rumour had it that she was really upset with Premier Bourassa, so much so that she was considering not running for re-election. I was pleasantly surprised when she accepted my invitation to lunch, where I intended to ask her to run on conviction and be our candidate in Jacques Cartier.

I was startled by the vitriolic frankness with which she declared her anger at the Liberal Party, of which she was still a prominent member. Yet she did not want to run for what she described as a one-issue party, though she agreed that what we were doing had a certain importance. Joan Dougherty eventually did run for the Liberals and was probably thinking of our lunch on election night when she lost to our candidate, Neil Cameron. She took her loss very badly and lashed out in a display of pique that ended her political career on less than a dignified note.

At that same pizzeria, I lunched with Graeme Decarie, the Chairman of the History department at Concordia University and a big wheel at Alliance Quebec, the federally-funded anglophone lobby group. He turned us down. I had lunch in Chinatown with Joel Hartt, Chairman of the Lakeshore School Board with the hope of having him run in the West Island riding of Robert Baldwin. He also refused. After the election he told me that on election night, while watching the neck-and-neck race between our candidate and the Liberal, Sam Elkas, he was very upset about having declined. I asked TV and radio personality Jack Curran to run in Nelligan riding and Geraldine Doucet, wife of the late Roger "O Canada" Doucet to run in N.D.G. They both thought better of it.

I had met Gazette columnist William Johnson for brunch at the former Beverley Hills Café on Decarie and asked him to run, but he felt that he could be more valuable to the cause of individual rights as a daily columnist. I asked former Federal Cabinet Minister Donald Johnston to run for us when I met him at a forum examining Quebec's two solitudes, organized by a group named "Entente Cordiale". He had always been a rare politician who acted on principle, and had recently resigned from the federal Liberal shadow cabinet over policy differences with his leader

John Turner, notably Turner's support of the Meech Lake constitutional accord. But he flatly refused our invitation.

I asked Bill Surkis, then the academic dean of John Abbott College to run in Robert Baldwin, as well as Romeo Brault, a former city councillor and West-Island Liberal mover and shaker. I asked Steve Olnyk, the normally outspoken mayor of Greenfield Park to run on the South Shore. In the end it was no, no and no. I asked Kenneth Cheung, president of the Chinese businessman's association, who once ran for mayor of Montreal, to run in Mount Royal. He would string us along for weeks until he too said no. Peter Blaikie was asked to run against Bourassa in St. Laurent; Bernard Lang, mayor of Côte St. Luc was asked to run in D'Arcy McGee, as was Hampstead city councillor and Canada Day organiser Barbara Seal. They all urged us to keep up the fight, but it was always thanks but no thanks as far as they were concerned.

The search for "name" candidates was deeply frustrating. Why were all these people turning me down? Despite the compelling urgency of our cause, it was obvious they felt we were destined to fail. History is littered with the husks of upstart political parties born of a single concept in the heat of a given moment. Alas, when it comes to the crunch of an election, few ever garner enough support for any real breakthrough.

On several occasions, I asked myself: why bother? Why was I spending so much time and energy on something that I had been warned, by people I presumed knowledgeable in such matters, had all the odds stacked against it ? Why was I, of all people, with no political background of any sort, getting so involved in the snake-pit world of Quebec politics ? My wife and parents certainly asked me the question over and over again. At 28 years of age; working in the profession I had always wanted to practice—for a highly successful firm in Montreal, and with the intention of starting a family, it just seemed to everyone around me that I was wasting my time and begging for disappointment

Still, the prospect of just dropping everything was even more disconcerting. Something about justice was involved here, we felt, and this alone for the time being was motivating us to take this thing to its logical conclusion—or at least as far as we could take it. There were a number of people counting on us by now, and throughout my life I was never one to give up easily. I was also learning a lot, circulating in a world that was completely new to me. I found myself immersed in an unfamiliar culture, mixing with people who were from many different backgrounds, origins and walks of life.

If nothing else, the horizons that this new experience was opening up for me were greatly revealing, after what had been a comparatively insulated upbringing. Not that I'd say there was anything wrong with the way I was brought up, but my lack of real contact with Quebec society outside the perimeter of "anglo-Montreal" was fairly typical of most English-speaking Quebecers who grew up in west-end Montreal during those years.

Despite this cultural insulation, I was very fortunate to have the type of upbringing that many would envy. By the time I was two years old I had two younger brothers, Warren and Glenn; eleven years later a third brother, Jamie, joined the rambunctious Libman brood. Growing up was therefore never lonely or dull; if anything, it was often quite turbulent. At our home, a "regular" baby-sitter was someone who dared come back a second time.

The stability of our home life made us a close-knit family, though in our growing-boy way the four brothers would never dare admit it, or indulge in any great outward displays of affection. The lives of both my parents revolved then, as they still do, around the well-being of their sons. Both were born here, of western European immigrant parents, and grew up where most of the parents of my generation did, in the midtown heart of Montreal's old Jewish neighborhood, now called the Plateau Mont-Royal. Both my father's parents came here just before the second world war; their respective families stayed behind in Europe and were wiped out in the holocaust.

While growing up, my father worked in his father's grocery store at the corner of Jeanne Mance and Villeneuve delivering orders on his bicycle during school lunch hour. To this day, I'm often asked if Chaimkeh, the grocer on Villeneuve, was my grandfather. Everyone knew him, it seems. He made a very decent living for his family and even owned a few apartment buildings. No matter what people needed during the war years, he was always able to get it somehow. Back then things like canned salmon or sugar were devilishly hard to come by and would fetch high prices. He had a very charismatic personality and was a brilliant and ruthless businessman. He would advertise apples for 10¢ each or, "two for a quarter." Sure enough, people would come into his store and take the "special" on two apples. He was very protective of his store, and one time he was hit on the head with a revolver after refusing to turn the contents of his cash register over to a robber. Thereafter he loved showing off the scars on his shiny bald head. My brothers and I were his pride and joy, and he never tired of taking us to all sorts of places. He died of a heart attack at the age of 55, when I was only five.

My father's personality is the complete opposite of his late father's. He is very quiet and likes to remain in the background. He attended Herzliah High School and then McGill University, an educational pattern that his four sons all eventually followed. He earned his C.A. degree in 1959 and became a partner in an accounting firm a few years later. He is in every way an accountant's accountant.

For my mother Goldie, there is no higher calling in this world than the role of motherhood; it couldn't have suited her more had she been born with apron strings. She grew up on De Bullion St. in very meagre circumstances. Her parents had married here, having arrived as children just before World War I. Her father delivered ice and worked as a presser in a "sweatshop," but a serious illness forced him out of his job when his family was still young. My grandmother, herself a victim of polio, had to become the breadwinner, working her fingers raw in another "sweat-shop" to feed her three children. The upshot of this adversity was that it drew the family together, and forged a unique and lasting closeness. At the same time—and of necessity—my mother grew up a very inde-pendent-minded young lady, having been a latch-key kid before the term was coined from the time she was eight. She envied her friends who had conventional home lives, feeling like the odd kid on the outside forever looking in. Her one dream therefore was to someday have a normal and stable family life that would bring her the joy and fulfillment of devoting herself entirely to making sure her own children never wanted for anything.

My parents met on a blind date in their late teens and married in 1959. I was born the following year, and when I was six months old, we moved to Ville St. Laurent. Six years later we moved to a bungalow in Chomedey, Laval, an ideal setting for a young family—The Suburban dream incarnate. Our home was situated on a crescent, and had a huge back yard which became the football field, baseball diamond and hockey rink for the dozens of kids in the neighborhood. A mutt named Fluffy completed the picture of a comfortable middle class upbringing.

Our mother ran in circles for us. She typed up our term papers, made our lunches every day and was constantly on top of our dirty laundry trail and the various messes that marked our passage through the house. On her car pool days she would bring homemade cookies for us and our friends. By the age of 24 she was a mother of three boys, and when she finally came up for air 10 years later, she had another one.

Providing a good education for the children was the number one priority for my parents. They felt that no price was too high to ensure a quality education and sent all of us to private parochial schools. They refused to have cable TV installed until we all finished high school. Homework was a must before play. The three of us were in consecutive grades and therefore shared a vast pool of friends. We were fairly good students, but like most growing kids coming to grips with adolescent peer group pressures, we got into trouble every once in a while for the typical juvenile pranks. We were very clean-cut however, and never even experimented with drugs and alcohol, and were critical of friends who did.

Since the entire neighbourhood was Jewish and the school system we went through was a private Jewish system, contact with non Jews, and especially francophone Quebecers, was practically non-existent. Playing in baseball or hockey leagues in Chomedey, there was occasionally a francophone on our team, but because of the homogeneity of the community in those days it was rare. Only when we played in tournaments or against teams from other leagues did we really encounter francophones our age. We also usually had a French Canadian teacher for French class who always seemed like something of an outsider on the teaching staff. In those days the curriculum only required about six hours a week of French instruction, so most kids graduating from English schools were far from bilingual, to say the least.

Politics was also something largely absent from my upbringing. The only two political events that stood out in my memory were Bill 22 and the election of the PQ in 1976. The only reason I remember these events is because they were topics of angry and heated conversation among our parents' family and friends. It was only in the run-up to the 1980 referendum, when I was already in CEGEP, that I began paying attention to politics on a regular basis. But even at that, politics as a career prospect was never even a remote consideration. To begin with, I was an extremely shy kid, and from the moment I knew what an architect was, it was what I wanted to be. I'd always been good at math and loved to draw, and architecture wonderfully combined the two. I used to draw cartoon strips about my classmates, with cameo appearances by certain teachers. More often than not, they were confiscated by teachers who failed to see the humor in my cleverest efforts.

Perhaps the only sign of any latent political inclination was my natural penchant for organizing. My pet projects included a very sophisticated hockey pool, Strat-O-Matic baseball league, and a complicated car pool among my friends—once we started getting our drivers licenses. My parents never overtly pushed any of us in a specific career direction, though my father had always wanted me to become a lawyer. I graduated from high school in 1978, with the caption under my yearbook photo expressing my desire to be "a rich and famous architect".

My brothers and I always used to compete to see who was stronger, who was faster, who had better marks. Sports was also a big part of my life. Not only was I a religiously devoted fan of the Expos, Canadiens and Alouettes, but my summers were taken up with playing baseball in various leagues. My brothers and I of course argued constantly about who was the better hitter or fielder. July and August were spent "up north" in a rented summer cottage on a lot with many houses near St. Agathe. We competed for the attention of different girls, and argued about who was better looking, or which one of us, certain girls liked the most. At sixteen I began working as a counselor at High Point Day Camp near our country house. The camp was also almost exclusively Jewish. My brothers worked at Camp B'nai Brith.

It was in Vanier College in St. Laurent where it dawned on me that I had lived a sheltered life. Not only were most of my classmates not Jewish anymore, but they came from many different ethnic groups. Nonetheless, Jewish students still congregated in their own area, as did the Italian students, Asian students, francophone students, and black students. Making close friendships with others outside your circle was therefore not easy.

Despite many complaints about CEGEP, I found the two years there important. For people who are unsure about what they want to do in life, it is a good parking space, a place to mature for an extra couple of years. For me the science program was quite interesting, but for someone coming from a private school, it was the cultural aspects that laid the essential groundwork for the transition to university.

As I was nearing the end of my two years in 1980, we were headed into a serious recession. I'd made the rounds of a few architects and a few professors of architecture at McGill and they all told me that architecture is an extremely unpredictable profession, and the way things were heading there would not be big money to be made in the field. Many friends I spoke to, warned me that maybe I should reconsider and aim for a more recession-proof profession, like medicine or dentistry.

I took their advice and applied to dentistry at McGill. The dental school took only one student a year straight from CEGEP, so my expectations were not high. At the same time I felt a nagging sense that I hadn't been really true to myself. When I was refused, it was almost a relief. I was accepted into my second choice which was the Bachelor of Science (BSc) program. I chose a major in mathematics because it offered the best opportunity for high marks, which would gain me acceptance into a professional program later on. During that year it became compellingly clear to me that my true calling was architecture. I realized that if I were to become a dentist, I would always wonder what it would have been like to be an architect. This clinched it for me, and after one year in the BSc program, I applied to the McGill School of Architecture. This time I stood a far better chance since my first-year marks were very high and the school accepted 48 new students a year.

I knew from how nervous I was with anticipation, as the date for early acceptances fast approached, that I'd made the right choice. When my acceptance came in the mail I was the happiest guy around. There is tremendous turmoil in any young person at that stage of life. When you're caught without really knowing what you will be doing for the rest of your life, and under pressure to decide then and there, it can get very frightening and nerve-wracking. When you get accepted into a career program, especially for a career that you passionately want to pursue, it brings on the most incredible feeling of relief. You take a deep breath as your future suddenly comes into focus and develops a semblance of permanence. Your self confidence also increases dramatically from that point on.

It was also that summer that I became the director of the day camp where I'd been a counselor at for the past four summers. This was the year that I apparently broke out of my shell. I grew out of my painful shyness by always having to speak and perform in front of 100 kids, staff and parents. The new sense of confidence fostered by the knowledge that my future looked secure made me a more outgoing person and much surer of myself within.

That September, I entered the McGill University School of Architecture. And though I had no inkling of it at the time, this was where some of the groundwork would be laid for my eventual political career.

Architecture students are put to an endurance test. You are given a number of design projects, and forced to meet very difficult deadlines that often end in "all-nighters". Your work goes up on the wall and you are called upon to make a presentation before the class, the professors and sometimes visiting architects. These sessions are appropriately called "crits" or short for critiques, since the professors don't hold back in their criticism. If a thick skin does not develop quickly, you could wind up a basket case long before graduation. First year was the most difficult because of the need to adapt to the rigours of mature creative expression, self discipline, humility, competitiveness and total commitment. Exciting as it may be on that first day to be listening to eminent professors discussing architecture, you soon realize that after being tops in math and art throughout your school life up to then, the 47 others in your class were in the same category in their high schools.

I was very quiet and unassuming in first year. Because you spend your days and nights in the architecture studio, which was in the McConnell Engineering Building in those days, the friendships you develop are important. The class was a melting pot. Almost a third of the class was francophone and there were also a number of Jewish, Chinese and Italian students. This was my first opportunity, at age 21 to really mix with other cultures. But then I wasn't the only one. For example, a classmate from La Tuque, in the upper St. Maurice region of

Quebec, told me that he had never seen a Jew in his life before arriving at McGill. This was quite an indication of what Montreal is all about and how rich this city is in its cultural diversity.

Our class was whittled down to 41 after first year.

In second year, my work area was next to the entrance of the studio, and adjacent to a French Canadian classmate, named Richard Jaeger. There was an alcove near our drafting tables which we annexed as a sitting area for break times and before long it became known as the "Richard-Robert Lounge". It became the social centre of the class and for the remainder of our four years he and I not only became very good friends, but became the goodwill ambassadors for the entire class. We organized architectural baking competitions, Halloween pumpkin sculpting competitions and multi-ethnic Christmas celebrations, recruiting different professors every year to dress up as Santa Clause.

The R and R Lounge was where I learned most about the lives of people of other languages and cultures. It offered the opportunity to be very casual, and I developed a very good relationship with my classmates, notably the francophones. I admired their courage, for many of them could barely speak a word of English before entering the School of Architecture, which was difficult enough in one's first language.

I graduated in the summer of 1985 with distinction and as a university scholar. Before jumping into the reality of full time work for the rest of my life, I went on a backpacking trip through Europe with Adam Adamakakis, a classmate of mine. We took all our notes on architectural history with us and marvelled while sitting inside the great cathedrals of Italy, and grand chateaux in France, reading our notes describing the architectural distinctions of every curve and corner of whatever building we visited. For a young and impressionable architectural graduate, nothing could have been more overwhelming and enriching.

My timing turned out to be fortuitous when it came to employment. I'd been lucky in previous summers as a university student to get architecture-related jobs. In 1983, I worked at Leonard Ostroff Design on a number of stores for the renovated Rockland, Fairview and Carrefour Shopping Centres. The following summer I worked for the Architectural Division of T. Pringle and Son where I had the opportunity to work on an industrial building for I.B.M. in Vermont and a few projects in Montreal for pharmaceutical manufacturers. In 1985, when I returned from Europe, I began to work for Pringle again. It was a large firm, bringing engineering and architecture under one roof. Working for a big company was again a departure from my usual milieu. Most of the employees were French and the drawings for projects in Quebec were all done in French, which was a real translation headache, since so much of the construction industry uses terminology from a North American standardized English vocabulary.

I also began preparing for my test at the Office de la Langue Française, which requires all professionals practicing in Quebec to pass a french proficiency test. Since architects must go through a two-year apprenticeship program before qualifying to write the provincial exams for their license to practice, I figured that I might as well get the French test out of the way, so that when I wrote my architectural licensing exams I'd have one less obligation to worry about.

It was at this time that I got a call from an old friend I had worked with at Leonard Ostroff who asked me if I wanted to be "fixed up," as custom had it, with his girlfriend's sister. He had mentioned to me months earlier, before I had left for Europe, that there were two available sisters, one who spoke English well and one who didn't. At the time I was seeing someone, so I didn't make much of it. He now told me that the sister who could speak English had moved to Paris, so if I was interested, the sister who spoke very little English was available for the proverbial fix. I figured why not; it would at least give me the chance to practice my French. I called her to ask her out and we arranged a double date. Her name was Malia Azeroual, and she was of Jewish Sephardic origin, having immigrated to Canada in 1974 from Morocco. She was slightly older than I was, and the ninth in a family of ten. When I went to pick her up, and rang the bell, two heads popped out the door—Malia and yet another sister, and I wasn't sure which one was my date. They said one minute and ducked back inside. As I stood there puzzled, I could overhear someone say, "Il est tellement jeune!" (He's so young!)

We soon started dating more seriously and my French was improving steadily, to the point where my exam at l'Office de la Langue Française was a breeze. A year later, we got married. I had proposed to her on Valentine's day, atop the downtown Sheraton Hotel. I carefully placed a ring inside the petals of a rose I gave her, and she accepted on the spot. I had also arranged to have a limousine waiting for us downstairs to whisk us off.

Professionally, I had moved from Pringle up one floor to Sofati, to work on their conversion of the old POM bakery building in Westmount into a luxury condominium apartment building. The president of Sofati was Quebec Inc. headliner Michel Gaucher, who had an M.B.A., an engineering degree and a law degree on his office door. When he strolled through the office his authority was palpable. We were a small team working on the project and when one of the younger architects did not

agree for artistic reasons to make certain changes, Gaucher came by and
told him that he should take his eraser and get the hell out of there.

I was the only English-speaking employee and was quickly becoming much more comfortable working in French and taking the little jokes
about being an anglo. We were then all transferred to Jacques Beïque et
Associes, who had taken over the project. This was a large architectural
firm in Old Montreal, and by then I was becoming much more familiar
with French Canadians from dealing with francophone engineers and
contractors and visiting construction sites. The ribbing was always good-
humored, and political animosity never surfaced in any way. In the mid
1980's the PQ and Quebec nationalist movement in general was becoming increasingly moribund, and the only political talk I can remember
hearing was about Claude Dupras, an engineer who did a lot of work
with our office and was a good friend of the boss, and who was running
for mayor of Montreal at the time.

I found it gratifying that I was being immersed in the French fact,
but at the same time I was starting to feel somewhat claustrophobic. I
would speak and work in a French language environment all day and
then come home and speak French to my wife, and watch TV in French.
I'd come a long way from Chomedey in a very short time.

At the time, a number of McGill graduates and former classmates
of mine were working at Tolchinsky and Goodz, an English-speaking
firm that seemed to be getting every major project in downtown Montreal. I applied for a job there in late 1986 and was hired. A few months
later I wrote the two day exams for admission to the Order of Architects
of Quebec (O.A.Q.) and was admitted with distinction in May 1987. Part
one of my boyhood ambition had been fulfilled in that I was now a
certified architect.

At Tolchinsky and Goodz I was handed a great deal of responsibility for some fairly large projects. Despite the long hours, it was a young
architect's dream to be given responsibility for projects on such a scale
in an office that was so busy that the senior architects had to rely heavily
on us. I worked on a number of high-rise proposals in downtown
Montreal, and headed up projects as diverse as an office building next
to the Ruby Foo's Hotel on Decarie Blvd, townhouse condominiums at Mont
Habitant, and a senior citizens retreat at Camp B'nai Brith in the Laurentians.

Though things appeared to be going well, I wasn't sure how far
into the future I could see myself staying in Quebec. This building boom
of the mid-'80s was bound to end eventually and it seemed that in the
long run there was a lot more opportunity elsewhere. A good many of
my friends, relatives, colleagues and classmates had been leaving Quebec in recent years. Virtually half the friends I grew up with were now

living in Toronto, a common situation for a great majority of English speaking Quebecers of my generation, most of whom already have one foot out the door of this province when they finish school.

When you graduate from CEGEP or university and envisage your future surroundings and prospects, your boundaries suddenly expand far beyond your neighbourhood or campus, which were almost entirely English environments. Your horizon now takes in all of Quebec, where the real world of business and the professions where English has steadily lost ground during the past three decades. There is a natural inclination for young anglos to be drawn to Toronto or the United States, where constitutional uncertainty or language laws are not the constant nagging preoccupation they are here. Despite my relative fluency in French, I also felt this magnetic pull. At the same time I didn't want to leave my family, and I also felt guilty about just giving up on Montreal, which was after all a wonderfully vibrant place to live. It was important for me to at least try to address what was really at the heart of the problem in Quebec for myself and for others like me. Furthermore, the English-speaking community had built up a wealth of institutions and organizations that don't deserve to die out through attrition. By leaving, you turn your back on the community that nurtured you.

In the relative isolation of the western part of the Island of Montreal, anglos enjoyed a life largely undisturbed by the prevalence of the French language in other parts of Quebec. For a long time most anglos didn't speak French because it was unnecessary. "We" didn't bother "them" and they didn't bother "us". When the PQ came into power in 1976, "they" started bothering "us" by imposing the linguistic straightjacket of Bill 101, whose stringent language requirements squeezed a lot of "us" out to be replaced by "them" in many spheres of activity, primarily in the province's economic life. I never really paid much attention to this new dynamic, but now that I was finished with school and part of the real working world, I became more conscious of these things. Although the sports pages were usually the first section of the paper I would normally read, I was spending more time reading the front section, and even the editorial page.

In the late '80's, a number of things were bothering me. The prohibition of my language on outdoor signs was bad enough, but by then it was something already taken for granted in everyday life. What irritated me more was the symbolism involved when, in 1987, the Liberal government decided to appeal to the Supreme Court the judgements rendered by the lower courts in Quebec, which had ruled that banning English signs was unconstitutional. This despite Premier Robert

Bourassa's promise in the 1985 election campaign that he would repeal the sign law imposed by the outgoing PQ government.

There was also the government's talk of changing the Quebec Cinema Law to prohibit the showing of an English film in Quebec until a dubbed French version was available. At the time, the government was also toying with the idea of extending francisation programs, thus forcing all businesses with more than 10 employees to operate fully in French, where up to now companies with fewer than 50 employees had been exempted from mandatory francisation. This would include internal memos, even if they were sent from one anglophone to another. The Bourassa line and the Liberal Party rhetoric was also getting decidedly more nationalist, as the other legislatures were dragging their heels on ratifying the Meech Lake constitutional accord.

A year earlier, the 10 Premiers and the Prime Minister had hammered out a package of amendments to the Canadian constitution at Meech Lake, the site of a federal government conference centre in the Gatineau Hills. The agreement would have designated Quebec a "distinct society" and extended its jurisdiction in certain areas. When former Prime Minister Pierre Elliott Trudeau brought the constitution home from Britain in 1982 and invested it with a new Charter of Rights and Freedoms, Quebec, then led by René Lévesque's separatist P.Q. government, was the only province that did not endorse the initiative, claiming the charter infringed on the National Assembly's power to protect the French language in Quebec. At Meech Lake, Bourassa had agreed to extend Quebec's full approval of the Canadian constitution, assuming the Meech Lake Accord amendments, based on five conditions put forward by Quebec, were ratified by all 10 provincial legislatures within three years. But the deal began running into stiff resistance throughout the country for a number of reasons. To pressure the other provinces to act more quickly, Bourassa was making hard-line nationalist noises and invoking the potential breakup of the country if the rest of Canada were to reject Quebec's "minimal demands" as set out in the accord.

Committed federalists in Quebec were understandably uncomfortable with this type of rhetoric emanating from the Premier and leader of the supposedly federalist government of Quebec. Unfortunately, the only serious political opposition at the time was the separatist Parti Québécois, which favored even tighter language restrictions. There was, therefore, no voice in the National Assembly willing to speak up forcefully for Canadian federalism or to utter so much as a peep about the rights of English-speaking Quebecers. But for me the straw that broke the camel's back was the nationalist backlash against the March 1988 annual report of Canada's Official Languages Commissioner, D'Iberville

Fortier, who had criticized Quebec's language laws by saying that Quebec's English speaking community was being "humbled" by them.

The PQ tabled a malicious motion of censure in the National Assembly condemning Fortier for this monstrous insult to the Quebecois people. Normally, these opposition motions are easily defeated by the government or are amended in such a way as to void the motion of any substantial import. In this case, however, the Bourassa government not only supported but amended the motion, in order to toughen the wording. The motion passed unanimously, supported by the vote of all anglophone MNA's, including John Ciaccia from Mount Royal, who apparently left his sick bed in Montreal to fly to Quebec City to vote in favour of the beefed-up censure motion.

The reasoning of the anglophone MNA's at the time was that they were positioning themselves for "the big one" — the imminent fight in caucus when the Supreme Court would presumably rule the sign law unconstitutional, a verdict expected later that year.

Gordon Atkinson, a political commentator on CJAD at the time, compared the Fortier Affair to the shot that killed Archduke Ferdinand, thereby sparking World War I. "The shot has rung out," he declared. "We must respond". I agreed, and how! I was driving my car on my way home from work, listening to Atkinson's radio editorial, and started shaking my head. Then I impulsively began to honk the horn in defiance. He had touched a nerve in me.

Something had to be done to light a fire under our community and let the majority know we were fed up and not going to take it any more. It was at this point that I decided to call some friends of mine to float the idea of actually doing something about it.

CHAPTER TWO
Bucking the Odds

*One good thing about being young
is that you are not experienced enough
to know that you cannot possibly do
the things you are doing.*
—Gene Brown

Most of my friends were not politically motivated. Now in their late twenties, they were preoccupied with building their careers and starting families. Getting involved in politics ranked somewhere with climbing Mount Everest on the scale of priorities. While contemplating where to start, I zeroed in on two friends with whom I sometimes talked politics. One was Gerald Klein, an outspoken accountant friend from school days with a feisty tongue and a go-for-it attitude. The other was David De Santis, a colleague at the architectural firm where I was working at the time, and with whom I had often spoken about political developments in Quebec. Both were equally turned off by the the Liberal government's retreat on language rights and agreed to participate in a discussion group.

In late March of 1988, I decided to organize a meeting in the office one evening to discuss either the creation of a new political party in Quebec or an alternative pressure group to Alliance Quebec. Though eight friends of mine had promised to attend, only Klein and De Santis showed up.

Nevertheless, we discussed the frustrating state of affairs confronting the anglo community, referring to articles we had clipped from The *Gazette*, in particular columns by its leading political pundits, Don Macpherson and William Johnson. I had listed four points which I proposed as the basis for our initiative:

1) To wake up English Quebec;

2) Not to criticize the francophone majority, but to defend our own rights and status;

3) Our efforts must get the attention of Premier Bourassa

4) Any strategy must be carefully planned and not go off half cocked.

It was decided that Klein would look into the financial aspects and the technical details of establishing an officially recognized political party. DeSantis would try to involve members of the Italian community and I would start to recruit more people from both my own circles and the broader anglo community to form the nucleus of an organization.

The Director General of Elections turned out to be graciously co-operative in providing us with all the information necessary to begin a political party. We read through the Electoral Act and tried to line up friends to join the cause. Deciding there was nothing to be lost in aiming high, we wrote a letter to "60 Minutes," the flagship of U.S. network public affairs programs, describing the language laws in Quebec and suggesting that the situation would make for a good story. They were polite, but not interested.

Getting friends to pitch in was like pulling teeth. I went for lunch with a number of people I knew, trying to rally interest in some type of movement, the form of which was yet to be determined. Some showed up at our occasional meetings, some said they would but never did. The meetings were not very large or eventful at first, as we pored over the nuances of the Electoral Law, kicked around recent events in the news and drew up ambitious lists of names. At each meeting it seemed as though we were repeating much of what had been discussed at past meetings to the two or three new people who had shown up. Everyone our age we contacted agreed with what we had to say. Like us they were fed up with what they perceived as prejudice against Quebec anglophones, yet most of them lacked any real spark for doing anything beyond carping and moaning about the crying injustice of it all. We began to think that at this pace nothing would ever really get off the ground. We needed to latch on to something, preferably a network of some sort with more politically experienced individuals.

That June, a public meeting was organized by a group called the Coalition of Canadian Quebecers (CCQ), which drew an impressive turnout at the Hellenic Centre in Montreal. It received widespread media attention and the rhetoric was consistent with what we had been discussing. The obvious problem with the meeting and the group in general was that it attracted mostly elderly people. In this respect it was greatly reminiscent of the defunct Freedom of Choice Party, founded in the late

1970s, as a protest against both the Liberal and PQ language policies. Largely unilingual, it was frowned on by the establishment pillars of the English community, and reinforced the worst anglo stereotypes in the eyes of the francophone media.

The organizer of the CCQ meeting was a woman named Carol Zimmerman. A few weeks later I called her to let her know that a group of young people had been meeting regularly and had been discussing, among other things, the possibility of founding a new political party. An answering machine responded that she was out of town and that I should call a woman named Gloria Freedman.

A meeting was set for August 4 in Côte St. Luc. Klein, De Santis and I met with Freedman, Lorissa Schouella, a lawyer named Bernie Sivack and Sam Goldbloom, an articulate businessman who was involved in the 1976 election with the Union Nationale, to protest the Liberal language legislation, Bill 22. We discussed the current language debate at length and I was impressed with the strength of their convictions and their resolve to do more than simply complain. We were also told that Carol Zimmerman had since been thrown out of the group for being too radical; already we were getting a taste of the divisions within Quebec's English community that belie its image as a political monolith, and would cause us no end of grief during the months and years to come.

As cordial as the meeting was, we got the distinct feeling that we were regarded as nothing more than nice but naive young guys. By the end I was wondering if they'd maybe pat us on the head instead of shaking hands on the way out. It was disconcerting to think that our very youth, however vigorous, would turn out to be a handicap in having some people take us seriously. Still, the meeting ended with an invitation for us to join their group, to add a young professional dimension that had been missing from the anglo activist ranks up to then. They were also of the opinion that a new political party would have very little chance of success because anglo voters for the most part were just too conservative to break with tradition to the extent that they'd risk their vote on an upstart party. D'Arcy McGee for example is far too "establishment" and set in its ways to elect anyone but a Liberal, we were told with absolute certainty. Nevertheless, they suggested we get in touch with Maurice King, a hands-on English rights activist from the Chateauguay Valley, if we were seriously committed to the idea of forming a political party.

We had another meeting with a group of friends and decided that a political party was the only way that we could really make a splash of any sort. A provincial election was due the following year, and being a party would distinguish us from existing anglo pressure groups such as Alliance Quebec and the CCQ, and get us closer to the centre of the action. We hadn't heard from the CCQ for a while since our meeting, so we assumed that we were on our own. Then, out of the blue, we received a call from them and were invited to a meeting at the headquarters of the Black Coalition of Quebec. Its president, Dan Phillip, presided over the meeting, which was also attended by Côte St. Luc city councillor Eric Helfield. There were seven of our core group present, and about seven others. The discussion went around the room and everyone said their piece about how wretched the language laws were and how something had to be done.

The meeting was marked by the uninvited arrival of the notorious David Parsons, a striking figure with the flowing beard and gleaming gaze of an Old Testament prophet, who had been going around town in a van painted with slogans denouncing Quebec a fascist state. His very presence filled the room with tension and the meeting ended shortly after he unleashed an impassioned rant about the fascists taking over Quebec, ignoring repeated calls to order from the chair. Once again we were encouraged to call this Maurice King fellow if we were still set on forming a political party.

We were badly demoralized after this meeting, from which we got the impression that this community would never get its act together. It was several weeks later that we had our next meeting prompted by a call from a Cliff Gover, who had attended the meeting at the Black Coalition. We met and talked some more about much the same things as before, but by this time there was a new focus to the discussion—the Supreme Court decision on the sign law which was expected any week now. We decided to meet the next week with someone Gover knew, who had written an article that had been published in Freedom House, an American publication devoted to human rights issues, dissecting the discrimination in the Education provisions of Bill 101. The author, Tony Kondaks, had written that limiting the right to educate one's children in the language of one's choice to people who had themselves been educated in English schools in Canada ultimately brought the issue down to blood lines, and thus constituted a form of apartheid akin to the institutionalized racial discrimination in South Africa.

The arrival in the group of Tony Kondaks, a self-employed businessman with a consuming interest in politics, and the tense anticipation surrounding the imminent Supreme Court decision, changed the dynamic of our meetings considerably. We began meeting more regularly after hours in the small boardroom of my architectural firm, gradually developing a political ideology focused on the primacy of individual rights. We also began to discuss more earnestly the specifics of obtaining authorization for a political party. First there was the name. I suggested the "Equality Party" which after much discussion prevailed over other suggestions such as: The Freedom Party, The Freedom of Choice Party, The Progressive Party, the Individual Rights Party, The Canada Party.

Then there was the question of who would be the leader. It was agreed that I would act as interim leader, partly because I was the most fluent in French. We chose Klein as the official representative. It would be his job to handle all the money and account for our spending to the chief electoral officer. The more difficult part was the requirement to collect 60 signatures of eligible voters endorsing the party seeking authorization from each of 10 different electoral constituencies.

We decided to put down on paper, in English and French, a series of points summarizing our movement's ideological foundation:

1. Opposition to Bill 101.
2. Bilingualism in both the public and para-public sectors.
3. Expression in the language of one's choice in the private sector.
4. Freedom to choose public education in either French or English.
5. Opposition to the Meech Lake Accord.
6. Opposition to the Notwithstanding Clause in the Canadian Charter of Rights and Freedoms.

We arranged to begin collecting signatures in Robert Baldwin riding which primarily encompasses Dollard des Ormeaux. The incumbent MNA was Liberal minister Pierre Macdonald, who was a controversial figure at the time for an offhand crack about not wanting to be served by "fat damned English ladies at Eaton's". On December 3 we arranged to meet at Dunkin Donuts on Sources Road. Kondaks, DeSantis and myself showed up and we went off to start what would be a painful and embarrassing mission.

We chose streets which we knew were heavily populated with anglophones. We began the humbling process of ringing bells and using the following line: "We are going door to door collecting signatures in order to start a new political party in Quebec. We are very upset about how Quebec anglophones are growing more and more to feel like second class citizens. The name is the Equality Party and here are the six points that form the basis of our platform." Some were easily riled when the Quebec government's attitude toward minority communities came up. Others only signed because they felt uncomfortable about saying no. At two separate doors we were asked if we were with the Communist party. Someone else told us that kids our age should have more constructive things to do. While most people eventually signed up, this experience was hardly an ego booster. We got a sense from most people that as soon as they closed the door, they'd probably roll their eyes and mutter about how these young guys are dreaming in technicolor. But even at that, when we knocked off after an hour and a half we had 48 signatures, well on our way to wrapping up Robert Baldwin.

The three of us and Klein met the following week in my office to fine-tune our statement of principles, which advocated the primacy of the Canadian Charter of Rights and Freedoms and opposition to any override provisions, such as the "notwithstanding clause," whereby provinces could opt out of certain provisions of the charter with a simple majority vote in their legislatures. By this time it had also been announced that on December 15 the Supreme Court would finally render its decision on the sign law.

Our initial intention, with an election expected the next year, was mostly to make an impact by stealing a significant percentage of the anglo vote from the Liberals. A message would thus be sent to the powers that be, and we could all go home satisfied that at least we spoke up and did something about it. The idea of actually winning a seat was so remote to us at the time that no one even dared suggest it.

However, the events of the following week changed our modest expectations. That week was most instrumental in deciding the fate of the Equality Party. The Supreme Court signs ruling, designated the Ford Decision, held that commercial expression falls within the orbit of freedom of expression. Therefore, the sections of Bill 101 banning English from commercial signs violated clauses in both the Canadian and Quebec charters of rights guaranteeing freedom of expression. Also part of the ruling was an implicit suggestion which seemed to be a recommendation to the Quebec government by the high court. The court ruled that preserving the French face of Quebec was an important and valid objective for the provincial government. It would therefore be a reasonable limit on freedom of expression for the government to legislate that French is obligatory on all commercial signs, or even its marked predominance, but banning other languages would be unconstitutional.

Here was the perfect out for Bourassa. He could say that his government had brought the case all the way to the Supreme Court. The verdict was clear and he had no choice but to abide by the decision, and thus allow other languages on signs. But to protect the French face of Quebec, all commercial signs would have to include the message in French, and that the French version would have to be in bigger letters or more prominently displayed than its equivalent in English or any other language. Unfortunately though, he caved in to opposition pressure, as Quebec nationalist groups took to the streets and the airwaves in a concerted campaign to denounce the Supreme Court ruling as a vengeful anglo assault on the survival of the French language.

The evening of the day the ruling came down, we were invited by the CCQ to a meeting at the First Baptist Church in Côte St. Luc, to explain the Supreme Court decision. Klein and I were asked to make a presentation about our efforts to organize a political party. There was a widespread expectation at the meeting that Bourassa would invoke the notwithstanding clause to override the Supreme Court decision.

Sure enough the following week Premier Robert Bourassa inflicted the ultimate betrayal on the anglophone community. In campaigning for re-election in 1985, he had promised to change the sign law to allow English on commercial signs. Three years later, after the Quebec Superior Court, the Quebec Appeals Court and now the Supreme Court of Canada all ruled unanimously that banning English was unconstitutional, Bourassa used the notwithstanding clause to neutralise the Supreme Court decision. His betrayal was couched in Bill 178, which maintained the English ban on outdoor commercial signs, yet allowed limited use of English with French predominance inside commercial establishments, though with many exceptions. He claimed that his "inside-outside" formula was necessary to maintain "social peace".

As far as our group was concerned, this was not only one of the greatest acts of political cowardice in Quebec history, but also an insult to all Quebecers and their respect for democratic values and the rule of law. His alleged reasoning assumed that Quebecers were inherently irrational and intolerant to the point where the sight of English words on outdoor shop signs would generate massive social unrest. We found it shocking that the French press did not condemn Bourassa's reasoning and come out in support of the Supreme Court decision and the principle of bilingual signs.

Politically however, Bourassa's decision made a lot of sense, and being the master tactician that he is, he was guided by the consideration that he could no doubt take the anglophone vote for granted. He knew that English-speaking Quebecers would be upset, yet with an election due the following year, it was the soft nationalist francophone vote that he needed to win. He must have figured, as he did in 1976, that the docile anglos would stick with the Liberals no matter what he did to them. After all, the alternative, in what was effectively a two-party system, was a rejuvenated Parti Québécois, its commitment to separation reinforced by Jacques Parizeau's hard-line leadership. Bourassa, who felt under constant pressure to prove his nationalist credentials, went so far as to boast at one point that never before had a Quebec premier ventured to suspend civil liberties as he had. For the anglo community, this was rubbing it just a little too deeply.

Daunting as it seemed, this political reality became a powerful motivator for us in light of what was happening. The anglophone community was outraged well beyond what most commentators realised. Anglophone MNA's within the Liberal Party caucus, who had promised all these years that once the Supreme Court decision came down they would be in a strong position to fight for our community, became objects of vilification and ridicule. Three ministers, Richard French, Clifford Lincoln and Herbert Marx, concluded they had no choice but to resign, despite intense pressure from their caucus colleagues and the Premier himself to support the legislation.

Alliance Quebec's low-key strategy of discussions behind the scenes and working within the system was blown away. Long suspect for being soft on language rights, the organization had no more credibility in the eyes of many anglos. If ever the time was ripe for a new political party to take off, this was it. We assumed that there were dozens of groups like ours discussing community action, and perhaps even preparing to launch a party much like ours. We therefore suggested that rallying all these groups would be in the greater anglo community's best interests, and would perhaps even stiffen Alliance Quebec's spine and force its leadership to pay attention to those they claimed to represent.

The approach we decided to take at the CCQ meeting at the First Baptist Church was that our community must stand together and stand tall. Of foremost importance was the need to show the government that our community and its vote could no longer be taken for granted. A new political party, even for only one election, was imperative. Our presentation seemed to get the crowd of about 50 revved up to the point where we took hope that this might lead to something after all. After the meeting, a number of people approached us who were willing to help.

There was widespread sentiment, however, that Alliance Quebec no longer fit into the picture. Many in the group had been active in Alliance and felt that any attempt to co-operate with an organization that had so clearly let us down would discredit our initiative and probably kill our chances of doing something new and bold.

Alliance Quebec was officially established in the early 1980's, the successor to a group that called itself the Positive Action Committee. The PAC was organized by a number of prominent English-speaking Quebecers shortly after the Parti Québécois won the 1976 election, which was a crucial turning point for the anglo community in Quebec. Not only did it provoke an exodus from Quebec of hundreds of thousands of English speaking Quebecers, but the election had the psychological effect of forcing the English community to see and define itself as a minority, as an interest group that would have to lobby on its own behalf instead of relying on its emissaries within a Liberal government. The community had always been prominently represented in the Liberal party, but it had no relationship to speak of with the PQ, and generally regarded it with mistrust and fear.

Alliance Quebec had been fortunate in the 80's to have very intelligent and capable leaders, all of whom were highly articulate and fluently bilingual, and could communicate English concerns to the francophone majority with a quiet effectiveness. This low-key approach, and the organization's eagerness to prove that the anglophone community was readily accepting the new reality of Quebec, led them to be overcautious at times in their efforts to avoid inflaming the debate. The trap of this kind of soft-pedaling moderation was that Alliance Quebec always seemed to wind up trying to do the government's work in finding the compromise solution on the language front.

For example, after Bill 178 was passed, Royal Orr, who was then the president of AQ, was a guest on Joe Cannon's popular morning phone-in show on CJAD, Montreal's leading English-language radio station. Orr acknowledged that perhaps the Alliance strategy had been misguided all along with respect to the sign law. Its position had been what the Supreme Court had seemingly recommended, that the French language should be predominant on all commercial signs, but that other languages could also be used. It would have been better had AQ positioned itself from the start at one extreme—that any merchant should have the freedom to choose any language for a store sign, even an English-only sign. On the other extreme would be the hard-line nationalists pushing for French-only signs. There would then have been more room in the middle for a logical compromise that would have been easier for the government to accept and defend.

Because Alliance Quebec—in order to appear moderate to the francophone majority, thereby enhancing its own credibility—consistently tries to manufacture its own compromise solutions, it gives the government less room to forge a compromise of its own that makes sense and saves face on both sides. This has always been a problem for the anglophone community as far as its spokesmen were concerned. As I was to learn over and over again later on, you get caught in the trap of wanting to seem reasonable. You become very concerned about projecting a respectably-moderate image to the powerful French media in the province, often to the detriment of the community you represent. You get treated with respect by the English media only if you win the respect of the French media, otherwise they will write you off as redneck crackpots, as we were to learn.

A few days after the CCQ meeting we met at my office with a number of the people who had expressed interest in our party at the meeting. There was now a much more focused sense of purpose, and we set out again the following weekend to solicit signatures in D'Arcy McGee, St. Laurent and N.D.G. ridings. We were now an active core of 10 people, who for the next month met every few days to refine our manifesto and then go out for an hour of soliciting signatures.

In early January 1989, a Montreal bookstore owner named Stephen Nowell made national headlines for covering up the English signs in his Sherbrooke Street store with black paper, and posting notices condemning the sign law. He organized a public meeting at Victoria Hall in Westmount that drew an astonishing crowd of more than 1,000 angry anglos and had to be held in two shifts. This kind of spontaneous activism by our community was practically unheard-of. Standing outside the doors, listening to the overflow crowd singing "O Canada" with a rare passion and chanting anti-Bill 101 slogans, one could sense that Bill 178 was a critical rallying point for the community, a tangible unifier that wasn't there before. The difference between now and the anger over the passage of Bill 101 by the PQ 10 years earlier was that the Liberals, as opposed to the PQ, were supposedly our friends.

Bourassa had promised us that he would give us back our language on signs. Claude Ryan, who, as publisher of *Le Devoir* had denounced the intolerance of the language laws, and who was our leader as the head of the NO forces in the 1980 referendum, was now the minister responsible for the application of Bill 101. It was said he had threatened to quit if Bourassa declined to invoke the notwithstanding clause; when asked, he neither confirmed nor denied it. Until then there was still an opportunity to rally our political opposition within the political structure of the provincial Liberals. Now there was a political catalyst to rally the community, but a new vehicle was clearly required.

Nowell's success held out the hope of some form of organized community mobilization on the grassroots level. He had called for a campaign of civil disobedience as well as a series of regional meetings. His large gathering at Victoria Hall allowed us to solicit over a hundred signatures and to recruit a number of people who were seriously interested in getting involved with our party. Our next two meetings had to be held in the larger boardroom of my father's office since we were now regularly drawing more than 20 people. The discussions were still largely ideological, as the manifesto was still being developed, but new people were arriving on the scene.

Among the newcomers was Lionel Albert, who had co-authored the book "Partition " during the 1980 referendum campaign, challenging the right of an independent Quebec to all of the province's present territory. He brought with him Neil Cameron, a history professor at John Abbott College. Also becoming a regular at these meetings was Jacques Renaud, recruited by Kondaks, a former nationalist allied with the radical Parti Pris movement, and author of *Le Cassé*, a controversial 1960s novel written in Québécois slang. He was now very much committed to the protection of human rights and had helped translate Kondaks' article for Freedom House into French. He became very caught up in our discussions about fundamental rights and the primacy of the Charter.

But we still lacked organizational direction, and it was at this point that we finally decided to approach Maurice King, who had been working toward forming a political party of his own in anglo areas of rural Quebec. He had been the mayor of Greenfield Park for 16 years and now ran the Chateauguay Valley English Speaking People's Association (CVESPA), a rural anglo lobby group with the kind of backbone Alliance Quebec too often lacked. The meeting at the pizzeria near my office was very valuable as he impressed upon us the importance of establishing ourselves in each riding where we expected to run candidates. In order to be on the ballot, a political party must field at least 10 candidates, therefore it was crucial to set up riding associations in each constituency. His fledgling Unity Party had already established itself in four ridings, and we were invited two weeks later to a meeting in Chateauguay where over 100 people showed up to hear a number of guest speakers denounce Bill 178.

The crowd was highly emotional, and we were called up to say a few words about our efforts in Montreal. People freely dropped money into buckets that were passed around and signed their names to riding lists. Most of the people were elderly, and made much of the fact that our youth would give the English rights movement a new level of credibility. Up to now it had been largely dismissed by the media as a bunch of geriatric cranks, but here were a group of young professionals in their late 20's who instead of taking the easy way out had decided to stay and fight.

It was clear that we had to get moving in setting up an organizational structure. Since our regular meetings now drew an average of 40 people, we started holding them once a week in the basement of the Van Horne Restaurant where everyone threw a buck into the hat to cover the $50 cost of the room. We formed committees to deal with things like membership, public relations, fundraising, communications, regional development and policy. Our primary strategy was to appoint two people in each of our target constituencies to take on the responsibility of setting up riding associations, and completing the lists of signatures needed for the minimum 10 ridings. We even chose a central executive that included myself as leader, Klein as president, DeSantis, Kondaks, Albert and Cameron as vice-presidents, and Gloria Freedman as secretary. By this time we were also attracting some media attention, if only in the form of passing references, thanks to Renaud and Cameron who were regular guest speakers at the public meetings organized by Stephen Nowell and had mentioned the imminent formation of a new party.

Nowell's idea of a civil disobedience campaign, which would have included things like paying Hydro bills with dollar coins or even pennies, never really caught on. His movement started to fizzle because there didn't seem to be a concrete objective or a tangible goal. A political party, on the other hand, provided both the opportunity for people to vent their anger and to get involved in building an organization with a clearly defined purpose. But things were literally heating up elsewhere, as the headquarters of Alliance Quebec in downtown Montreal was torched by an arsonist who was never caught, while anonymous police sources falsely alleged that mild-mannered Royal Orr himself had set the fire.

As the situation intensified, things were starting to look more and more promising for our party. The regular meetings were steadily getting bigger, though they were also becoming somewhat repetitive. There were too many people showing up just to blow off steam and hear themselves talk, and you'd hear the same things over and over again. To bring our efforts into focus, we decided that the party would be officially launched riding by riding. All riding representatives were assigned to organize public meetings to launch their individual riding associations two weeks apart. This would give the impression that we were spreading like wildfire.

We decided to begin the process on March 13 in N.D.G. with what would be a typical riding meeting. The interim presidents of the soon-to-be N.D.G. riding association, Earl Wertheimer and Ron Silverman, booked the Monkland Community Centre. An anti-Bill 178 rally to organize a political party would be publicized in the local media and with fliers distributed door to door. They were in charge of organizing the event, local publicity and enlisting volunteers, while I was assigned to line up three guest speakers and send out a press release the day before the event. Outside the auditorium doors, we would set up a table for printed literature and for filling out membership forms. The admission was $1 per person to help defray the cost of the room.

As it turned out, the typical meeting would draw several hundred people. We would ask for volunteers to come back on the same day the following week to the same building for a smaller meeting to set up the nucleus of the riding association. Between 30 and 40 volunteers would normally turn up at the follow-up meetings. We repeated the process every two weeks in different ridings, in church basements, hotels, and community centres.

By now the CCQ crowd had broken up, with most of its activists gravitating toward our initiative, including its original hard core with whom we had met, and who had looked down on us as naive young dreamers.

The morning before the N.D.G. kickoff I attended a B'nai Brith Covenant Breakfast where Royal Orr was the guest speaker. I brought with me the envelope with all our required signatures from the 10 ridings in it because I needed a commissioner of oaths to sign the papers, and I knew that at a B'nai Brith function there would be an abundance of lawyers and accountants. I approached Royal Orr after the meeting to let him know what we were up to and asked if he would sign one of our forms. He was polite but didn't seem too impressed. He refused to sign, saying he was from the Eastern Townships, assuming this automatically put him out of our range.

The next night was opening night for the party. The required signatures had been sent to the chief electoral officer, along with all the other necessary information. Some 5,000 pamphlets were printed up by DeSantis' brother and distributed in N.D.G. by a dozen volunteers the previous week. The local weeklies had carried stories announcing a meeting to form a new political party, and I had gone into my office to send out faxes the day before when my bosses weren't around, informing the major media outlets of the meeting. The *Gazette* ran a small story on page A4 that day with the headline "New party to promote bilingualism".

When I arrived at the Monkland Centre a half hour early that night, there was already a cluster of people signing their names at the table near the entrance. The room began to fill and by show time the 300 seats were filled. Klein and I were the first two speakers. He launched into a vicious attack on Robert Bourassa and Quebec's language laws, bringing the crowd to its feet. I noticed Jeannie Lee of PULSE news standing at the back with her cameraman, her coat still on. When she saw the impact the speech was having on the crowd, she took off her coat and instructed the cameraman to start rolling.

Our first guest speaker was Geraldine Doucet, widow of the late singer Roger Doucet, famed for his stirring renditions of "O Canada" in both official languages. She had been in the news recently for sending an open letter to the media saying that Bill 178 had prompted her to want to leave Quebec. She belted out "O Canada"and revved up the crowd even more. Jacques Renaud and Neil Cameron were the other speakers, and both kept the momentum going. The meeting was a huge success with over 100 people signing up. On their way out they demonstrated their sincerity by filling up the collection buckets at the doorway, and we wound up raising several hundred dollars. It seemed like we had hit on a winning formula.

The media reviews the next day were encouraging. I found it peculiar hearing our party being discussed on the radio all of a sudden, with the occasional reference to my name. *The Gazette* carried an editorial a few days later that was surprisingly positive, saying that "the party is a healthy sign that many anglophones are willing to explore new ideas and new forms of political action". However, in the last two paragraphs they raised the spectre of our party's potential to split the Liberal vote, and therefore help elect the PQ as in 1976. This fear was to plague us throughout the campaign, though it made no sense at all. Our intention was to run only in ridings where there was a large anglophone vote. In these ridings the PQ stands zero chance, even with a split in the Liberal vote.

We were suddenly being called for interviews from all over the place. *The Canadian Jewish News* was doing a feature on Klein and myself. CJAD Radio asked me to do an interview on the morning talk-show with news director Gord Sinclair. (The program would shortly get a new host in the person of none other than Royal Orr. He had recently left Alliance Quebec, where Peter Blaikie took over as the chief spokesman on an interim basis until a new president could be found.) This was to be my first ever live interview and I was as nervous as a groom on his wedding night. Not only that, but I was to do the interview by phone from my office, and I was fervently hoping the boss wouldn't come around to my desk while I was on the air.

Sinclair was his trademark sceptical, cynical self. But I got across the line that we quoted over and over in those days, about how we must be vigilant because "never in history has a minor violation of rights which has gone unchecked, not led to a more substantial violation of rights and freedoms." That week, Gloria Freedman set up a phone line in her house, and procured a post office box for the party. We also had a graphic artist start work on a logo.

Our second rally was coming up, this time in St. Laurent riding, significant because it was Robert Bourassa's home riding. I was supposed to have an operation on a deviated septum a week before the rally, but the operation was postponed until one day before. I insisted on being discharged from the hospital the next day, and was able to deliver the opening speech that night, albeit with an uncomfortably swollen proboscis.

The rally was held on a rain-drenched March 28 in the banquet hall of an upscale restaurant called the Buffet Crystal. When I walked in I couldn't believe the activity. TV cameras and reporters were everywhere. There was a large crowd around the membership tables and all 300 seats were already taken. We had again distributed several thousand flyers the week before, and from our first meeting we'd learned the old trick that you must always book a room too small for the anticipated attendance. It looked impressive when they had to open up a side wall to allow the nearly 500 people fit in.

We focused our attack on Bourassa, and Klein made news by calling him a "pathological liar" and a "separatist". Renaud, Albert and Kondaks were the guest speakers. In response to a question from the audience, I said the party recognizes the right of any merchant to put up an English-only sign. A sign of how seriously the meeting was being treated was that I recognized columnists Don Macpherson of *The Gazette* and Bernie St. Laurent of the *Montreal Daily News* sitting at the back of the room, tapping away on their lap-top computers. Macpherson's subsequent column labelled us a throwback to the "freedom of choice" anglophone protest movement of the mid 1970's, and predicted that anglos would not feel comfortable about endorsing the party's "reactionary, narrowly ideological approach to language". His last line was "he (Bourassa) has little to worry about from the Equality Party."

Though Macpherson was wrong, as it turned out, this first assault of negative press caused considerable panic among most of the active party members. *The Gazette*'s senior political writer, Hubert Bauch, in a long piece in the Saturday edition that weekend, referred to the party as "the redneck anglo-rights fringe". The negative reaction in the French media also lead to Jacques Renaud's hasty retreat from the party, which in itself made headlines a few days later. He was concerned about Lionel Albert's contentious remarks that the federal government would be justified in sending troops into the province because of Bill 178. This was the first serious schism to develop in the party. There were a number of people who felt that we should moderate our position, in particular our policy stand that a merchant should be allowed to post a sign in English only.

After all, the Supreme Court of Canada had suggested that it was justifiable for the government to legislate that French be obligatory (or even markedly predominant) on all signs, so long as other languages weren't forbidden. Many of us felt that if we were to modify our position, supporting the Supreme Court recommendation, then at least we would be sending out a message to the francophone majority that we recognized the need to preserve Quebec's predominantly French face. The harder-line elements of the party insisted that any merchant should have the god-given right to advertise any way he wants on his own store. They reasoned that if a store-owner is stupid enough not to advertise in the language of 85% of the population, then he has every right to go bankrupt.

I was getting calls at the office the entire morning of the Macpherson column, so I decided that we needed an "emergency meeting" to resolve the issue. A few days later, over 80 emotional and what were described in reports as "colourful" people crammed into the Van Horne Restaurant basement for what turned into a non-stop five-hour marathon. In the end the group voted in favour of modifying our position , prompting a handful of the hard-liners, including Tony Kondaks, to pull out in a huff. Still, I was relieved. I felt that a compromise such as this was crucial to get Renaud back and to stall the growing perception of the party as a redneck, reactionary protest movement that was bound to fail. I worried that I was becoming too preoccupied with what the press was saying about us, but as far as I was concerned, the only way to get our message across in such a short time was via the media. If they ridiculed us, so would the populace. All politicians become media slaves to a large extent. So much of what you say, and how you say it, is governed by what you think the media reaction will be, and how you can best impart a spin to the media reports that favors your side. At the same time, I was able to square the shift in our position with my own conscience because the Supreme Court decision agreed with it anyway.

We had another 10 days to get our act together before the next rally, to be held in D'Arcy McGee, where the incumbent, Herbert Marx, had resigned as Justice Minister over Bill 178. He would be an easy target, if he were to swallow his pride and run again, but rumour had it that he would land a judgeship and bail out of politics.

Now that we had moderated our stance I was working to get Renaud back on board. June Weiss and Rafael Chalkoun, regulars at our meetings who had become good friends with Renaud, got the four of us together in a room, and late into the night we hammered out a new program to clarify our position. It was entitled "For a Better Quebec / Pour un Quebec meilleur.

It stated that "the Equality Party of Quebec seeks to create an atmosphere of tolerance, respect and good-will between Quebec's linguistic and cultural communities. . . The party will contribute to the development of a more just and more democratic society in Quebec, a society in which the aspirations and rights of all citizens are fully respected."

Renaud agreed to come back if the party activists adopted the plan. At the regular meeting a week later we got it through with overwhelming support. Compromises were worked out on minor sticking points, and all was well again. The most intractable of the hard-liners had already left the party the week before, and it made for a much smoother meeting. The platform was sent out to the media and got good play in the French press, which also printed the text of Renaud's earlier speech at the St. Laurent meeting.

On April 7th we got word that the Equality Party had received authorization from the Director General of Elections as an officially recognized political party in Quebec. We could now officially sell memberships and issue tax receipts for all contributions. At the D'Arcy McGee rally a few days later, Renaud's return and fiery speech to the crowd of 300 was big news, as was the champagne that accompanied the unveiling of the new party logo and the announcement of our official status. We were decidedly back on the rails.

The following week I was invited to be an in-studio guest on the midnight CJAD open-line show with host Chris Mota. It was to be my first such experience, but any butterflies quickly dissipated as, despite the late hour, the lines were soon blazing with passionately offended anglos, all of whom were gung-ho supportive of our efforts. This was my first real taste of general public sentiment toward our party. We had been in the news, as The Gazette, PULSE, NEWSWATCH, and CJAD had covered all three of our riding rallies. We had good turnouts and genuine enthusiasm at our meetings, but we still lacked a real feel for where the average voter stood. Those two hours on the air gave me the first clear indication that there was grass-roots support out there. The press was starting to see the possibility of us making a dent in the political landscape and stories even began appearing about how the Liberals were having to respond to us. Another sign of solid support was that we were raising some serious money and had already sold over two thousand memberships at $5 apiece.

On April 25th we held our fourth rally, launching the Robert Baldwin riding association and signed up about 150 new members. There was another boisterous, standing-room-only crowd of 400 people. By now I was becoming much more comfortable speaking in front of crowds. Their enthusiasm and emotional commitment to the issue stimulated a certain adrenaline flow in my system, and it was becoming easier to find the words that would move a roomful of people. I began most speeches by asking how many people had seen their children or grand children leave Quebec. The fact that well over 50% of the crowd generally raised their hands always set an emotional context for the rest of the speech. Another successful line was the warning that "to vote Liberal is to kiss the foot that kicked you."

We had meetings lined up in Brossard, Chomedey, Mount Royal, Outremont and St. Louis riding in downtown Montreal. Follow-up meetings were continuing in N.D.G., St. Laurent, D'Arcy McGee, and Robert Baldwin, drawing more and more people every week. At the first Mount Royal public meeting an articulate francophone, Jean Pierre Isoré took to the microphone and encouraged all francophones to join the crusade to fight for individual rights. He very quickly became a force in the party. We also began holding policy workshops in the old Ramada Inn on Decarie Boulevard. These sessions served a dual purpose. On the one hand the label of "one issue party" was starting to get on our nerves and we felt that a policy statement on social issues was required to reinforce our mainstream credibility. More important, it was a way of keeping the party activists keenly motivated. In a political party it becomes all too easy to center policy decisions in the small circle surrounding the leader. However, most volunteers want to be involved in policy discussions, and regard this as their payback for the hours of organizational dogwork they put in. A leader who organizes policy discussions and gives even the impression that he is genuinely interested in the views of the rank and file, is usually assured of a solid following.

All the while, I was meeting new people every day, doing interviews and at the same time trying to keep my mind on my job as an architect. The receptionist at the office was constantly complaining to the boss about the number of calls I was getting. Mr. Tolchinsky, with whom I was working closely at the time on an office building next to the Ruby Foo's Hotel on Decarie Boulevard, voiced his displeasure every so often about the amount of time I was spending on the phone on political business. His patience grew very thin one Saturday when he answered the phone at the office. On the line was a *Gazette* reporter who was downright rude to him when told that I wasn't available.

The media coverage of our activities usually featured a slightly condescending twist, though we provided them with an angle to the extent that we were keeping the language issue at the forefront of the pre-election debate. But our prospects of winning a seat were still considered somewhat less likely than a UFO landing at the Fairview Plaza parking lot.

In late May I was asked to speak at the Alliance Quebec annual convention, in a forum on the choices for anglos in the upcoming election. On the platform with me were Heather Keith-Ryan, who would be running as an independent anglo-rights candidate, John Ciaccia, representing the Liberals, and Jacques Parizeau himself, the new leader of the PQ. I asked Keith-Ryan, former president of the Townshippers Association as we were walking toward the auditorium if she would consider running for the Equality Party, but she felt that her chances were better as an independent. Since Ciaccia had voted in favour of Bill 178 for the purpose of maintaining his seat in cabinet, most anglos were furious with him. Parizeau, meanwhile, was the leader of the party that intends to break up our country. But while between them they stood for most of the things I most ardently opposed, I found that it's hard to despise a person when you're thrown together in a civilized setting, making idle small talk while waiting for the meeting to start.

I was genuinely impressed with the way Parizeau handled himself on such unfriendly turf. Ciaccia was interrupted by boos throughout his address and tried to diffuse some of the anger by taking a light-hearted, shoulder-shrugging approach. To my mind, he just didn't seem to get it. The issue was far too important for any politician to try to downplay to an anglophone crowd. This motivated me for my speech, which was far less polished than the others but which hit the chord to which this crowd was attuned. According to the Toronto *Globe and Mail* the next day, I received a "rousing welcome," yet *The Gazette* did not even mention us. The suspicion began to set in that *The Gazette* was beginning to worry that our party might in fact do something to break new ground, and had therefore decided to tone down its coverage of our activities to the extent that if there was nothing bad to say, then they would just ignore us.

A lot of us thought that the arbiters of *The Gazette*'s political line, people like editorial page editor Joan Fraser, national editor Jennifer Robinson and provincial affairs columnist Macpherson, were concerned about how it would look to francophone Quebec, if such a rag-tag "redneck" group were to succeed in capturing the anglophone vote. What they seemed to be missing was what we were encountering regularly at the grass roots—that their own readers were seriously steamed and wanted to ventilate their anger. Our movement, with young, clean-cut, and seemingly sincere newcomers at the helm was saying the things the average anglo wanted to hear.

We were setting up membership booths in shopping centres, sending speakers to different groups, and continuing to set up riding associations in Outremont, Argenteuil (Lachute), Westmount, Laurier (Park Extension), Two Mountains, Marquette (Lachine) and Marguerite Bourgeois (Lasalle). We also raised enough money to rent a fairly large office in West End Montreal and hire two staffers to answer the phones. A number of volunteers were also on hand to process memberships. As the election call neared, my lunch-times were still largely devoted to courting potential candidates. While the frustration of finding credible name candidates was gnawing at me, there was no shortage of political"driftwood", or people who wanted to run just for the hell of it. One guy asked whether the truth would "get out" that he'd served time in prison, because he'd never told his present wife about it. Someone else wanted to run in order to prove to his mother that he was not "a useless human being" as she would often call him. Many of the "career political candidates" who would run for every fringe party on the political map knocked on our door, as did a whole slew of deluded souls who thought that they could just run, be elected as an MNA and live the good life.

I was encouraged to attend Premier Bourassa's nomination meeting in his home riding by our St. Laurent riding association, which felt I could make waves by showing up. When I walked in, Deputy-Premier Gérard D. Lévesque was warming up the packed hall. I was escorted against my will by our riding president to a seat that was right in front of the Premier and his wife. I felt very uneasy, figuring that everyone, including the Premier, must be thinking that I was some brash young kid out to make a scene. After the meeting, as people were milling about in a media scrum, I came face-to-face with Bourassa for the first time. He extended his hand and said, "Mr. Libman, I saw that you were sitting right in front of me. Good luck." I couldn't help asking myself if this charming man could be the same person who aroused so much impassioned anger?

Uncomfortable as I was in that odd situation, it provided an angle for the media to bring up the language issue, since Bourassa that evening had tried to stick to economics in his speech. His riding had a significant percentage of anglo voters and he would do all he could to focus on anything but the language issue. Despite our high hopes for the riding, especially in light of the fact that Bourassa had twice been personally defeated in his home ridings in past elections, this meeting showed me what political organization was all about. The slick orchestration, the glitzy posters and literature, the upbeat music, the flashing lights, the proliferation of walkie- talkies and the crowd of well over 500 people made our rallies look pathetically Mickey Mouse. This was my first taste of an event organized by a major political machine and my heart sank. Our St. Laurent riding association drew very enthusiastic supporters, yet compared to this juggernaut, we looked like a rowboat floundering in the wake of the Queen Mary.

Battle lines were also developing in some of our stronger riding associations over who would run in the election. In St. Laurent, for example, riding president Lew Gauthier was chosen by riding members at a hastily organized nomination meeting where he defeated three other aspirants from the riding association. He installed security systems for a living and felt that an ordinary, hard working St. Laurent resident was what the population of the riding wanted. I had originally hoped that in Bourassa's riding we could land a showcase candidate. However, Peter Blaikie had refused, as did Jacques Renaud and Michel Décary, who was head of the Quebec chapter of the Canadian Federation of Independent Business.

For some reason the media was speculating that I would run against Bourassa when in fact I now wanted to parachute Romeo Brault, an articulate and perfectly bilingual former Liberal riding president, who finally agreed to run after the other potential "name" candidates had declined. Meanwhile, Gerald Klein wanted to bring in his accounting partner's husband, an immigration lawyer named Ciro Paul Scotti. Lew Gauthier resisted, and then defiantly backed Philip Chrysafidis, another lawyer who was on the party executive, but whom I wanted to run in Laurier. He had been ready to run in Laurier, but backed off when he was allegedly approached by a few individuals who warned him that if he ran in Laurier against Liberal Christos Sirros, then he would never have another Greek client for the rest of his life.

As it turned out, Romeo Brault decided that he would not run for the party unless he was the leader. We put this to the membership at an emergency General Council meeting in early August where I received an overwhelming endorsement from the party, and the decision was made to drop the word "interim" and elect me as the leader of the party heading into the election. It was resolved that Chrysafidis would run in Marguerite-Bourgeoys, and much to the dissatisfaction of the riding volunteers, Scotti was to be the candidate in St. Laurent. Other ridings were also involved in similar battles between the central executive and the membership. We saw candidates as a group of individuals who would be carrying the image of the party, and therefore had to know the issues well. The riding associations and their volunteers, on the other hand, took pride in democratically choosing a candidate they felt was something of a local entity. Any intrusion by the leader was seen as strong-arming the very volunteers who were the bedrock of our movement. After extensive consultation and many long, heated meetings, most of these conflicts were resolved. We were always unified by our primary objective, which was to make a strong showing in the election.

On August 8 we held the final rally in our series of riding association launches at the Holiday Inn Pointe Claire where we officially initiated the associations in the West Island ridings of Jacques Cartier and Nelligan with a packed house of more than 600 people. The media was there in full force as the election call was expected the next day, and the election fever around the membership tables and donation buckets was palpable. We were still being heckled at many of the meetings by the same "anglo hard-liners who claimed that by supporting a position that obliged the use of French on commercial signs, we had abandoned all principles of equality. Tony Kondaks even heckled this very meeting for that reason, but these attacks from the anglo far side ultimately served to enhance our image as a party that could be politically pragmatic and able to compromise.

That evening we unveiled what we called our "Three cornerstones" which were the focal point of our election material:

- Individual rights and freedoms
- Bilingualism
- Canadian unity

The next morning, Premier Bourassa called the election for September 25, less than seven weeks hence. That morning I asked Tolchinsky and Goodz for six weeks leave without pay beginning the following week, fully expecting that I would be returning to work as an architect on September 27.

CHAPTER THREE
Chasing Stars

Those who expect to reap the blessings of freedom
must undergo the fatigue of supporting it.
—Tom Paine

With the election campaign now officially underway, many party members became somewhat frantic. We had yet to line up candidates in a number of key ridings and had still not confirmed any of the "star" candidates we had been promising to the media. I kept reassuring everybody that things would fall into place, and that there were a number of irons in the fire.

Two weeks earlier I had received a call from Eric Helfield, a lawyer and Côte St. Luc city councillor whom I had met through the CCQ. He asked me to call a lawyer named Richard Holden, whom he had met in court that day. Holden had mentioned to Helfield that he was really angry about Bill 178 and was thinking of running as a candidate. He knew that Helfield had been involved with our party so he asked him to have "one of those kids" give him a call.

Holden had some name recognition as a libel lawyer and a certain notoriety as a political gadfly, especially in Westmount where he had grown up. He was the lawyer who had fought Sun Life's head office move to Toronto in the '70s and had recently been asked by Peter Blaikie to take over Royal Orr's lawsuit against the TVA network for reporting that Orr himself might have started the fire at Alliance Quebec's headquarters. Blaikie had originally been asked to take the case, but because the same TVA network was one of his firm's clients, he had to decline. Holden had run federally in 1979 for the Conservatives and provincially as an independent in 1962 to challenge the Lesage government's plan to nationalize the province's power companies. He was soundly defeated both times. At Holden's press conference announcing his candidacy in 1962, he fainted dead away at the microphone. The next day, a photo of his unconscious form, sprawled on the floor, made the front pages of Montreal's newspapers. (Though not *The Gazette*, where Holden had some influence with management and got the picture spiked; the only acknowledgement of the incident in *The Gazette* report was that at one point during the proceedings the candidate had become "indisposed".)

I called Holden and we set up a lunch meeting for the next week at Winnie's bar on Crescent Street. When I told Doug Robinson, he was pleasantly surprised. Robinson said that while many people regarded him as a "putz," he felt that Holden was a highly credible candidate. He was a product of the Westmount establishment, had considerable experience and extensive connections and was considered politically in tune with modern day Quebec.

Winnie's was a favored lunch-time hangout for political pundits and players, who sit around the bar and banter about the day's events and trade the latest gossip. When I arrived accompanied by David De Santis, our interim Westmount riding president, Holden was perched on a barstool. It was obvious that he was a seasoned regular in this company, on an easy first-name basis with everyone at the bar. He was larger than I expected, his face alight with a ready smile and a ruddy glow.

To our disappointment, Holden told us that he had initially thought about running as a candidate in the election, but after serious consideration, and after talking to Peter Blaikie who encouraged him to run only as an independent, had decided to decline. He claimed that he was too fat and out of shape, and that just thinking about the prospect of day-to-day campaigning at his age was too tiring. Despite our entreaties for him to reconsider, it was to no avail, and we resigned ourselves to the prospect that we would have to find someone from within our own riding association to run in Westmount.

Over the next few days, however, all that would change. At a Montreal press conference during the first week of the campaign, Premier Bourassa was so anxious to showcase the Liberal party's "star" candidate for Westmount that his haste resulted in a public relations disaster. William Cosgrove was one of the vice-presidents of the World Bank in Washington, where he had resided for the past 16 years. Bourassa felt that Cosgrove, by virtue of this position, fit the candidate profile for anglo Westmount so ideally that he'd be a shoo-in.

At his coming-out press conference, however, Cosgrove looked ill at ease, was inept at answering questions and had trouble explaining his qualifications for provincial office after a 16-year absence from Quebec. But what buried him was a cynical question from Barry Wilson of PULSE

News who asked Cosgrove if he knew what Bill 142 was—the legislation providing for English health care services throughout the province. Cosgrove obviously didn't have a clue, though Bourassa could be heard frantically prompting him under his breath. The embarrassing exchange was gleefully broadcast by the English media. Not only was it an example of condescending arrogance by the premier for making assumptions about stereotypical Westmount anglos, but it was a sign of how out of touch Bourassa was with the anger sweeping through the anglo community. When questions were raised as to whether Cosgrove was even eligible to vote in the election after his sixteen year absence, it only heightened the element of farce surrounding his candidacy.

But it also had other ramifications. The next day, Richard Holden called me back and invited me to lunch, this time at Woody's pub, another downtown watering hole favored by the political crowd—and the Montreal landmark most recently immortalized by Mordecai Richler, who featured it in his notorious New Yorker article on Quebec nationalism. Over the phone Holden did not want to tell me to what I owed the pleasure, but said that it was very important. When I arrived, the company around the bar included Nick Auf der Maur, the storied downtown city councillor and man of many political stripes, Tory backroomer and senator-in-waiting John Lynch Staunton, former Conservative Member of Parliament Egan Chambers, and Colonel Pierre Sevigny, the former Diefenbaker-era Conservative cabinet minister best known after all these years for an unfortunate acquaintance with one Gerda Munsinger. Holden effusively paraded me around the bar, introducing me to one and all. Auf der Maur joined Holden, Robinson and myself for lunch along with two of Holden's buddies, businessman Irwin Steinberg and Ron Seltzer, the publisher of the now-defunct *Downtowner* weekly newspaper.

Drinks were going around, and political discussion about the election campaign and general good cheer were the order of the day. They informed me that if I wanted to be a serious politician I'd have to kick my boring habit of drinking straight orange juice all the time. After lunch, Holden got serious. He told me that after seeing the Cosgrove press conference he was seriously reconsidering, now that he might actually have a chance to win. He still had some reservations, however, and continued to be very reticent. Almost on cue, his cronies began to egg him on. Finally, after feigning much personal angst and indecision, he relented and agreed to be the Equality Party candidate in Westmount. To my considerable surprise, after all the elaborate hesitation, he proceeded to pull out of his briefcase a fully prepared contract for me to sign, setting out a series of conditions for his candidacy: He would do his own advertising; the party would make no demands of him before noon any given day; he would not be obliged to campaign door-to-door until after Labour day, and could continue to support the Meech Lake Accord, despite the party's stand against it.

I accepted the first condition, assuming he would at least use the party logo. The second and third conditions posed no serious problem. As for Meech, I proposed that if he stayed quiet on it, I would never oblige him to renounce it in public. This would later come back to haunt me, but with the election campaign underway, and without a candidate in Westmount, I was only too happy to sign the deal. We shook hands and decided to announce his candidacy at a nomination meeting two nights later. His nomination announcement would be our first. Nick Auf der Maur would be his campaign manager, and had already devised some hard-hitting campaign literature lampooning "Wild Bill Cosgrove: Quebec's one millionth visitor". I left Woody's very enthusiastic about the potential impact of Holden's candidacy. Holden and his friends stayed on for the rest of the afternoon to toast his leap into the fray.

Gordon Atkinson had become well known to Montrealers over several decades as a sportscaster with the CBC, and was now doing the news and editorial comment every evening on CJAD radio. His fire-and-brimstone style had gained him a large following among disaffected anglos. Shortly after Bill 178 was passed, I had mustered the nerve to call him and tell him that I really appreciated his editorials. I also asked if he would meet a group of young guys to discuss our idea of forming a political party dedicated to minority language rights. Much to my surprise he agreed and came to meet us in my office the following weekend, during a lashing snow storm as it turned out. With his six-foot-plus stature, white handlebar mustache, fur hat and cane, he cut an impressive figure; with his booming voice on top of everything else, his presence in the small conference room was almost overwhelming.

Gordon Atkinson instinctively takes a shine to anyone who seems to admire him, especially if this is expressed in gushing tones. We were very appreciative of his coming to see us and sincerely flattering about his editorials and his pugnacious style. It therefore made for a very hearty meeting where Gordon was in full performance mode. There was actually very little of significant value in what he told us that day, except for how all the media were spineless wimps and lazy scum. However, the meeting sowed the seeds of a future relationship and a bond that was almost paternal. On the radio, Atkinson continued to bash the Bourassa Liberals and occasionally broadcast editorials lauding our efforts once the party began making news. Something told me that one day I might well be able to land him as a candidate by stroking him the right way at the right time. In the meantime, he made himself available for consultation.

In the summer of 1989 I decided to ask him if he would be the keynote speaker, along with author William Weintraub, at a major rally to launch our Westmount riding association at Victoria Hall on Sherbrooke Street. He was hesitant, but agreed to speak as long as his speech could be non-partisan and more of a historical retrospective of Montreal and the language debate. My hunch was that if we had a good enthusiastic crowd to egg him on, his restraint would go right out the window. Sure enough, my hunch was bang on.

We had a Scottish piper start the meeting off, followed by a school choir singing "O Canada". The hall was packed with more than 500 people who constantly interrupted his speech with cheers and applause. His opening line was the slogan of the French Revolution: "Egalité, liberté, fraternité." From there he became completely swept up in the moment, roaring, pounding his fists and wiping his brow with a handkerchief. If anything, it was the most vitriolic partisan attack on the Liberal government and the Premier that I had heard since we began holding political rallies. He called the Premier a "coward," a "scoundrel" and a "pipsqueak". He spoke of "cultural and linguistic genocide" against English speaking Quebecers. He drew parallels between our upcoming election battle and the two wars in which he served our country "with dignity and with honour". The thoroughly delighted crowd rewarded him with a prolonged standing ovation.

I had arranged for a number of people to approach him after the meeting to encourage him to be a candidate for the party, but I was beginning to wonder if it was such a great idea, considering how easily and how recklessly he could let himself be carried away in the heat of the moment. Nevertheless, the news coverage the next day, as well as the highly positive reaction from the party rank and file during the following days, dispelled my fears and convinced me that a name candidate like Atkinson would be a major boost for the party. All I heard from members of the Westmount association and around the office for the next couple of days was how Atkinson brought the house down at Victoria Hall.

A few weeks later I invited Atkinson to dinner at a Sherbrooke St. restaurant with a few other potential candidates we were courting, including Jacques Renaud and Michel Decary. The wine flowed and the mood was relaxed and upbeat, and as we strolled over to the Ritz-Carlton for nightcaps, I made my pitch to Atkinson. I heaped praise on him, emphasizing how he had fought all his life for just and patriotic causes, first as a soldier in two wars and then behind his microphone.

Here, I continued, was a glorious opportunity, in the twilight of his professional career, to bring his lifelong battle to the very arena where it mattered most at this time. This was his chance to move out from behind his microphone and stand up for our community, to fight for our country against the separatists, right there on the floor of the National Assembly. You could see the wheels turning in his head, and the glint in his eye told me that he sorely wanted to run. But even after more drinks at the Ritz, he still refused to commit himself.

He did suggest, however, that if he were to run, he would like to take a shot at D'Arcy McGee, since he had a large following in the Jewish seniors' community, having been closely involved with the Allied Jewish Community Services Council on Aging. But I knew that in D'Arcy McGee it was essential to have a Jewish candidate since it was the only riding in the province where the Jewish community had the numbers to ensure the election of one of their own to the provincial legislature. I urged him to consider running in N.D.G. instead.

Shortly thereafter, our N.D.G. riding association was scheduled to hold a meeting where all their potential candidates were to present themselves to the association membership. I convinced Atkinson to show up and say a few words, just in case he might eventually decide to run. He agreed to participate, and with his stentorian voice and rotund rhetoric in a room barely large enough to contain him, he clearly won over the crowd. That night it again looked as though he was willing to take the plunge, but he still seemed troubled about something. The next day he invited me to the United Services Club on Sherbrooke Street for lunch and a private tete à tete. I went thinking that he would tell me then that he'd be a candidate.

The United Services Club is a beautifully appointed refuge on Sherbrooke Street in downtown Montreal, with lush wall coverings and elegant furnishings. Just off the main entrance is the Queen Elizabeth room where an imposing portrait of the Queen keeps a watchful eye on things. Members of the upper crust anglo establishment relax in these plush surroundings, making jokes about lawyers and politicians. After a hearty lunch, spiced by tales of Atkinson's wartime adventures, we got down to the nitty-gritty. He began by telling me that he felt insecure about his limited ability to speak French.

He then dropped a stunner: he would run for the Equality Party, but only if I would find him a guaranteed job if he lost the election, at salary equivalent to what he was making at CJAD. It must also be media-related, he specified. He believed that running for the party would taint him politically to the extent that he could no longer work at a station like CJAD. This was a tall order for a 28 year old kid, still damp

behind the ears and with no media connections whatsoever. Here I was
being asked by someone who had been in TV and radio for over 40 years
to find him a suitable media job. I wondered if he was really serious.
Maybe he was just testing us and would run anyway. I left in somewhat
of a quandary. How in the world could I deliver such a tall order?
Strangely enough, my first idea bore fruit.

The owners of *The Suburban* newspaper, a weekly distributed
throughout the western part of Montreal, had been very supportive of
the party. I had met them recently through Gloria Freedman who was
friends with Amos Sochaczevski, one of two brothers who owned the
paper. I decided to approach them about Atkinson's stipulation, and
they invited the two of us to a meeting. Atkinson was well known to
them already, being a contributing writer for the magazine *Montreal
Business* which they owned as well. They actually agreed on the spot that
if he were to run and lose, they would guarantee him a management
position at *The Suburban*. Brimming with enthusiasm as we were walking
to the car, I asked Atkinson where and how he would like us to officially
announce his candidacy. I felt that it was crucial at this stage to unveil a
"star" candidate as encouragement for others to come forth.

But Atkinson was still reluctant to declare. He was still concerned
about his poor French, and he was committed to leave for Europe the
following week to host a trip sponsored by CJAD. The nomination
meeting to select a candidate in N.D.G. would take place during that time
and without a firm commitment on his part to run—which he couldn't
give before fulfilling his obligation to CJAD—I figured his chances of
being chosen in absentia were limited.

Nevertheless, he agreed to let his name stand. At the nomination
meeting the moderator read Atkinson's CV and spoke a few words on
his behalf, and despite his refusal to commit himself officially, which the
other contenders played against him, he was chosen to be the candidate
by the 250 delegates, on the strength of his appeal as a media personality
and much behind-the-scenes arm-twisting on our part.

When he was tracked down by the media in Europe the next day,
he sounded very much like a candidate. In a live interview with CJAD,
he went on at great length about how honored he was to have been
chosen and how important it was for our community to have strong
spokesmen at this critical juncture in our history. We had hoped to make
the official announcement the following week, when he was scheduled
to return. When he did return, however, he was still not willing to make
a hard commitment. To put additional pressure on him we announced
that we would be officially naming our N.D.G. candidate four days later
at a public meeting. If he were to back off, Neil Cameron, who had

finished second in the voting at the N.D.G. meeting would be our candidate. As the day approached, and despite my insistent urging, he was still wavering. Finally, very early on the morning of the meeting, my telephone rang at home. I picked up the receiver and without even having said hello, heard that booming voice at the other end of the line: "Sound the trumpets. Ring the bells. You have your candidate in N.D.G.".

That night Gordon Atkinson did not disappoint. He roused the 200 party faithful at the Monkland Community Centre to their feet several times. His nomination papers were easily filled with the 100 signatures of N.D.G. residents necessary to nominate him as an official candidate, and the drama surrounding his candidacy gave the party's election campaign a significant boost.

Before the meeting we picked Atkinson up at his downtown apartment on Sherbrooke Street. I pulled out the blank copy of his nomination papers that were to be filled out that night. As the leader of the party, I had to sign the nomination papers of all candidates, and date of birth is one of the blanks to be filled in on the form. This is how I discovered his true age, which had been a source of some confusion. After he filled it in, I looked at him after doing the quick arithmetic. I asked how this was possible. Up to now the standard media reference had been to "75 year old broadcaster Gordon Atkinson". He chuckled and told me that whenever he's asked by a journalist how old he is, he responds "How old do you think I am ?" Whatever their response, he says "you're right". One reporter guessed 75 and it seemed to have caught on. For the record, Gordon Atkinson was born in August 1922.

Apart from N.D.G. and Westmount there were a handful of other crucial ridings where we actually had a chance to make a good showing. Robert Baldwin, Jacques Cartier and D'Arcy McGee were all within reach because of their high concentration of anglophones. D'Arcy McGee was the seat of the Jewish community. Encompassing Côte St. Luc and Hampstead, where Jewish numbers held sway in any election, it had most recently been represented by Herbert Marx and before him Victor Goldbloom; both had held senior cabinet posts under Robert Bourassa, making it all the more imperative for us to find a credible candidate in what was generally regarded as the safest Liberal seat in the province. Our attempts to find someone of matching stature came up empty. The first thing that came to mind whenever we broached the idea to any prospective candidate was that running against the hand-picked candidate of the governing Liberal party would invite ostracization by the Jewish community establishment. It was obvious that the community leadership would be backing the Liberal candidate—if not publicly, then by quietly twisting arms to maintain a Jewish Liberal in cabinet as their direct conduit to the powers-that-be.

I had believed for a long time that I would end up running in Robert Baldwin. Primarily consisting of Dollard des Ormeaux, it had a younger demographic profile with a substantial Jewish population. D'Arcy McGee, I believed, wanted an older, more established person.

It was my mother who first suggested that I consider running in D'Arcy McGee myself. She believed that I had a natural affinity with the high percentage of senior citizens in the riding — the highest percentage of any riding in Quebec — who would identify me with their many kids or grandchildren who had left the province, and appreciate that I was staying in Quebec to fight for them. As we were having trouble finding a candidate for the riding, I had suggested that Sam Goldbloom, the riding president, could do very well. But a number of riding association members privately told me that they were very much against his candidacy, and that it was crucial that D'Arcy McGee have a standard bearer who was a professional. They were also warming to the idea of my candidacy. John Kohos, who had helped start our Mount Royal association, crunched some numbers and was also convinced that my chances in D'Arcy McGee were very good.

When the Liberals had chosen their candidate, Gary Waxman, a youngish labour lawyer, and Community Relations Director at the Canadian Jewish Congress, it seemed to open the door for me to run there. Despite being the established community's hand-picked candidate, he did not fit the model of the elder statesman to which the riding elite was accustomed, and did not have a very high profile in the community. There was still much speculation that I would run against Bourassa in St. Laurent. Two days before I was to officially announce my candidacy in D'Arcy McGee, I appeared on CANADA AM and the host tried to get me to announce that I would be running against the Premier. When I was evasive, she wrapped up the interview saying, "well, that sure sounds like a yes to me". In fact, this was never a serious consideration.

My decision to run in D'Arcy McGee got the party members in the riding very excited. They knew that it would be a high profile campaign, and they were getting psyched for it. They had set up membership booths in the two shopping centres in the riding and had already signed up over 1200 members from the riding alone by the end of the summer. But on the day of the election call, Robert Baldwin was now left without a candidate. A number of our supporters in the very active riding association would have liked to run, but were not considered serious contenders. After several well-known West-Islanders had turned us down, out of the blue I received a call from Adrian Waller, a professor, author and former journalist with *The Gazette*. He told me that he had been following our exploits and might be interested in being a candidate for our party. Doug Robinson and I drove out to see him the weekend after the election was called.

His shingled house on the quiet Lakeshore seemed the classic setting for an author. Inside the house, books and papers were strewn all over the place, and the smell of tobacco from his pipe hung pungently in the air. On the coffee table, fragile-looking tea cups were quaintly arranged on a tray, along with dry cake. Adrian Waller himself looked very distinguished, spoke with a plummy British accent and waxed poetic about Canada and the language issue. He asked us about as many questions as we asked him. After minimal encouragement he agreed to run, as long as his personal cost would be minimal. We assured him that we had raised enough money to pay the lion's share of campaign expenses for most of our candidates, though they would still have to do some of their own fundraising to make up the rest. We shook hands on his porch and invited him to a meeting a few days later when all the candidates would be gathering for the photo shoots for the campaign material.

The other riding where we had a good chance was Jacques Cartier, which includes Pointe Claire and Dorval. For several weeks, dentist Bill Shaw, who was also a former MNA, had been bringing in supporters to the riding. When the executive decided to hold a nomination meeting, Shaw won hands down.

At the time I was still fighting the perception that we were a "redneck," reactionary group. Despite being fluently bilingual, married to a francophone, and quite in tune with Quebec politics, Shaw was considered by the media to be the quintessential anglo extremist and language hard-liner. He had collaborated with Lionel Albert on the book "Partition" in 1980, detailing how Quebec could be carved up if it separated from Canada. For this he was consigned to the crackpot fringe by the establishment prints, both French and English. I believed that having him run would give the media and our opponents, rightly or wrongly, a pile of ammunition with which to slag us during the campaign. I had a very long and emotional meeting with the Jacques Cartier riding executive and laid out my bottom line—that I could not authorize Shaw's candidacy. The one unassailable legal power that a leader has is the right to refuse any candidate. To run for a political party, your nomination papers must bear the leader's signature, and I refused to sign for Shaw.

I suggested Neil Cameron to the riding association as the alternative to Shaw. After Cameron lost the nomination to Atkinson in N.D.G.

I asked him to think about running in Jacques Cartier. He taught on the West Island and, therefore had something of a following in the riding. At first he was lukewarm toward the idea, since he lived in N.D.G. and did not drive a car. I encouraged him with the demographic breakdown of the riding, showing that its non francophone population was over 70%. It was not until the morning after Atkinson finally accepted the nomination in N.D.G. that Cameron agreed to run in Jacques Cartier. The next step was convincing the riding association, many of whose members were still steaming over my refusal to endorse Bill Shaw.

Cameron, who knew Shaw personally, spoke to him privately. To his credit, Shaw rallied behind Cameron and the party's cause without holding any outward grudge. With this foundation for a united front in place, it was no problem for Cameron to win over the riding association.

Now that we were positioned in the key ridings, with the largest concentrations of anglo voters, the serious campaigning could get underway.

CHAPTER FOUR
Courting the Vote

Every election is a contest between heritage and impulse,
as the verities of the past compete with the risks of the future.
—Peter C. Newman

When Robert Bourassa called the election for September 25, senior Liberals were so confident of winning the English vote that they were quoted as saying that no special election handouts were necessary to woo the anglophone community. The mainstream media and political observers were also expecting the community to vote like sheep, and conventional wisdom heartily scoffed at the prospect of a breakthrough by the Equality Party.

The day after the election was called *The Gazette* reported that the Equality Party still lacked the money, organization and volunteers to make a serious dent in any Liberal ridings. Graeme Decarie suggested that "the only choice for anglophones is to spoil their ballots. Then it would be impossible for Bourassa to say, 'See? The English are quite happy in Quebec.'" Nonetheless, he predicted that English speaking voters would vote Liberal en-masse. He said, "Like idiots they'll vote Liberal. It's disappointing. I wish they would show more gumption."

We had been able to raise funds, but were obviously outclassed on a level playing field with the two major parties. The first priority for our modest war chest was to rent and furnish local committee rooms for each of the candidates as well as the basic posters, literature and flyers. Expensive television or radio ads were well beyond our reach. To compensate for this, we were easily able to take advantage of our novelty factor in this campaign. Polls showed clearly that the Liberals were going to win the election and for the English media many of our activities were newsworthy. We capitalized on this interest with our strategy of unveiling our candidates riding by riding to maximize the party's media exposure.

We had a number of former Liberal party workers spread out throughout our associations who knew the organizational ropes, but at the core we needed direction. It was crucial to put a campaign steering committee together, and to that end I hand-picked a group of individuals I felt most comfortable with. Doug Robinson, Mort Taffert who had been a party strategist, Howard Krupp from our Robert Baldwin riding executive committee, Martin Segal from our N.D.G. riding association, my father, who was also my official agent in D'Arcy McGee, and Gerald Cooper, who became the party's treasurer, were to co-ordinate the party's financing, preparation of election material, posters, brochures, pins, etc. and to steer the campaign from the central office.

The key piece of material was a small colourful brochure highlighting the party's three policy pillars: individual rights, bilingualism and Canadian unity. There was a section where we responded to the "most commonly asked questions," taking great pains to reassure people that voting for our party would not split the vote in such a way as to help the PQ. Some 500,000 of these brochures were distributed to all our candidates who were instructed to drop them at as many doors as possible throughout their ridings. All election material was standardized except, of course, Richard Holden's. He did however use the coloured brochures.

Well into the campaign, with candidates lined up in the key ridings, I continued to meet potential candidates for other ridings where we didn't have much of a chance but nevertheless needed a standard bearer. In these ridings I felt that if it would make the riding happy to choose their own candidate, so be it, as long as the prospective standard-bearer was not an obvious disaster. Money was being collected at the grassroots level by passing the bucket around and selling memberships at local meetings, and through small-scale solicitation. Our brochures had a tear-off portion soliciting donations and we received a considerable amount in the mail this way. We also had a few women, including my mother, who were successfully raising larger contributions by telephone. But we still lacked a prominent community figure to co-ordinate a special-names fundraising initiative.

Howard Krupp put me in touch with his uncle, the owner of Brown's Shoes, Morton Brownstein. He had expressed an interest in helping us out. He was one of the merchants who fought the sign law all the way to the Supreme Court for his community. Here was someone who had paid his dues in the language wars without ever expecting anything in return except the satisfaction that what he was doing was right. Unlike some of the other plaintiffs he is perfectly bilingual and was even willing, out of respect for the French face of Quebec, to accept a compromise whereby an anglophone merchant should heed a four-to-one rule whereby the French would be four times the size of the English on a sign (in keeping with the four-to-one French-English ratio in Quebec) as long as English is not prohibited.

He was most supportive of our initiative and felt that it was very important for the community to make a statement in this election. He organized a large fundraising cocktail at a downtown hotel attended by a number of affluent members of the Jewish community. Sam Berger, the former owner of the Alouettes football team, and his son David, the federal Liberal M.P. for St. Henri-Westmount, were among those on hand. David Berger was the first elected figure to come out publicly for our party and courageously defended his actions before the media and members of his own party, pointing out that our policies on individual rights, bilingualism and Canadian unity were consistent with federal Liberal policy. He was rebuked by federal Liberal leader John Turner as was John Karygiannis, an Ontario M.P. of Greek origin, who supported Phil Chrysafidis, our candidate in Marguerite-Bourgeois.

Brownstein's initiative proved to be a windfall for our fundraising drive. The one thing he asked of the party was that we not run a candidate in Outremont. He had developed a close relationship with Liberal candidate Gerald Tremblay, a rising star in the party in whom he saw great potential both as a cabinet minister and a friend of the Jewish community. Outremont usually elects a Liberal, but not by much, and with its sizeable anglo community, an Equality candidate could well take enough votes from the Liberals to allow the PQ candidate to slip through the middle. As it turned out, had we run a candidate—and got the same percentage of the anglo vote as in other ridings, Tremblay would have lost to the PQ. Thanks to Morty Brownstein, his political career was saved.

The party had rented a large office on Royalmount. It was not a glamorous election-central of the sort that a major party would sport, but it had all the classic necessities. A large meeting room, press conference area, a couple of private offices, a waiting area and a work area. Once we got the phones plugged in and posters tacked all over the walls, it soon started humming like a typical political campaign office.

A few days after the election was called we held our first major press conference at headquarters to launch the campaign. Before a massive half-fleur-de-lys, half-maple-leaf prop that provided a striking and colourful backdrop, I introduced our executive and reiterated our party's commitment to its three policy cornerstones. I co-chaired the press conference with our new vice-president, Jean Pierre Isoré, who was doing a lot of public speaking for the party, especially in French, and therefore garnering considerable coverage in the French media. A very intelligent and intense individual, but often volatile, he was nonetheless giving our party a much needed francophone face. Jacques Renaud was still making the occasional speech at our meetings and providing me with material for my own speeches, but had assumed a much lower profile as a result of intense pressure from friends and colleagues about what they viewed as his heretical involvement with the party.

Our campaign launch was widely covered and seriously treated by the media. In the French election coverage, language was not a huge issue. There were many other items dominating the election campaign agenda, notably the Liberal government's economic performance, a nurses' strike, and the government's fumbling attempts to find a place to store PCB wastes. Our party was not perceived as resembling any threat to the Liberals, but the French media used us as a news peg for their occasional language stories.

The English media were covering us on a fairly regular basis, as the language issue was very much on the minds of the anglo community. With TV cameras now present at all our nomination meetings and press conferences, we started to look much more serious and decidedly real. The upstart *Montreal Daily News*, then taking a scrappy run at *The Gazette*'s local anglo daily print monopoly, had twigged that something was seriously afoot in the anglo community and began to cover our every move. They even had a small photo of me along with Bourassa and Parizeau at the top of their daily election coverage page. I was also given the opportunity to write a regular column during the campaign, alternating with PQ and Liberal spokesmen.

We still had problems with *The Gazette*. There were times when we felt we were not getting the coverage we deserved on some of the issues we raised or events that we organized. This caused many party workers, on their own, to call the paper to complain. Tact or subtlety was not always a governing trait with many of our party members, and this only encouraged *The Gazette* to take us even less seriously. When *The Gazette* did write about us, the coverage was often condescending or tended to belittle our efforts, leaving us wondering in frustration if we weren't better off when they just ignored us.

We may not have been the slickest or most professional of operations, but I felt that with its highbrow attitude, *The Gazette* was also belittling the convictions of most of its own readers, and, in the process, alienating itself from the grassroots of our community. The paper was duly critical of the Liberal party for the passage of Bill 178, and for generally turning its back on the anglophone community. Yet its editorial line still held that the Liberals were a more viable place than our party to park the anglophone vote. Our rhetoric and many of our political positions were considered too extreme and uncompromising. *The Gazette* still failed to see the overall significance of the protest vehicle we provided as an outlet to show the governing Liberals that our community must not be taken for granted, and at this time in history it could not have been more important for our community to make this clear.

The Gazette's coverage of our launch, for example, focused on the party's position that all Quebecers should have the right to choose the language of education for their children in either of the two official languages of Canada, and that francophones were losing out by being denied this right. Unfortunately, calling for the government to relax Bill 101 to allow everyone free choice in the language of education was obviously a political non-starter in today's Quebec. The reigning powers in the paper's editorial ivory tower therefore deemed it a preposterous suggestion.

This despite the fact that enrolment in English schools in Quebec had dropped from 250,000 in 1971 to 100,000. Bill 101, barring all immigrants from sending their children to English schools, clearly denied the community adequate opportunity to replenish itself. Moreover, polls have consistently shown that 90 per cent of the anglophone community favours a policy of freedom of choice. So when provincial affairs columnist Don Macpherson wrote in the *Gazette* that we were "fighting long-lost battles" it showed quite clearly that the English establishment media is too often blindfolded by what is politically correct or feasible in the nationalist climate of Quebec as opposed to what is morally right. Macpherson's readers would have a lot of trouble identifying with his harsh criticism of us for supporting the restoration of a freedom to all Quebecers that exists everywhere else on the planet where two educational systems operate in the same jurisdiction. Despite the unlikelihood of this policy seeing the light of day in the foreseeable future we were resolved not to lose sight of the fact that the strength of a democracy depends on the willingness of citizens to speak up for what they believe is morally right, and to back up their words with appropriate action.

A more experienced party and leader would have been greatly preoccupied with avoiding bad press, and tried to shape every statement to conform to accepted and expected norms. We, on the contrary, were just saying what we believed, and speaking from the heart, something experienced politicians would call recklessly naive, but which our target constituency fortunately found most refreshing. We were tapping into a wellspring of sentiment that many would express privately in their homes, but which they had never heard coming from a public platform.

Momentum was building and even many of the anglo hard-liners, who had been disillusioned when we moderated our position on commercial signs, were returning to the fold. Tony Kondaks had come back very apologetic about heckling public meetings a few weeks earlier, and offered to work full time on my campaign, doing numbers-crunching and polishing speeches. I welcomed him back on the promise that he would keep his dogmatic inclinations in check.

Throughout the campaign I would travel everywhere in Mort Taffert's white van with Robinson, Kondaks, my D'Arcy McGee campaign manager Sam Goldbloom, my bodyguard Danny Fry, and, on most evenings, my wife. Fry had originally been an activist with the CCQ but he started working for us when things started rolling for the party, as did their entire organization. He was a huge guy with a square jaw and moustache that said he meant business. He was a former history teacher and had been a part-time bodyguard for pop star Roch Voisine and other show-biz types.

Since the election call, the office had received numerous death threats, some targeting me personally. Despite my discomfort with the idea, my father hired Fry to be at my side at all times. We developed a close friendship and I would bounce ideas off him once in a while. He heard the same speeches over and over again during the campaign and would occasionally try to relieve the boredom by trying to break my concentration onstage. When I would look over to him at the side of the room, he'd be there mouthing the words as I spoke. He also developed a close affinity with Goldbloom. Goldbloom, who was an excellent speaker and crowd warmer, would always introduce me the same way by asking with a flourish, "Where are the youth ?," referring to the thousands who had left. He would then wheel around, point to me and say, "Here is one young man who has decided to stay and build a better Quebec." Knowing how Fry and I were so used to hearing this daily routine, Goldbloom after a while couldn't keep a straight face when he delivered the lines.

The day after our first candidate announcement—that Richard Holden would be our standard bearer in Westmount—it was my turn to be nominated in D'Arcy McGee. I was to be introduced at my nomination meeting by Jacques Renaud.

I arrived at the Centennial Park Chalet in Côte St. Luc with what I felt was an extremely emotional speech. Reading it in the van on the way to the hall, I was starting to get really revved up, and even more so when I saw the corridor leading to the hall bustling with party members

Before the 1989 vote, Robert Libman with Richard Holden and Mordecai Richler.

Election night victory. From left to right: Goldie Libman, Doug Robinson, David Libman, Robert Libman, Sam Goldbloom.

November 1989. At the National Assembly, sworn in as an MNA with theLibman family in the background.

The four Equality Party MNAs just after taking the oath of office, From left to right: Richard Holden, Robert Libman, Gordon Atkinson, Neil Cameron.(Photo: Marc Lajoie)

Summer of 1990, sitting in front of the microphone at CHRC radio in New Carlisle, where René Lévesque began his career.

Summer 1990, with Cree Chief Billy Diamond, fishing the Rupert River near James Bay.

An official portrait of Robert Libman with Michel Bélanger and Jean Campeau, co-chairs of the Commission on the future of Quebec, now opponents during the 1995 referendum.

Spring 1994. A world away from Quebec politics, with Nobel Peace Prize laureate and acclaimed writer Elie Wiesel.

eagerly anticipating my arrival. The hall itself was jammed to capacity. When I walked in everyone jumped to their feet waving "Libman" placards and chanting my name. These are the precious moments, the reward in politics, when you get swept up in the heady enthusiasm of a cheering crowd and the adrenal sense what it is to have power. Politics is often a thankless occupation. The pace is grueling, the hours are long, the sacrifices to be made are many and a lot of garbage get heaped on your head. But any regrets, any doubts, are washed away in the sheer glory of moments like this.

The powerful image that being introduced by a prominent francophone like Jacques Renaud projected; the media presence, the overflow crowd, the banners, the posters, the balloons, all gave the evening a perfect savour. There were people in the crowd of all ages. My speech hit the proper notes. I argued that the Jewish community had always been a barometer of human rights violations, which was precisely why this riding, which was predominantly Jewish, must lead the way in this election.

Even an impartial observer in the crowd that evening would have concluded that I might actually stand a chance of winning the riding. I was whisked into the van afterward to go to another meeting, and in the van I asked for the first time whether anyone really thought I could win. The answer from everyone except Robinson was unanimous. "You're damned right." Robinson warned about getting cocky, reminding everyone that the campaign had started just a week ago.

The night after the D'Arcy McGee meeting we introduced our candidate for Chomedey riding, Jean Paul Barbucci, whom I had met only a few days before. The local riding association was very high on him because he was half-francophone and perfectly bilingual, and had been very active on the local municipal scene. That evening, however, he seemed to take our bilingualism message far too literally. Throughout his speech, he would deliver his lines in both English and French, often switching to one language in mid-sentence to repeat what he had just said in the other. The French media happened to be well represented that evening and had a bit of a field day with his presentation. La Presse, calling it grotesque, quoted the following extract from his speech: "J'ai déjà été engagé gratuitement, free, pour un parti politique, for a political party... Quand on m'a approché, j'ai dit pourquoi pas moi? Why not me?"

This was an example of the potential pitfalls with a slate consisting mostly of inexperienced candidates. Discipline among the candidates was definitely a problem, and something I would have to broach carefully with this group of individually-minded people, most of whom I barely knew. But what mistakes they made mostly stemmed from an excess of honesty, and given the temper of the times, this worked in our favor to some extent. There was so much disdain for the governing Liberals at the time, along with a growing disenchantment with established politicians of any stripe, that a group of ordinary people running a very grassroots-type movement such as ours was widely perceived as a welcome alternative to the slick machinations of the mainstream parties. Nor was this sentiment restricted to Quebec's anglo community. Out west, at the same time, the rough-hewn Reform Party was tapping into the same motherlode of voter disenchantment with establishment politicians of all stripes to become a new force on the federal scene.

As the campaign wore on, we were starting to make noticeable progress in the polls, primarily among anglo voters. Talk began about a debate between Premier Bourassa and PQ leader Jacques Parizeau. When the subject of an English debate was raised, the major media outlets were calling for my participation, much to my surprise. This gave us a solid credibility boost, especially when a Saturday *Gazette* editorial on the subject said that "the Equality Party is emerging as one of the few strong voices for linguistic equity in Quebec," and that "Premier Bourassa has largely disqualified himself as an interpreter or representative of the concerns of a large part of the English community." This was quite unexpected coming from The *Gazette*. Being given such a platform would be a tremendous opportunity for the party, though I admit I was daunted by the prospect of going up against two of the most experienced and erudite politicians in recent Quebec history.

The following Monday I was invited to a meeting atop the Maison Radio Canada in east end Montreal with the producer of NEWSWATCH, Roch Magnan, and Mike Donegan and Bob Bennedetti from PULSE news. Robinson and I expressed our eagerness to participate in the televised English debate without really putting any conditions on the table, so awestruck were we to even be considered at this stage. But in the end the debate went down the drain as the Liberals and PQ were never able to agree on a format, allowing me to breathe a secret sigh of relief, even as I publicly denounced them as cowards.

Another development in the first few weeks of the campaign was an announcement by Alliance Quebec that anglophones should not vote for either the Liberals or PQ. And while they never came out and said vote Equality, most analysts perceived it, rightly or wrongly, as an indirect endorsement of the party.

Alliance Quebec founding stalwarts like Michael Goldbloom, Eric Maldoff, Alex Paterson and Royal Orr probably choked on their corn flakes when reading about the Alliance's recommendation in the newspapers. They were acutely uncomfortable with the prospect of our party making a big dent in the anglo vote, which would amount to a defeat for the strategy of muted rapprochement with the nationalists and their cozy relationship with the Liberals. So many former AQ officers or employees had gone on to run as Liberal candidates that it was becoming known among cynics as the Liberal party's anglo farm team.

The bold Alliance announcement was possible only because Peter Blaikie and Graeme Decarie were minding the store between Alliance presidents. Peter Blaikie is a rare anglo with candour who is widely respected by the community establishment. As unpredictable as he is overpowering, he doesn't give a hoot about offending the Liberal party or the anglo establishment when he feels like it. What the rest of the community establishment had to realize was that this election was different from all the others. Any attempt to work quietly within the Liberal party had been proven a sham by Bill 178. Bridge-building can only work if both sides show a will to co-operate. Instead, the Liberals had blown up the bridge, and if the anglo community were to vote for the Liberals despite what they had done, our community would be exposed as a spineless laughing stock.

The strategy of unveiling candidates one at a time, practically every evening, was working splendidly. It was easy to co-ordinate and generated the free publicity we so badly needed. Each riding association could, at this stage, easily fill a room with more than 100 people, and a news release was was always sent out a day before, inviting the media.

Philip Chrysafidis was announced as our candidate in Marguerite-Bourgeoys (LaSalle) at a meeting attended by a significant representation from many cultural community groups. In St. Laurent, Ciro Paul Scotti was introduced as the candidate. And while the riding executive had resigned when we confirmed that Scotti would run, they relented a week later, citing the party's overall mission as being more important than any other consideration.

Gerry Klein was starting to feel a little squeezed out by this point. In an election, the candidates get most of the attention while party officials fade into the background. As party president he felt that he should be given much more prominence, despite the importance of showcasing our candidates. His reason for not wanting to run himself was his inability to speak French, but he wanted to play a major role in the St. Laurent campaign, where his friend Scotti was the candidate, and insisted on being the keynote speaker at the nomination meeting. In his speech that night, he went to great lengths about how in South Africa discrimination based on race is called "racism," whereas in Quebec, discrimination is based on language, and should thus be called "linguis-

ticism". This speech naturally got us raked over the coals by the media
the next day as we were accused of comparing Quebec's language laws
to apartheid in South Africa. Raphael Chalkoun, our French-language
communications director, threatened to quit over Klein's remarks.

I had no choice but to distance myself from Klein's statements and
to suggest that instead of making public speeches for the rest of the
campaign, he should concentrate on administrative matters and research
on the Meech Lake accord. This angered Klein to no end and marked the
beginning of a deterioration in our personal relationship, as well as his
enthusiasm for the party. Throughout the campaign he would complain
about being left out in the cold, and the more he tried to impose himself,
the more tension he created within the party, alienating many of the rank
and file who were too busy to indulge bruised egos. There were some in
the party who were righteously fired up by Klein's speech and felt that
South Africa-type rhetoric was the kind of thing the party should es-
pouse more avidly, and a number of them quit the party in a huff when
I publicly disavowed Klein's remarks. Not because there was nothing to
be said for the concept of "linguisticism," but because the parallel to
South Africa had nothing to do with daily life in Quebec.

The St. Laurent nomination meeting was also marked by an attempt to crash the event by the leader of the fringe-separatist Parti
Indépendantiste, Gilles Rhéaume. He was the nationalist language
zealot, and former president of the venerable Société St. Jean Baptiste,
who once tried to urinate on Wolfe's statue in the middle of the winter,
but experienced difficulty completing his "statement" due to the extreme
cold weather that day. Rhéaume and his small group were barred from
the meeting room and eventually escorted out of the building by the
police.

We were successful in recruiting immigration adjudicator and
longtime Liberal Richard Lord to run for us in the riding of St. Anne. As
a well known activist in the black community, his candidacy clearly
improved the image of our party as one which could now rightfully
claim to be the only one to represent such a wide cross section of minority
community groups with its slate of candidates.

During the week before Labour Day we held a massive rally on the
West Island to unveil our three candidates. The grand ballroom of the
Holiday Inn Pointe Claire was full, and having to open two additional
partitions to hold everyone made for great TV. Waller was introduced
as the Robert Baldwin candidate, Cameron in Jacques Cartier and Jean
Pierre Isoré in Nelligan. We spoke that night of riding a wave to victory
and of how the Liberal party had betrayed the anglophone community's
attempts to be full participants in Quebec society. A number of our

candidates and party volunteers were on hand from many different ridings that evening and all left more fully inspired than ever before to take the campaign down to the wire.

Jean Pierre Isoré lived in Mount Royal and had helped build our Mount Royal riding association. Yet, despite my urgings to run in the riding, with its large anglo and allophone population, he was convinced by the president of our Nelligan riding association, Joanne Iacono, with whom he had become very close friends, to run in Nelligan, which takes in Kirkland, Beaconsfield, and St. Genevieve. The riding is majority francophone, and its riding executive felt that it should be represented by a francophone candidate despite the long odds against Isoré. We also had francophone candidates in Verdun (Roger Mercure) and in Groulx (June Paquette-Vernham). In the downtown riding of St. Louis, we had engineer José DiBona; Rudolph Neumayer in Deux-Montagnes; Bruce Calder in Marquette, which encompasses the city of Lachine; and Peter Vernham, facing off against Claude Ryan in Argenteuil.

It was felt by many Italian members of the party that the St. Leonard area, where there is a large Italian community, should have the opportunity to vote for our party's message. David DeSantis therefore ran in the riding of Viger and Tony Cipriani, the son of my landlord, ran in the Jeanne Mance riding.

Labor Day was a landmark date in the campaign, beyond which loomed the home stretch. On that day, we held a major press conference at the Ruby Foo's Hotel in Mount Royal riding with all of the 18 candidates we had chosen thus far. But we were still missing a candidate for Mount Royal itself, where it was imperative to find someone to challenge John Ciaccia, the only anglo minister who did not resign over Bill 178. With only a few days before the nomination deadline, our leading prospects were still reluctant to commit.

At that press conference we went to great pains to explain why our party was not a threat to split the vote to the extent that it would elect the PQ. Gordon Atkinson was among the speakers and toward the end of his standard barn-burning number, he got a little more carried away than usual. With his arm pointed in my direction, he boldly referred to me as the Lech Walesa of Quebec. I was caught by surprise and shrugged it off by claiming that I didn't even speak Polish. Needless to say, it got us lampooned in the media, and the dubious honor of being caricatured for the first time in an Aislin cartoon on *The Gazette*'s editorial page; Bernie St. Laurent calls me Lech to this day.

Labor Day weekend saw the release of the first serious poll of the campaign. It was conducted by the highly respected Sorecom polling firm, and to our great delight—and considerable amazement—it showed

Equality ahead of the Liberals in support among decided anglophone voters, with a 45-40 per cent margin. This set off shock waves in the media and got us much greater coverage. It also prompted a number of stories about the growing concern among anglo Liberal candidates and how the Liberal party was rethinking its earlier decision not to woo anglo voters with any special election goodies. But the more the Liberals would turn on the charm or hold out more promises to the community in exchange for its support, the more it worked in our favour. It proved that the more our community expressed its independence and firmness the more the governing Liberals would listen. It served to drive home our message that the government will listen to us only if we show that we cannot be taken for granted.

In D'Arcy McGee the campaign continued to go very well despite my numerous commitments in other ridings. I had a committee room in the "shmall," which is the affectionate nickname for the Cavendish Mall in Cote St. Luc. My opponent's office was two floors below. Gloria Freedman and my mother were coordinating the day to day operations of the office, which was constantly buzzing with volunteers milling about. This being my first election, I knew very little about the mechanics of a local campaign, but fortunately enough we had a large number of former D'Arcy McGee Liberals onside who were familiar with the stand-ard election-time drill.

I had a calendar on the wall which was filled with speaking engagements at the local synagogues, churches, seniors' residences and apartment buildings, as well as a schedule for door-to-door canvassing and community events at which it was imperative to make an appear-ance. Much to the chagrin of my organizers who felt I was wasting my time, I also spoke at several elementary schools, invited by teachers who wanted to spark their students' interest in the upcoming election through first-hand contact with an actual politician. My organizers changed their tune quickly after seeing the number of people I bumped into who said their little boy or girl told them they had to vote for that nice Robert Libman, who had come to see them that morning and given them a campaign pin.

Despite some concern that I was spreading myself too thin by spending so much time in other ridings, as leader of the party I was benefitting from exposure that no local candidate could ever expect. I was now recognized wherever I went in the riding, and getting very positive vibes about my chances. Yet every time I stopped for a minute to think about it, the prospect that I could actually be elected to the Quebec National Assembly just didn't seem real. It was strange seeing myself on the evening newscasts almost daily and reading about myself in every morning's papers. I would get the feeling that they were talking about a whole different person.

Gary Waxman, my Liberal opponent in D'Arcy McGee, was very capable and knowledgeable on the issues. However, when he was chosen to run in the surest Liberal seat in Quebec, he never expected a real contest, nor did he anticipate the vitriolic reaction he would encounter. As a result he constantly appeared nervous and ill at ease during the several debates organized by community groups in the riding. His campaign was based on the need to work for change from within the governing party as the only way for the community to get due consideration from the government.

Our first public debate, took place in the same Centennial Park Chalet where I was nominated a few weeks earlier, and once again it was packed to the rafters. Before I arrived, a fight almost broke out between my supporters and the Liberals over whether partisan banners would be allowed in the hall. The organizers decided against it. Besides Gary Waxman, the PQ candidate Jacques Carraire—a student who was running his threadbare campaign out of a basement—and Graeme Decarie were on the panel of speakers. Decarie was there to present the Alliance Quebec view that the Liberals did not deserve the anglo community's support.

Waxman got a rough ride from a crowd that was largely in my favour. It was easy to rip into his "working-from-within" arguments, pointing out how the likes of Herbert Marx, Clifford Lincoln and Richard French all had to resign because the Liberal party had spurned their best efforts to play the establishment game. When he spoke of safeguarding our community institutions by voting Liberal it smacked of blackmail and he was booed and heckled, which badly rattled him. I stuck to our central themes of how our community desperately needed politicians who could speak up for our community without a muzzle, and how voting for "Bourassa's candidates— Bourassa's puppets" as I called them—would send the signal that our community will always be compliant. All our candidates were instructed never to refer to our opponents by name, but always as "Bourassa's candidate" since he was so despised by our community. Anglo Liberal candidates themselves downplayed, or even eliminated, references to their leader in their campaign literature.

Though Waxman knew some of the issues better than I did, he came away from the debate as the clear loser and suddenly became deeply concerned about the possibility that D'Arcy McGee might break with its tradition of always voting Liberal. I was still very cautious. Despite a surge of optimism among our supporters after that evening, I was still not convinced that our community would actually have the guts to vote for me. Once they were in the ballot box, would they really foresake the Liberals to vote for such an inexperienced and unknown kid?

The next day would be my most difficult test. I had been invited for an interview with the editorial board of *The Gazette*. That morning I had been rigorously grilled with possible questions by Holden, Robinson and Kondaks. The strategy was to always veer back to the party's cornerstone policy positions and hope not to be drawn into issues that I did not know very well. We were hoping that the resultant story in the paper would focus on how important it is for our community to have alternative representation in the National Assembly, and that none of the ridings where we were running were likely to go PQ because of a split anglo vote.

I attended the interview with Doug Robinson. It was the first of a series of meetings the board was to have with the leaders of the three major parties, and eight or so of the paper's editors and political writers were on hand to grill me. The atmosphere was stiffly formal. I felt ill at ease throughout, and at times somewhat out of my league. I was not completely familiar with the Meech Lake Accord at the time, and it became an important topic of conversation. The meeting was interrupted by the arrival of Joan Fraser, the editorial page editor, who sat down and took the floor with the following question: "Mr. Libman, how could your party expect to be taken seriously when you can compare Quebec to South Africa ?" My heart sank.

I don't believe I scored many points that day, and after reading about the interview in the paper the next morning, it seemed as though there was a clear intent to set us up. What turned out to be the sticking point, and what was played up the next day, was a cynical manipulation of our party's position on bilingual services in the public sector. Reporter Alexander Norris wrote a front page story that implied that our party was less committed to providing health services in English than the Liberal government's Bill 142 supposedly provided. Our party platform guaranteed bilingual services in the public sector throughout the province "where numbers warrant." Though never fully implemented, the Liberal's Bill 142 provided for the availability of English language health and social services throughout the province, with no stipulation about numbers. *The Gazette* therefore jumped on this, and its front page headline the next day proclaimed: "Equality wants English services only "where numbers warrant.'"

The article also dwelled on how we lacked policies on many other issues, and how I refused to elaborate, saying only that many policy issues would be worked out eventually.

Norris had collared me after the interview and wouldn't leave me alone unless I told him our position on abortion. To get him off my back, I offered what I stipulated was my personal opinion only, and on condition that it be off the record. The next morning, there it was int The *Gazette*. Also after the interview, national editor Jennifer Robinson wanted to know why Richard Holden would want to run for us. If he was just doing this on a lark, was he now worried that people were predicting that he might actually win? I walked out of there with the definite impression that The *Gazette* held neither myself nor the Equality Party in any great esteem.

With only two weeks left before election day, we had to submit all nomination papers for our candidates. All our leads for a candidate in Mount Royal had come to nothing, so now we had 24 hours to find not only a candidate, but also 100 people in the riding to sign the nomination papers.

Nat Bernstein, the popular president of a large synagogue in St. Laurent had been a solid supporter and he volunteered to be what he himself called the sacrificial lamb. But by then we had no other choice. We had to have someone to go up against Ciaccia for his spineless compliance with Bill 178. We managed to get Bernstein's papers filled out by the official deadline and headed into the stretch with 19 candidates.

Polls continued to show our party with strong support among the anglophone voters. This prompted the Premier to turn on the charm and start addressing anglo voters much more frequently in the campaign. First he praised the community for making "remarkable progress integrating into the new reality of Quebec." When this was widely dismissed as figuratively patting the anglos on the head, Bourassa began to get defensive and fell back on the old scare tactic of warning that a vote against the Liberal party was a vote for the PQ.

My Liberal opponent tried the same thing during a televised debate on the McKenty Live television show. He warned that the Liberal party had won 57 seats with a margin of 2,000 votes or less in the last election, when the true number was only 17. At an all-candidates debate that evening I accused him of lying and fear-mongering. There were a number of all-candidates debates throughout the West Island where the Liberals were desperately trying to stem the wave of momentum in our favour with the same argument, but to no avail. When Liberal candidates like Joan Dougherty warned anglophones not to "hurt themselves" by voting Equality, they were often met with derision by crowds who were growing increasingly scornful of the Liberal party. I knew at this point that we would do a lot better than anyone had expected. With a week to go I was starting to believe for the first time that unless we made a major blunder, we actually had a chance to win a seat or two.

My first reaction, when I picked up *The Gazette* a week before the election, was that my fear had come true. On the front page was a story about the Revenue Department pursuing Richard Holden through the courts for a bundle of unpaid taxes. That afternoon, Holden and I were to appear at a press conference to unveil a series of statements about a whole range of issues. The idea was to defuse some of the criticism of us as a "one issue party". But the only issue the media wanted to address that day was Holden's tax problem. Outwardly unabashed, Holden responded like a real political pro, waxing indignant about how the Liberals were so concerned about losing the Westmount seat that they planted private information with the media. Because he was English, he continued, the francophone bureaucrats in the tax department were out to nail him with questionable claims. He later joked that in a riding like Westmount, where people who have it know the value of money, he could get a significant sympathy vote for his troubles with the taxman. Holden's response turned the tables on the Liberals, who became defensive and began adamantly denying any involvement. However, for an untrusting anglo electorate, it fuelled their cynicism toward the Liberals.

In the last week the party was getting heavy media coverage as we were becoming the story to watch in a campaign whose other major imponderable was whether the Liberals would win 90-plus seats like the last time, or slide into the 80s; in either case, they would have a comfortable majority of the National Assembly's 125 seats. Amid all the attention, I was starting to worry that we might be peaking too soon and that the momentum could fizzle out in the last few days. I was reassured when the banner headline in *The Gazette* on the Saturday before the election announced, "53% of anglos support Equality: poll." We could not have got a better headline had we written it ourselves. Anglophones still nervous about breaking from tradition and supporting our party now had a bandwagon on which they could jump. The question remained as to whether the sobering confines of the voting booth would give them cold feet. I was gratified that *The Gazette* editorial that weekend also urged my personal election in D'Arcy McGee.

On the last day of the campaign, we held a multi-vehicle parade through the streets of D'Arcy McGee. The atmosphere was electric. Sitting on the back of a red convertible, my wife and I felt intensely positive vibes from the upraised thumbs and spontaneous cheers along the route. We wound up in the committee room afterward with a training session for all the volunteers and poll captains, followed by a reception to thank them for all their hard work. It was an emotional moment as we all wished each other good luck for the next day. We had done all that we could, and it was now in the hands of the voters. That evening I called all our candidates to offer a final word of encouragement.

On election day morning my wife and I were picked up early by Sam Goldbloom and Danny Fry. I had several troublesome death threats over the past few days, so Fry recruited two other burly campaign volunteers for the security detail that day. Harold Cummings had offered us a rental car for the day, and we set out on a tour of the 200-odd polling stations in D'Arcy McGee to shake hands with the scrutineers and returning officers. That night I was to watch the results at Goldbloom's house and then make my way over to the committee room and then on to the Buffet Crystal in St. Laurent where what we hoped would be our victory celebration was to take place.

After our tour of the polling stations, I arrived at the committee room at about 4:00 pm and sat down with Kondaks to go over the two speeches, one for victory and one for defeat, we had prepared for later that night. We could not agree on whether in case of a big victory, I would invoke René Lévesque's memory by repeating his famous line when he won the election in 1976. On that fateful evening he said that he had never been so proud to be a Quebecer. Our idea was to add, "and a Canadian." We decided to let the actual moment determine whether I'd go for it or not. At 6:30, it was time to head over to Goldbloom's place. My wife and parents would stay at the committee room and I would meet there later.

I left with Robinson for Goldbloom's house. As we were entering the elevator I asked him what he thought. "It's in the bag," he said confidently. This was the first time he had ever shown emotion of any sort or had gone out on any kind of limb in terms of predictions. I told him I didn't think so. It still seemed too unrealistic.

This was the first time during the whole campaign that I actually started to get butterflies in my stomach. Every Monday evening, a brief surge of nervousness would come over me as I ticked off one less week before election day. But nothing compared to what I was feeling now. Every meeting, every speech, every interview of the past year had all led up to tonight. I had thought all along that our sole intent was to make a ripple and send a message. And while we had certainly done that with our spirited participation in the campaign, it suddenly felt as though everything was riding on this evening's result.

At that moment, I had no interest in being with anyone, not even my wife or any other members of my family. An extraordinary sense of loneliness came over me, but I wouldn't have wanted it any other way.

It was all out of my hands now. There was nothing more to do that could earn me one more vote. Having to sit there, helplessly watching the results on TV was a form of exquisite torture.

At eight o'clock the television coverage began. We were switching back and forth between NEWSWATCH and PULSE. My heart jumped when at the bottom of the screen the category called "other" started showing numbers. The anchor desks started buzzing with talk that the Equality Party seemed to be making a major breakthrough in the West Island.

When the first counts came in, Atkinson, Holden, Waller and Cameron, as well as our candidate Scotti, running against Bourassa in St. Laurent, were all leading by small margins. Still no word from D'Arcy McGee. Then, at about 8:30, they flashed a partial tally from D'Arcy McGee showing me leading almost two-to-one. It all happened so suddenly that it took several seconds to sink in that I was headed for election.

All our expectations were being surpassed. Once the formality of projecting the expected Liberal majority had been dealt with, all the newscasts began focusing on the story of the evening, which was none other than the Equality Party. I couldn't help but laugh as the telecast went to remotes at our election headquarters where excitement among our supporters was approaching delirium. The anchor desks had first projected a victory for Atkinson in N.D.G. PULSE News switched to Atkinson's headquarters where bagpipers were filling the air with good cheer. I was next to be confirmed victorious in D'Arcy McGee, prompting Brian Britt of PULSE News to announce that "Lech and his dad are going to Quebec City."

At about 9:00 pm I left to make my appearance at the D'Arcy McGee committee room to greet our volunteers. As the car pulled up to the mall we noticed a throng outside the doors. CJAD was now projecting an Equality victory in four ridings with a possibility of five. I was surrounded by the three bodyguards who ushered me into the elevator past dozens of people who rushed to the ground floor as word spread that I was in the building. As the elevator door opened on the fifth floor, pandemonium erupted and I was engulfed in a crush of TV cameras and microphones. A path was cleared so my wife could get to me.

We walked into the small committee room where people were packed in like canned sardines. Microphones were being thrust in my face from every conceivable angle. The warmth and enthusiasm exuded by all the workers and supporters was overwhelming. I thanked them all, but before I could quite finish I found myself having to respond to the clamoring media horde.

I told the reporters on hand that in my speech later that evening I would be stressing the importance of all communities working together to find a balance between the protection and promotion of the French language and the respect of everyone's civil rights. I declared that Premier Bourassa would never again trample on fundamental rights, and that our community had shown it would never again let itself be taken for granted.

That said, and while still waving to the chanting crowd, I was swept out the door, back into the elevator and then out to the car. We were now headed to Election Central at the Buffet Crystal where party members from all our ridings were gathering. But even then I still had no idea of what to expect when I got there.

There was the same emotionally-charged aura of anticipation around the entrance of the Buffet Crystal. Again I was whisked in, this time with my wife in tow, by the three bodyguards. I was escorted to the large doors at the side of the grand hall, and could hear Gordon Atkinson's voice booming over the public address system. Then I heard him say: "Robert is in the building." A roar went up and I was propelled forward by a surging mass of people. I wasn't even moving my feet. It was like riding the rapids in a canoe, being swept along, not altogether sure where the white water would take me.

The noise was deafening. All I remember is being flung upward and landing on a raised platform, crowded with familiar faces and a podium sprouting a thicket of microphones. Below was a grand ball-room, overflowing with a heaving sea of people. I came face to face with Gordon Atkinson and we hugged each other like World Series winners. He whispered in my ear: "We're off to Quebec City, Lech." I then turned to face the crowd, which was going berserk by now. People started chanting, "Four more years — Four more years." As I tried to speak they roared even louder.

The crowd finally settled down enough for me to be heard, and right then I couldn't resist going with the René Lévesque quote from 1976. I felt that this moment of anglo pride was significant enough in the context of our community's history that francophone Quebecers should be made to recognize it. The way to pull this emotional trigger was to go to the source of pride for many francophones, René Lévesque, though subtly and with a twist. I said that I had never been so proud to be a Quebecer—and a Canadian—as I was that night. First in English and then in French. The loaded phrase struck a powerful chord. It brought the house down that night, though I was scolded for it in the French press the next day. I went on for another 10 minutes, with every sentence drawing a roar from the crowd.

It was one of those very rare moments, however fleeting, when you feel on top of the world and that absolutely no one could knock you down. As far as I was concerned, there wasn't a worry in the world that night. It all seemed so easy. I even suggested that "if the Equality Party could achieve so much in a few months, imagine what we could do in four years". But even with the roar of the crowd ringing in my ears, I felt strangely detached from the whole frenzied scene. Part of me still wasn't quite convinced that all this was real.

By the end of the evening we had won four seats—D'Arcy McGee, Westmount, N.D.G. and Jacques Cartier, and came very close in Robert Baldwin. We finished second in five ridings. We had garnered close to 130,000 votes, and the Unity Party had amassed another 30,000. It seemed somehow much too good to be true.

But it wouldn't take long for the full force of reality to start setting in.

CHAPTER FIVE
Coping With Success

The problems of victory
are more agreeable than those of defeat,
but they are no less difficult.
—Winston Churchill

On the morning after election day I woke up just before my alarm went off, after barely three hours of sleep. Amid the giddy euphoria at the Buffet Crystal the night before, I had agreed to do an early-morning radio interview at the CBC building.

Looking into the mirror with shaving cream on my face, I saw the same person I saw every morning. My job at Tolchinsky and Goodz came to mind, and it occurred to me for the first time that I had been thrust into a new career. The old one, the career I loved, had trained for and had just got down to practicing, would have to be put on indefinite hold. After last night, I was no longer the architect I knew, but a full-time politician, a profession I had so often scorned.

At this moment, I realized little of the significance of what had transpired and was blissfully unaware of what awaited me. With no training and the barest of experience, I was about to jump feet first into a very public and very serious world that for me was mostly foreign terrain. As it all started to gradually sink in, I grew increasingly uneasy. My wife, who woke up as I was getting ready to leave the house, seemed equally oblivious to how our lives had been altered. We talked about routine things, much like every morning, as if nothing had changed.

Apart from this morning interview, I had nothing else planned. I anticipated a fairly quiet day during which I could start dismantling the committee room and to get some badly needed rest.

I picked up Danny Fry on my way to the CBC studio and he told me that the Equality Party was the lead news story on all the English radio broadcasts, and that he had never heard so many good things said about the party. I had The *Gazette* in the back seat, rolled up and still unread, so I pulled over to the side of the road for a few moments to have a look at it. Under a big headline declaring: "Libman triumphs" was a large photo of me hugging my wife. The accompanying story included virtually all the quotes we had hoped to see in print. It recounted how my committee room had been a joyous mob scene, and confirmed that we had been THE big election night story. Danny Fry pounded me on the back and said, "We did it, boy."

When we arrived at the CBC building, it was in full post-election bustle. As we were led through the halls to the studio, several people approached me to offer congratulations, which I found somewhat surprising. As we were waiting to go into the radio interview, a CBC TV reporter grabbed me and asked if I could stick around afterward to do a short interview. I agreed, though I felt uneasy about going on TV unprepared, never mind wearing a casual shirt with a checkered blazer.

On my way out of that interview I was met by more cameras and CBC reporters asking me if I would tape interviews for the six o'clock news in both English and French, and a few other short items. More than two hours after my arrival, I finally got out of the building, only to encounter another scrum of reporters outside the CBC building. I recall asking Danny afterward where on earth they all came from and how did they know to find me here ?

I had to deal with this onslaught of reporters before I had even had a proper chance to fully size up what had happened or to consult advisers and the other members of our newly elected caucus on our media spin. I couldn't figure out why they were there in the first place since they'd been all over me the night before. An experienced politician would normally hold off the media for at least a few hours by announcing a formal press conference later in the day. Not knowing what to expect, I had walked into a media feeding frenzy. Fortunately, most were so taken by the novelty of our achievement that I could do no wrong that day.

I tried to reassure those who were terrified that the turn of events in this election might poison relations between French and English Quebec that they could relax, that this one didn't even rate a Valium compared to 1976. I emphasized that the anglophone community had shown that it could no longer be counted on to take violations of its rights lying down. But I also stressed the importance of forging links between the two linguistic camps.

When I finally arrived at the committee room just before noon, Gloria Freedman was running around in a panic trying to deal with a restive pack of about a dozen reporters waiting for me to show up. Lights blazed and cameras rolled when I walked in. On my desk was a daunting pile of messages from yet more journalists. There were requests for interviews from at least five other Canadian provinces and from papers as far afield as the *Chicago Tribune* and *The Detroit Free Press*. On a wall in my office, someone had stuck up *The Gazette* headline from that morning, as well as the *Toronto Sun's* front page with a headline that said: "Anglos jolt Bourassa."

I managed to juggle interviews with four reporters at a time, while being constantly interrupted by well-wishers who came by to congratulate me.

The French-language press blossomed with editorials and analysis about the anglophone vote. Until now the French media had failed to appreciate the insult to anglophones that Bill 178 represented, and no francophone opinion leaders had denounced the law for its discouraging impact on the anglo community. This election made them pay attention. As such, the party had achieved its initial objective of sending that very important message to all of Quebec society that the language laws trampled individual rights and insulted anglophone Quebecers.

In the late afternoon, as things began to calm down, I just sat at my desk for about 20 minutes doing absolutely nothing. I had dozens of phone messages and dozens of other calls I wanted to make, but I just didn't know where to start. I hadn't even had a chance to speak to any of the other candidates or elected MNAs. But by then I just wanted to go home and relax a little, and analyze the election results without anyone breathing down my neck.

There was an obvious and remarkably consistent correlation between the demographic breakdown of the ridings and our success in those ridings. The higher the percentage of anglophones in a riding, the greater our percentage of the vote. According to a demographic analysis of the election results by Pierre Drouilly, a Université du Québec sociologist, the party's share of the anglo vote approached 70 per cent in all ridings where we ran a candidate, a proportion he called "massive" in a *Le Devoir* article. Our share of the allophone vote was close to 15 per cent. He also noted significant support for the Unity Party among anglo voters in rural ridings, though it failed to win a seat. Its insurmountable obstacle was that there were simply not enough anglophones to swing the outcome in the ridings the party contested. (See Table 1)

TABLE 1:   Equality Party Candidates and their results

RIDING	CANDIDATE		VOTE		LANGUAGE		
		E.P.	Lib.	Diff.	French	English	(Other)
1. D'ARCY McGEE	Robert Libman	58%	35%	+6,069	15%	58%	27%
2. N.D.G.	Gordon Atkinson	43%	35%	+2,090	22%	55%	23%
3. JACQUES CARTIER	Neil Cameron	44%	41%	+802	26%	63%	11%
4. WESTMOUNT	Richard Holden	41%	38%	+513	31%	48%	21%
5. ROBERT BALDWIN	Adrian Waller	41%	46%	1,384	32%	49%	19%
6. NELLIGAN	Jean Pierre Isoré	30%	47%	6,035	46%	42%	13%
7. MT. ROYAL	Nat Bernstein	28%	53%	5,165	33%	31%	36%
8. ST. LAURENT	Ciro Paul Scotti	24%	52%	8,392	45%	25%	30%
9. MARGUERITE-							
BOURGEOYS	Phillip Chrysafidis	24%	50%	6,551	46%	31%	23%
10. VERDUN	Roger Mercure	23%	39%	3,438	63%	32%	5%
11. CHOMEDEY	Jean Paul Barbucci	19%	53%	11,006	55%	19%	26%
12. ST. LOUIS	José DiBona	17%	41%	5,219	50%	26%	24%
13. MARQUETTE	Bruce Calder	17%	49%	8,695	65%	26%	9%
14. ARGENTEUIL	Peter Vernham	15%	52%	10,135	82%	16%	2%
15. ST.-ANNE	Richard Lord	14%	41%	6,032	68%	25%	8%
16. 2 MOUNTAINS	Rudolph Neumayer	7%	46%	13,207	89%	9%	2%
17. JEANNE MANCE	Tony Cipriani	7%	65%	15,366	56%	5%	39%
18. VIGER	David DeSantis	7%	61%	15,016	64%	7%	29%
19. GROULX	June Paquette Vernham	4%	48%	15,595	89%	6%	5%

Note: 5-9   Finished second
          10-19   Finished third

* primarily yiddish but most respondents identify with the anglophone community

The next morning I got a call at home from Herbert Marx, the former justice minister and my Liberal predecessor in D'Arcy McGee. I was somewhat taken aback as he congratulated me and invited me to his house a few days later to discuss the riding and my new career

I finally had a chance to call Atkinson, Holden and Cameron, all of whom had been through a hectic post-election day in their respective ways. Holden had held court at his favourite watering hole, entertaining journalists and cronies amid copious liquid indulgence. Atkinson did a string of interviews from his committee room, and Cameron diligently went to teach his morning class at John Abbott, where he got a standing ovation from his students. We arranged to hold our first caucus meeting later that week.

I went in to the party's central office with my pile of messages from the day before, only to find another stack of phone messages and telegrams waiting for me. It was another day filled with interviews. A *Gazette* reporter followed me around for most of the day, which included a visit to my office at Tolchinsky and Goodz. Since the National Assembly would not be in session until the end of November, I had arranged to come back to work for several weeks to close up the projects I had been working on. I was warmly applauded and gently teased when I walked into the office. Being escorted by a bodyguard was a little much for my architectural colleagues.

Murray Goodz called me into his office. Though his partner had been complaining about the amount of time I was spending on the phone, he told me that Tolchinsky had finally confided to him that it had been worth it. We arranged that I would be back at work the following Monday.

Wherever I went these days, people were recognizing and congratulating me. It was a new and exciting experience, and I saw how readily a naive ego could become inflated under the circumstances. It was easy to get caught up in it all to the point of feeling invincible. The prospect of building the party into a powerful political force seemed like something that would naturally fall into place.

Within 36 hours of the election victory, I received at my doorstep a package from the National Assembly, containing a guide for MNAs and business cards already printed. The guide detailed everything you had to know about salaries, expenses, tax free allowances and allocations for an office and staff. It was entirely in French.

Each MNA gets an office in Quebec City and receives about $20,000 a year to maintain a riding office back home. In addition they get $100,000.00 a year to hire staff for the riding office and the office at the National Assembly. I had already agreed to hire Tony Kondaks to be my executive assistant in the riding, but now I had to find space and a secretary for each of the two offices. Most of this would be readily resolved thanks to my meeting with Mr. Marx.

I walked up the steps of a modest home on Sheraton Drive in Montreal West, noting that it was one street outside the D'Arcy McGee riding boundary. I was greeted by Mrs. Marx, who, it turned out, had gone to school with my mother. She congratulated me and even kidded me that members of her own family might have voted for our party. Herbert Marx was very casual, talkative and surprisingly frank as we sat in his basement for well over an hour. He talked about the Quebec City media, about how much easier it is to be in opposition, and about his strategy for holding press conferences on different issues. He also suggested that to ease the transition, it would probably be a good idea to hire his former secretary of six years, who was now out of work and who knew all the ropes. He proposed that I consider renting his old riding office in the Cavendish Mall in Côte St. Luc, which is the hub of the riding.

I took him up on both suggestions. Being such a novice, and with enough to worry about running the party, I wanted the riding office to start functioning without delay. Simone Dayan was a francophone Jew from Morocco. As an MNA, having a francophone secretary is a must and the fact that my riding was over 75% Jewish, made her an obvious and easy choice.

The size and location of Marx's office was also ideal so I signed a lease with the Cavendish Mall for four years. One thing I questioned when I first inspected his office was why he had a remote magnetic lock on his door. The response did not surprise me. When he was Justice Minister under Bourassa, the Appeal Court upheld the lower court ruling that banning English on commercial signs violated the Charter of Rights and Freedoms. When Bourassa decided to challenge this decision before the Supreme Court of Canada, it was Marx who was responsible for the appeal, and had to do the legal spadework on behalf of the government. D'Arcy McGee residents were furious with him and often harassed him at his office, while others threatened to storm the building. He had no choice but to take precautions. I found it ironic that I would have this additional security device in my office for that reason.

When I returned to my drafting table the following week, I had serious difficulty concentrating on what I was doing. The work somehow just wasn't the same. Working out foundations and drawing drainage or window details didn't have quite the meaning it did before. A few days later, much to my surprise, I received a paycheque from the National Assembly, dated from September 26th, the day after the election. Already on the National Assembly payroll, unable to properly concentrate on the work, and eager to deal with the host of issues and new responsibilities that awaited me, I decided to leave my job the following week. Saying good-bye was difficult and leaving the drafting table for the last time was like leaving home for the second time in my life. I wondered when, if ever, I would be back.

In the days following the election, talk began to focus on whether we would be granted official status in the National Assembly. The rules clearly say that you must elect 12 members or capture 20% of the popular vote to qualify for official status, which guarantees question period privileges, more statutory speaking time and additional research funding. Bourassa, in his post-election press conference, did not sound very receptive, warning that we would not be getting any favours.

Jacques Parizeau on the other hand, who held his press conference a few days later, gleefully called the Equality Party his new "objective allies," giving us a warm, yet tongue-in-cheek welcome and vowing to do everything he could to get our caucus official recognition. His game was obvious. The stronger we got, the more seats we would eventually take away from the Liberal Party and the better his chances would be of winning the next election. Since the only votes we were likely to steal would be federalist votes, there was no danger for him if our party's status were to be enhanced.

The first caucus meeting of all four Equality MNAs was at Atkinson's private club on Sherbrooke Street, and a media pack was gathered outside when we arrived. We met in the Queen's room under Her Majesty's unswerving regal gaze. We went over the MNA guide, discussed the perks and just reveled in the excitement of the past few days.

Holden, whose knowledge of parliamentary procedure and protocol proved most helpful at this point, had prepared a series of letters for my signature to the Secretary General of the Assembly and the two other party leaders, requesting meetings to discuss housekeeping matters, including research budgets, office locations and speaking time.

Holden now also insisted on speaking out about Meech Lake, having received a call from his longtime friend Senator Lowell Murray, who was the Conservative leader in the senate and Brian Mulroney's point man in the Meech Lake Accord ratification drive. Bourassa's post election press conference focused on the urgency of passing the Meech deal and the potentially disastrous consequences for the country if the accord were to collapse.

The accord had been effectively hamstrung when Manitoba Premier Gary Filmon withdrew his province's support the day after Quebec adopted Bill 178. When "178" was passed, many who feared the concept of the "distinct society" clause wondered aloud whether violations of individual rights similar to those in Bill 178 were what the Quebec government had in mind when it referred to a "distinct society". Our electoral success, based as it was on an anglo backlash against the legislation, reinforced this perception in the rest of the country. Holden was therefore determined, after prodding from his old Conservative pal, to soften our opposition to the accord. I reminded him of our agreement over lunch when he decided to run, but he maintained that it was I who had agreed that he would be able to diverge from the party line in this case.

He insisted that our disapproval of Meech was due to a lack of understanding, and pulled out three order forms for a Meech Lake primer that Murray had sent him, insisting that we all order a copy. After the meeting, the media naturally seized on the potential rift over Meech Lake after Holden brazenly declared that we were reviewing our position.

On October 11 the Premier named his new cabinet. I had a pile of messages from the media asking for comment on the new ministers. I had no idea who many of them were and had to scramble to get a hold of Doug Robinson to fill me in on the backgrounds of those that he knew. It became apparent that we needed an experienced professional media relations person to keep us on top of these things. We assumed that the media attention would not subside, and if we could hire a francophone to be our liaison with the press, a much more positive image could be fostered. Holden's girlfriend put us in touch with Yvette Biondi, a bilingual francophone who had some experience in the publicity department at a local community newspaper. She agreed to take on the job of press attaché for the caucus and, in her words, improve our standing in the francophone community.

We had arranged for the four new MNAs to officially visit Quebec City for the first time on October 13 to look into lodging and to arrange the logistics for our swearing-in ceremony. Atkinson suggested that we go in style and rented a white stretch limousine from Murray Hill for the day. A Radio-Canada television crew wanted to follow us around in Quebec City that day and we agreed, as long as they promised not to show any footage of the limo.

On our way to the provincial capital, comfortably ensconced in the plush seats of the long white limo, we were getting along as well as could be. For at least half of the ride, Neil Cameron explained to us the origins of "Whigs" and "Tories," or something along those lines. Atkinson loved to relate anecdotes about his experiences in World War II and Korea, and Holden liked telling stories about the Conservative party and Brian Mulroney, who was his daughter's godfather. It was as if I was the young impressionable student and these three "elder statesmen" were my mentors. A peculiar situation, considering the fact that I was supposedly the boss or leader of these three characters, all old enough to be my father, and in Atkinson's case, my grandfather.

When we arrived in the provincial capital, our car was ushered into the parking lot under the "bunker"—as everyone in the National Assembly ambit calls the low-slung concrete pile on Grande Allée that houses the Premier's office. We were led through the underground tunnel the

Premier uses to go directly from his office to the Assembly chamber across the street when he wants to avoid reporters.

We had a lengthy meeting with Assembly deputy Secretary-General Gérald Laliberté and members of his staff, discussing matters ranging from the new marble in the bathrooms to free French lessons for MNAs to proper parliamentary language. They told us how the transcribers of the National Assembly journals had been working overtime practicing their typing skills in English, anticipating a much greater use of the language. All the officials at the National Assembly with whom we dealt always bent over backwards to accommodate our needs and requests. They provided us with piles of documents and took us on an extensive insider's tour of the Assembly complex. I couldn't help but marvel at the wonderful architecture and sumptuous detailing throughout the building.

Speaking of sumptuous, the highlight for my three colleagues was lunch in the grandly-appointed Café Parlementaire, the National Assembly restaurant where some of the finest chefs in the province toil to satisfy the culinary demands of Quebec's 125 MNAs.

As we waited at the entrance to be seated, a fly was buzzing around and landed on an apple that was part of a decorative display. Atkinson wanting to show off to our hosts the success of his Berlitz French lessons he had allegedly been taking for the past few weeks, remarked: "Regardez le mouche". Mr. Laliberté corrected him, saying, "Mr. Atkinson, pardon me but it is 'la' mouche". Atkinson turned to him with a seriously impressed look on his face and said, "Mon dieu! You have really good eyesight!"

As we strolled through the beautiful restaurant towards our table, all eyes turned to us, and there was a sudden hush in our wake. A few days earlier, a cartoon had appeared in *Le Soleil*, the Quebec City newspaper, showing four aliens in a flying saucer hovering above the Old Capital's skyline. The flying object was identified, however, with the words Equality Party written on its side.

After lunch we met the press. My colleagues were in glowing good spirits, having washed down their lunch with a few hearty tipples. Much of the media attention focussed on the niche we planned to carve for ourselves in what has traditionally been a two party system. They also seemed quite taken with the fact that Gordon Atkinson had ordered his lunch in French.

After the media scrum, we inquired about rates for MNAs at the various hotels in the area and visited a few rooming houses. As we would be in Quebec City only three days a week, we determined that the most practical alternative would be to stay at the Hilton Hotel, which was adjacent to the Assembly complex and connected by an underground tunnel. On our way back home, my colleagues decided that we should make a happy-hour pit stop at the Café Madrid near the halfway point between Quebec City and Montreal.

Many key issues were still to be resolved, such as the location of our offices, the sum of our research budget and question period speaking time, which would be determined mainly by the Premier and his cabinet, in consultation with the Official Opposition. Holden was delegated to negotiate these matters on our behalf.

We were still enjoying a honeymoon with the media. They still regarded us as a novelty, and just about everything we did was being covered. After our highly publicized first trip to the capital, Don Macpherson wrote, "Almost everybody seems to have fallen in love with the Eeks. The province's English media have been carrying almost daily bulletins on the activities of the Equality Party members, resembling those that Buckingham Palace issues on the doings of the Royal Family."

The following week, Holden and I were back in Quebec City, this time by plane, to meet with Jacques Parizeau and the PQ House leader, Guy Chevrette.

We arrived at Parizeau's office and were warmly greeted by his staff who ushered us into his grandly-appointed office. As we waited, Chevrette arrived with his chief of staff, Charles Grenier. I had been uneasy about meeting Chevrette, the PQ pit bull in the National Assembly, who often gave vicious speeches about how the anglo community was the best treated, most pampered minority in the world. I figured that he must have cursed the living daylights out of me for our party's breakthrough in the election. Much to my surprise, I couldn't get over how pleasant and friendly he was in this cordial setting, jovially kidding around and even calling me by my first name.

Parizeau arrived with his chief of staff, Hubert Thibault. The PQ leader was much more formal than Chevrette, yet very much down-to-earth at the same time. He was definitely not as large as his TV image suggests. Before even sitting down, he launched into a discourse on how unbelievable it was that a political party could get only four per cent of the vote and still win four seats. He lamented the fact that in the early seventies, the PQ would score well over 20 per cent of the vote yet only capture a half dozen seats.

Comfortably installed on the couch in Parizeau's office, I couldn't help thinking that here I was, sitting down with these two leading Quebec separatists, whom I regarded as two of my worst political enemies—people who would love nothing more than to break up my country. Furthermore, I was being impeccably polite and exchanging casual pleasantries with them. It gave me an odd feeling, almost like an out-of-body experience. Part of me was there, going through the motions, and part of me was somehow removed, gazing down in wonder at the sight of myself carrying this off, and thinking that politics can be a very strange game at times.

Parizeau readily agreed that as far as additional research funds were concerned, location of our offices and other minor details, he would support us. As far as working out a compromise for our participation in the 45-minute daily question period, they would discuss it at the PQ caucus meeting the following month. What we wanted was to have one guaranteed question a day, which of course would mean one less for the PQ. Ultimately, however, it would be up to the Premier and cabinet to make the final decisions, since allotting us a guaranteed question a day was tantamount to granting official status.

We also had an opportunity to interview a few potential secretaries in Quebec City that Simone had lined up for us through the Human Resources Department. When an MNA loses an election, his or her secretary's name goes into a pool from which newly elected MNAs are encouraged to choose. The first woman I met impressed me right away and I hired her on the spot. Carmen Catellier had been Joan Dougherty's secretary for eight years, before which she worked transcribing debates for the National Assembly journals. She was therefore able to type over 120 words a minute, and having worked for a West-Island MNA, spoke English and knew something about the anglo community. I shared her with Neil Cameron, while Holden and Atkinson hired a perfectly bilingual Quebec City anglo, Lauretta DeTony to work for them. By sharing two secretaries between the four of us, we had sufficient funds to also hire a young lawyer who had just graduated from Université Laval for the Quebec City office. Chris Mostovac was a West Island anglo, now living in Quebec City, who would be our researcher and liaison with the staffs of the other two parties in the legislature.

When we returned to Montreal I put in a call to the Premier to set up a meeting to discuss the outstanding issues. He and I had exchanged letters of congratulation after the election, but had still not spoken to each other. He took the call and I once again offered my congratulations, mentioning that he was now one term short of equalling Maurice Duplessis' record of five terms as Premier. He knew the purpose of my call and suggested that we meet on the weekend, which would be far less hectic. He also suggested that we meet away from his office to avoid journalists, and therefore invited me to his house in Outremont the following Saturday afternoon at 3:00 pm.

We happened to be in a good bargaining position for an important technical reason. According to the National Assembly's statutory calendar, the government has until November 15 to introduce bills for the fall session solely on the strength of its House majority. After that date, any new legislation slated for passage that fall requires unanimous consent to be tabled. Since the election was in late September and the Assembly was not to reconvene until November 28th, our approval was necessary to allow smooth passage of any law the government wanted to introduce before Christmas. Since Holden had been our point man in these negotiations, I asked him to join me at Bourassa's house.

Before the meeting, I went to my office to put in a few hours of work. At 2:00 pm I received a call from a very agitated Premier, who had a gaggle of journalists and photographers camped on his front lawn. He abruptly cancelled the meeting and said that I should get back to him during the week to reschedule it. I told him that I had no idea how they found out, since I had been very discreet about the meeting. I was leaving for Club Med in the Bahamas the next morning on a much needed vacation with my wife who was now almost three months pregnant. I would have to call the Premier when I got back, only two weeks before the session was to begin.

From Club Med, I called the office a few times. Over the phone, Kondaks read me a condescending editorial by Bernie St. Laurent in the *Montreal Daily News*, criticizing us for not being discreet about our meeting with the Premier and reminding us that we were now in the big leagues with less room to fool around. Ironically, it was Holden's buddy Auf der Maur, then working at the *Daily News*, who had tipped off the media. Holden had apparently let the cat out of the bag about the meeting, probably during one of his liquid lunches. The meeting was never rescheduled, and while we wound up with good offices and ample additional research funds, we were never able to strike a satisfactory deal for a daily slot in question period.

That week on the beach at Paradise Island, was the first time in almost a year that I was really able to just sit back and think about the whole thing. I was getting quite excited about the opportunity to sit in the National Assembly and ask some of the questions, raise some of the issues, and provoke some of the debate that had been too long suppressed because the anglos in the Assembly had to toe the Liberal party line. I looked forward to it as an unprecedented opportunity for our community to really be heard.

Once back home, I was invited to a whirl of community functions along with my wife, who was becoming increasingly uneasy about all the attention. I was also in demand for speaking engagements at various synagogues in the riding. In these speeches I was often critical of the Jewish community establishment, accusing it's leading lights of having been out of touch with grass-roots sentiment during the election campaign. This prompted the community leadership to seek a meeting with me, which led to a more positive relationship between myself and some of its key figures, though largely on a personal and informal basis. Officially—and publicly—however, I was never really welcome. I was still a new and unpredictable factor, and there was great concern over how the community would be perceived by the Liberal party if it embraced me too fondly.

At this time also, we entered into negotiations with the Unity Party leadership, and it was readily agreed that a merger was desirable.

A week before our first National Assembly session was to begin, we officially opened my riding office at a large wine and cheese party, where I gave out certificates to all 200 of my campaign workers. Later that evening, my wife and I flew to Quebec City for the swearing-in ceremony the next day.

For the past few weeks, Atkinson and his new political attaché, Liza Bouchard, who was his campaign manager and one of the founders of the N.D.G. riding association, had been organizing a bus trip for party supporters to attend the ceremony. It was to be held in the lavishly ornate "Red Room" of the National Assembly, which used to house the Quebec legislature's appointed upper chamber before it was abolished in the mid-1960s.

It was to be a special day for me. My parents and brothers would all be there, including my brother Warren who was now living in Seattle. After winning the Gold Medal at the McGill University School of Dentistry he was accepted to the University of Washington to specialize in prosthodontics. Much of his American education was paid for by a scholarship from Quebec's Ministry of Education, yet he is another young Quebec anglo who will not be back in Quebec. As much as he wanted to be near his family, the prospect of returning to all this uncertainty and, as he put it, "language and constitutional fatigue," was something he didn't want to inflict on his children.

In a driving snowstorm, our convoy of 10 buses made their way along the Jean Lesage Autoroute between Montreal and Quebec City. More than 400 party supporters poured into the Red Room to witness the ceremony, prompting *Journal de Québec* columnist Normand Girard, the dean of the National Assembly press gallery, to write that the members of the sovereign council of New-France were surely spinning in their graves. Never had the Red Room seen as many anglos as were there that day, he wrote.

The atmosphere was electric as we stepped forth one after the other, surrounded by our respective families, to stand behind the stately desk and pledge our allegiance to the Queen and to the people of Quebec. We would then sit down behind the desk and sign the official register, with the cameras clicking away. After all four of us had been sworn in, we took turns at the podium to say a few words. Atkinson brought the house down when he roared "Bienvenue chez nous".

The following week, at its pre-session caucus meeting, the PQ reversed its earlier position. Instead of extending us a gracious welcome, they opposed any concession to our party with respect to additional speaking time or a guaranteed daily slot in question period. When the media descended on me to respond, I called Parizeau's earlier press conference, where he playfully welcomed us to the Assembly, an exercise in buffoonery. Parizeau chortled when the media informed him of my adjective and publicly congratulated me for "starting rather well". I threatened to play hardball if necessary, by resorting to obstructing bills requiring unanimous consent, only to be contradicted later by Holden who said: "An architect doesn't understand rules of procedure. I don't see tying things up at all".

That week we also finalized the agreement with the Unity Party to merge with us under the Equality Party name the following spring, thus increasing our membership to 16,000 from 11,000, and our organization from 19 riding associations to 35. Neil Cameron warned me that we might one day live to regret this decision, but at the time it seemed that it would give us fresh momentum. Cameron feared that we were expanding into ridings that would never elect an Equality candidate, but where we could very well wind up helping the PQ by splitting the federalist vote in the next election, something we had taken great pains to avoid during the past election.

We were scheduled to make our National Assembly debut the following Tuesday, opening day for the first session of Quebec's 34th Legislature. On the Monday I flew to Quebec City for a meeting with Holden and the House Leader of the Liberal Party, Michel Pagé. Pagé, being not only a lawyer but one who appreciated a good scotch, hit it off with Holden right away. He seemed far more interested in small talk about the legal system and just about anything other than the business at hand.

Knowing full well that the PQ had balked at allowing us guaranteed time in question period, which would mean one less question a day for the PQ, Page came on like he was our best friend in the world. Of course he had no major objection to our party having a question a day and promised to discuss it with the Premier and the PQ leadership.

Insincerity was written all over his face, but Holden was greatly impressed and considered Pagé a potential friend. We also met with the new Speaker, Jean Pierre Saintonge, who promised that in the absence of official status he would be as generous as he could in giving us our share of questions.

The Gazette headline on the morning of the session opening proclaimed: "Equality debut highlight of fall legislature session." In the story, they referred to me for the umpteenth time as the "boyish looking architect". Similarly, the latest edition of l'Actualité magazine featured a piece about our caucus entitled, "La bande des quatre" (The gang of four). It described me as having the air of a high school class president as opposed to the aura of a provincial political party leader.

This kind of thing always made me grind my teeth, but I was coming to realize that there are some things you just can't change overnight.

CHAPTER SIX
Behind the Scenes
at the National Assembly

If you think it's easy to be a politician,
try to straddle a fence and keep both ears
on the ground at the same time.
—*The Globe and Mail*

The Quebec City Hilton Hotel is right across the street from the National Assembly. Residents of the 17th floor, where I was to live while the Assembly was in session, are offered a continental breakfast every morning, and the smell of the fresh croissants awaiting in the lounge wafts down the corridors and into the rooms. On this first morning, I spent at least an hour sipping coffee and reading the newspapers, all of which carried stories speculating about "the new kids on the block." After breakfast I took the tunnel connecting the hotel with the National Assembly to meet with my three fellow caucus members.

On the morning of the first day of the legislative session the four of us held our first press conference in what's called the "Hot-Room." Several rows of desks slope down toward an elevated table equipped with microphones, with a light blue curtain as a backdrop. Off to the side is the recording engineer who registers every word for subsequent transcription. On this Tuesday morning, all the places were full as the press corps was eager to put the new boys through their paces. When they call it the Hot Room, they're not kidding, both literally and figuratively. Intense TV lights glare down from the ceiling as you sit face-to-face with dozens of journalists, with no escape but your own wits. They wanted to know what our plans were for the fall session and whether we had struck a deal for speaking time and research budgets.

Holden and I had resolved to ease up on any threats about blocking legislation and to express satisfaction with most of our arrangements. We had been given very good seats in the legislature. Holden and I would occupy two front row seats facing the speaker, with Atkinson and Cameron, directly behind us. The government had been fairly generous with our offices and research budget. We had no official commitment for question period except the speaker's promise that he would use his neutral discretion to be as fair as possible with us.

The reporters took great delight in some of Atkinson's turns of phrase in French, which prompted favorable comment that our supposedly unilingual MNAs, Cameron and Atkinson showed a surprisingly unexpected ability to get by in French.

The National Assembly exudes considerable pomp and majesty in itself, but on special days, such as the opening of the Legislature, the regal atmosphere is positively infectious. The first day is marked by the ceremonial throne speech delivered by the Queen's representative, the Lieutenant-Governor, who sets forth the government's legislative agenda. This is then followed by the Premier's inaugural address, which elaborates further on the government's plans. Afterward, everyone retires to the gilded Red Room for cocktails and schmoozing.

The National Assembly is heavily guarded. Since Denis Lortie's shooting spree in 1984, Sûreté du Québec guards, armed with guns and metal detectors, have been posted at every entrance. Security guards are also posted throughout the building at the end of every corridor. All 125 MNAs receive a circular gold pin which affords ready access throughout the Assembly complex. As we received our pins that morning we were told that it doesn't hurt to wear them around town. If a maitre'd in a restaurant, for example, recognizes the pin, you are sure to receive special treatment.

It was quite an experience this first day. All eyes seemed to be on us, as though we were members of some exotic species. When the bells rang, indicating the start of the session, I got butterflies in my stomach. The four of us slowly walked upstairs together. As we approached the entrance to the legislative chamber, colloquially known as the "Blue Room," lights blazed and cameras rolled.

When we entered the Assembly to take our places there was a buzz in the visitor's gallery above. All the other MNAs were exchanging greetings and patting each other on the back. I just sat down, feeling like a complete outsider, yet marvelling at the beauty of the place. You couldn't help but feel as though you were at the centre of Quebec's political universe, and be smitten by the history that had been made within the walls of this chamber where I now sat as an "Honorable

Member". I began poring over my short speech to welcome the new speaker, which would be my first words once the session was called to order. Just then a smiling Gérard D. Lévesque, the dean of Assembly members, interrupted my thoughts. He came right over and grabbed my hand, warmly welcoming me to the National Assembly. He was the Finance Minister and had been an MNA for more than 30 years, and here he was, on my first day, making such a friendly gesture to put me at ease.

The first order of business was the pro-forma election of the speaker, who had been named by the government and informally endorsed by all parties beforehand. The speaker and two deputy speakers are chosen by the Premier from the ranks of the new government's MNAs. While the speaker is a member of a political party, he or she must be completely neutral in all functions. After the Premier and Leader of the Official Opposition welcomed Saintonge to the chair, I was given two minutes to say my first words in the National Assembly, extending my own congratulations to the new speaker. But it was also an opportunity to subtly suggest that he be conscious of giving our party its fair shake.

Lieutenant-Governor Gilles Lamontagne then entered, following his Gendarme who follows the Sergeant-at-Arms, who carries the ornate mace that rests on the Assembly table while the house is in session. Both the speaker and Lieutenant-Governor read portions of their speeches in English, which prompted a number of MNAs to turn their eyes in our direction.

Sitting in my comfortable and richly-crafted chair, I felt distinctly out of my element. It all seemed so incredibly foreign to me. I couldn't help but keep looking up at the fresco painted on the ceiling, or admiring the elaborate architectural detailing all around. I was struck by the presence of the crucifix above the speaker's chair, something that had not been part of my upbringing up to now. While relishing the moment, I tried not to be too dazzled by the thought that I was sitting in a front-row seat in this historic chamber, mere feet away from some of the most prominent figures in recent Quebec history about whom I had been reading for years in the papers: Claude Ryan, Robert Bourassa, Jacques Parizeau, Lise Bacon, Daniel Johnson and Marc-Yvan Côté.

When the Lieutenant-Governor rose to leave, we all stood. As he moved toward the large oak doors just past our desks, he exchanged a knowing glance with fellow World War II veteran Atkinson, who was decked out with the Knighthood of the Order of St. Lazarus around his neck and rows of medals and ribbons across his chest.

It was now time for Bourassa to speak. He made a brief reference to our party, welcoming us and hoping that we could bridge any differences on language. His speech, which focused primarily on the importance of ratifying the Meech Lake accord, was directly aimed at the rest of Canada. He warned of "unforeseeable consequences" if the rest of Canada were to reject the accord. With just over six months before the ratification deadline, he wanted to turn up the heat on the three holdout provinces, Manitoba, Newfoundland and New Brunswick. Bourassa also spoke about the economic challenges that lay ahead and boasted about how his government had been able to cut the deficit in half during its tenure. He spoke of job creation, in particular the many jobs that had been generated by the installation of a number of metals manufacturing plants in Quebec since the last election.

After his speech the Assembly was adjourned until the next day when Parizeau, as leader of the Official Opposition, would respond to the inaugural address. It was confirmed that my opening speech in response to the inaugural address would lead off on Thursday's sitting. As everyone got up to attend the opening-day cocktail, I innocently headed toward the washroom in the corridor leading off the back entrance to the Blue Room behind the speaker's chair, and walked right into a media scrum. It turned out that this is the spot where the media ambush politicians on their way to question period. Unprepared as I was, I used the occasion to express concern about Meech Lake and the possible interpretation of the distinct society clause and its impact on linguistic minorities. This was broadcast on television that evening with the backdrop of a sign that said "HOMMES". I realized I would have to get wise to the ways of the Assembly jungle if I wanted to avoid these little pitfalls.

On my way back from the washroom I bumped into the Premier who was also behind the speaker's chair, getting ready for the reception. He welcomed me warmly. I apologized to him for the foul-up over the meeting at his house a month earlier. As we walked together in the procession to the Red Room, he said he hoped we were satisfied with our seating and office space.

At the reception, there were very few people I knew. Certainly, most of the MNAs at this stage would not take the initiative to approach me. I stood around with Cameron and Atkinson as Holden circulated. He had an ardent newfound affinity for Michel Pagé, the Liberal house leader; since our earlier meeting, Holden had taken every opportunity to heap him with generous praise, to which Pagé was most receptive. As far as I was concerned, Pagé was a classic political smoothie. You got the crawly feeling that he had an ulterior motive for everything he said or did. Observing from afar, I couldn't help but suspect from the way he buttered up Holden, that he saw in him a foil he could wield to divide and undermine our party.

The next morning, Parizeau was in the spotlight. His speech kicked off the two-week debate in response to the inaugural address, which takes precedence over all other matters at the beginning of a session. The Premier, sitting right across from Parizeau listened and made facial gestures, depending on what was said. There is very rarely any real personal animosity between political opponents. While they took little digs at each other, many of the shots during both speeches were cushioned by a touch of humor. I found it fascinating to watch the chemistry between the two. Both possessed a genuine respect for what the other represented in the context of Quebec history, though Parizeau considered Bourassa to be wishy-washy and Bourassa considered Parizeau to be too aristocratic. Each satirized the other's personal character weaknesses in their speeches.

Because the Equality Party was not granted official status as a parliamentary group, we were technically four independent members. There was however, a tacit recognition of our party as a distinct entity and a designated caucus. This eventually translated itself into more frequent recognition by the speaker in question period and regular participation in debates on motions that require the unanimous consent of the House. On this second day the PQ tabled one of these motions to mark the 1837 Patriote rebellion. We could easily have blocked the motion by refusing our consent, but Atkinson wanted to make a fiery speech about how anglophones fought side by side with francophones in the Lower Canada uprising, which Quebec nationalists have appropriated and greatly misrepresented for their own ends. He paid hommage to "the bravery of the men and women who fought to defend the principles they cherished." This caught many MNAs by surprise, having never heard it put this way.

The quasi-recognition of the four of us as a group brought us into consultation with the house leaders of the other two parties on a daily basis. Every morning Chris Mostovac would speak with Chevrette's and Pagé's chiefs of staff to go over the agenda for the day and what motions, if any, would be tabled by the parties. On more serious issues, Holden who had been designated as our house leader, would speak directly with Chevrette and Pagé.

I also had opportunities above and beyond those of an ordinary MNA. On special or solemn occasions, such as the welcoming of the new speaker, or the delivery of eulogies for the victims of the massacre at the École Polytechnique, or the evening the Meech Lake accord expired, I got to say my piece along with the Premier and Parizeau.

I also was usually granted additional speaking time in certain debates. For example, in the debate on the inaugural address, the Premier and Leader of the Official Opposition are allotted up to two hours each of speaking time. I would be given up to 40 minutes as opposed to all other MNAs who got 20 minutes each. This was always worked out in negotiations with the other house leaders, generally in the neutral zone behind the speaker's chair. The speaker would allot us our time and the rest was split between the other two parties. If one side doesn't use up all its time, the other party can use it. It is the house leader of each party who usually determines which MNAs speak and for how long and in what order, with government members alternating with opposition members. It is all very orchestrated. Most MNAs sit in their offices and watch the Assembly proceedings on closed circuit TV. When their turn looms they make their way to the chamber. The Blue Room therefore rarely has more than 20 or so MNAs present at any given time, except for the 45-minute question period when the house is generally packed.

On the day of my opening address the Liberals readily agreed to give me 40 minutes, but the PQ was still angry at me for referring to Parizeau's antics the week before as buffoonery and would only agree to the 40 minutes if I would begin my speech by apologizing for my remarks. It was comply or lose half my speech. Grudgingly I complied.

My speech focused on language rights and Bourassa's increasing nationalist stance. Jacques Renaud had written some powerful material about the critical importance of respecting fundamental rights and freedoms in a healthy democracy. The speech was at least two-thirds in French, with sections in English geared to furnish the anglo media with sound bites. The speech got wide play that focused on my challenge to the Premier to stop wavering about where he stood on federalism.

The daily sitting of the National Assembly is broken up into two parts: "Les Affaires Courantes" (Routine Business) and "Les Affaires du Jour" (Orders of the Day). The Affaires Courantes period includes ministerial declarations; tabling of bills, documents, commission reports and petitions; complaints of breach of privilege or contempt and personal explanations; deferred votes; motions without notice; notices concerning commission proceedings; and the question period, which is the theatrical highlight of the legislative day.

Question period is the 45 minutes every day when the opposition can ask any minister any question falling within his or her jurisdiction. All MNAs are usually present and the seats in the press gallery are full. When you get up to ask a question all eyes are on you, so you had better not fumble. You are allowed a short preamble before your principal question, followed by two or three (depending on the speaker's indulgence) complementary questions with which you try to pin down or embarrass the minister. It takes a lot of concentration and nerve to pull this off well, and you have to be very quick on your feet. Some MNAs practise for question period in front of a mirror, working on facial expressions, arm gestures and body language.

Giving a speech in the National Assembly is a lot easier than rising for question period, when you can get your ears pinned back if you haven't done your homework; the governing rule for question period veterans is never ask a question to which you don't already know the answer. Regular speeches on legislation under consideration are part of Affaires du Jour, which takes up most of the daily sitting. It is much more relaxed because most of the seats are empty and the media are rarely present. All media offices however, as well as those of the MNAs, are equipped with TV sets tuned to the National Assembly channel at all times. It allows you work in your office while keeping an eye on what is going on in the Blue Room. On the Assembly's in-house cable service there are also channels that repeat the newscasts over and over again, in case you missed something important, and all offices also have radios which pick up the proceedings in all committee rooms. This way you can follow any debate anywhere in the building from the comfort of your office. When there is a vote in the House, strident bells ring throughout the building for several minutes, giving MNAs ample time to make their way to the chamber.

Every word uttered in the National Assembly or in committees is transcribed in the *Journal des Débats*, the Assembly's official record. A few hours after speaking you receive the photocopied first draft of what you said and are given an opportunity to correct mistakes in the transcript, though not, unfortunately, in what you actually said. English text is often in need of repair. The final version of each day's proceedings is printed a few days later and distributed in booklet form. Videocassettes of all your speeches in the Assembly are also made available.

The day of my speech in response to the inaugural address was also my first opportunity to join in question period. My heart was pounding as I nervously rose a few times before the speaker finally recognized me. The official opposition gives a list to the speaker every day showing the order of their MNAs for question period. In our case, if one of us had a question, we would have to pop up in the hope of catching the speaker's eye. Over the years, Saintonge was eminently fair in according us questions. His decisions on whether to recognize us would be based on the number of questions on that day's list and how long it had been since we asked our last question.

My first question was about the Health Minister's white paper on the proposed reorganization of the health and social service system. Of concern to minority communities was the plan to replace the boards of directors of individual institutions with one board of directors for all institutions within a given territory. This could have a negative impact on the identities of institutions serving minority communities. For example, if an institution that specifically serves the anglophone community is in a territory that is majority francophone and has a number of French language institutions, then the territorial board that would oversee all the institutions would consist mostly of francophones and would not necessarily be sensitive to the special needs of the minority institutions.

This bureaucratic concept could work well as a model in most parts of Quebec where there are no specific institutions serving minority community groups. In Montreal, however, where there is much cultural diversity, the structure would be detrimental. I asked the minister if he was aware of the concerns of minority communities for the autonomy and identity of their institutions and what compromise solutions he would be willing to examine.

The Health Minister replied that there would be extensive public hearings on the white paper and that all these concerns would be aired and discussed. He made no specific commitment, which is typical of question period replies. Rarely is a question answered squarely. Skating around an issue and avoiding any promises or commitments is the norm for ministers in this forum. If the question makes an insinuation that catches the media's interest, or highlights an issue that the media will follow up, or if a minister is thrown on the defensive or embarrassed in any way, then the opposition member has succeeded.

Our offices were grouped together on the ground floor, occupying both sides of almost a full corridor of the main Assembly building. We were each given a private office, as well as one for each of our two secretaries. We also had a research office, a separate office for our chief political attaché, an additional office for visiting staffers and even a cosy lounge, which we decorated with enlarged Aislin cartoons lampooning the Equality Party.

Cameron also stayed at the Quebec City Hilton. Holden and Atkinson preferred to stay at the Chateau Frontenac where they shared a suite. It did not pay to rent an apartment since the National Assembly only sits six months a year. From mid October until the end of November it sits only from Tuesdays through Thursdays. From the beginning of December until the Christmas break, it sits five days a week. The session then breaks until mid March. Until the end of May the Tuesday through Thursday schedule is in force. From the beginning of June to the 20th, the house is back in intensive session five days a week before the summer break, which lasts until mid October.

On Tuesdays and Thursdays, the sitting begins at 2:00 pm, breaks from 6:00 pm to 8:00 pm, and then resumes until 10:00 pm. On Wednesdays, the Assembly sits from 10:00 am to 1:00 pm and from 3:00 pm to 6:00 pm, after which most MNAs go out for a hearty dinner at one of the many fine restaurants in the old capital. In the intensive session in June and December, the Assembly often sits right through the night to pass all the legislation on the order paper before the long breaks. My usual routine was to hop on a plane to Quebec City every Tuesday morning, stay over Tuesday and Wednesday nights and fly back to Montreal on Thursday evening.

In between sessions there are sometimes commission hearings or meetings in Quebec City, but it is usually time devoted to constituency affairs in the riding office. During sessions, Mondays and Fridays are set aside for riding business.

A number of other MNAs also stayed at the Hilton, though for some reason none of them were members of the PQ. There are two executive floors, the 17th and 18th, where most of us stayed, which are accessible only with a special elevator key. The executive lounge serves breakfast in the morning and has an open bar all day, serving hors d'oeuvres from 5 to 7 pm every evening. It was a pleasure to unwind in the lounge most evenings, with its soft couches, television set and a sweeping view of the city. Political affiliations notwithstanding, good friendships grow easily in these comfortable and congenial surroundings.

It is in this type of environment, as I had discovered with the Richard-Robert Lounge at McGill, where one learns the most about people of other cultures and walks of life. Your guard is down, you are in a mellow frame of mind and your politics are your own, not your party's. You could often have a greater political impact on a political adversary in bars, lounges and corridors than in the bear-pit arena of the Assembly. There were a number of Liberals who confessed to me during these encounters that the language laws were completely unnecessary, were unfair to anglophones or were an embarrassment. Yet, they all felt that it was necessary to maintain a pronounced nationalist posture to keep the PQ in check. If they talked of changing language laws, the PQ would capitalize on it to their electoral advantage. Yet they all predicted that the laws would be changed one day when the time was right.

I spent a lot of time with Jean Claude Gobé, the MNA for Lafontaine, and Cosmo Maciocia, the MNA for Viger. Also part of the group at the Hilton were Jean-Pierre Bélisle, the MNA for Mille-Iles, Rejean Lafrénière of Gatineau, Albert Houde of Berthier, Robert Lesage of Hull, Pierrette Cardinal of Chateauguay and a few others. Our den mother was Thérèse, the cheerfully friendly hostess at the 17th floor lounge, who made sure that we were always happy as could be in our home away from home.

I usually returned to my office in the evenings. If I was in the mood for some bonding with other MNAs, I would wander into the Blue Room during the evening sitting. In the evenings, the atmosphere is very loose. Many politicians like to hoist a few at dinner, which makes for a jolly ambiance. There is generally one MNA standing and giving a speech and about 15 others sitting in small clusters. Everyone sits anywhere, and pays only scant attention to what is being said. There is a lot of kidding and joking around. Fortunately, according to regulation, the camera recording the proceedings for the National Assembly TV channel can only focus on the person speaking and cannot pan the Assembly to catch other members hobnobbing or snoozing in their seats.

Sometimes the MNAs giving speeches like to capitalize on the jovial atmosphere and embellish their points, or say things that go a little too far, or take a few humorous shots at some of the other MNAs who are doing house duty. Sometimes speakers wander off on tangents to kill time, saying things that have nothing to do with the topic at hand.

There are always a few MNAs who are masters of rhetorical banter and the tongue-in-cheek quip. André Boulerice and Yves Blais, for example were two PQ MNAs worth the price of admission any evening for their nimble wit. Guy Chevrette of the PQ, who is probably the finest parliamentary performer I have ever seen, can speak for hours on any given topic with a brilliant caustic edge, intellectual depth and incisive partisan slant.

On the Liberal side, Réjean Doyon and Ghislain Maltais often sparkled during these evening sittings. They would stand up without any notes and rant for 20 minutes, point fingers, wave their arms and get all red in the face. Agriculture Minister Yvon Picotte had his own crude way of riling up the house as did Jean Garon, the former PQ agriculture minister, who would constantly annoy even members of his own party. When he went into one of his rants you could barely understand a word he was saying. On the other hand, listening to Claude Ryan was always an education. Despite always having to put on the earphones to amplify his soft voice, his use of language and the way he strings thoughts together to make an important point is the political equivalent of grand opera.

Finally, there was no one more vicious, more powerfully articulate and more successful in question period, than the PQ MNA for Saguenay Lac St. Jean and intergovernmental affairs critic, Jacques Brassard. His inflection and uncanny ability to zero in on the point of vulnerability in question period had the Liberal government constantly reeling on constitutional issues. Part of the reason that the Premier and intergovernmental affairs minister, Gil Remillard had so much trouble handling the Meech Lake Accord in the months leading to its demise was the constant barrage from Brassard. After a short time, it became obvious that Parizeau, as leader of the opposition, did not have the skill to do well in question period. His cerebral, professorial style often causes him to stray from the point or elaborate too much while formulating a question. It became clear that he was no match for Bourassa, who could sidestep and twist a question into a pretzel with ease. When Parizeau rose to ask the Premier a question, Bourassa always seemed relaxed. This was not the case with Brassard. When Brassard would rise and tell the speaker: "M. Le President. Ma question s'adresse au Premier Ministre," you could see Bourassa tense up and sit straighter in his chair. Armed with a rapier wit, Brassard had that instinctive knack of being able to hone in on the jugular, always putting his victim on the defensive. The Liberal house leader often tried to throw him off by interrupting and calling for a ruling on whether Brassard's preamble was too long, too argumentative, contained unparliamentary language, or whatever. Anything to rattle him.

It was quite an experience to be learning the ropes by watching these seasoned political pros. It was also the ultimate French immersion program. I was thoroughly enjoying the experience, and for a 29 year old, the salary was also most satisfactory. In my first year the base salary for an MNA was $55,000. In addition, there was a $400 tax free travel allowance every month and an additional annual $10,000 tax-free supplement for expenses. All travel expenses to and from Quebec City are covered, as were accommodations in Quebec City for up to $12,000 a year.

There was an additional supplement for ministers of about $40,000 a year, for parliamentary secretaries and Committee Chairmen of about $11,000 a year, and, for members of other bodies, such as the National Assembly Bureau, an additional $5,500 a year. I was among a pool of substitute parliamentary committee chairmen and therefore received an added supplement of $5,500 a year. If a committee of which you are a member sits on a day when the Assembly is not in session, there is a daily $140 honorarium for those who attend. And of course, there is a very lucrative pension plan.

All MNAs have unlimited use of fax, telephone and photocopying equipment in both their offices, courier service between Quebec City and Montreal, unlimited car-phone time, unlimited calling card privileges, access to the partly-subsidized National Assembly restaurant and even a supply of briefcases.

All employees of the National Assembly are there first and foremost to serve the 125 MNAs. The restaurant staff and the printing and photocopying room personnel are always eager to please. The National Assembly library staff do research upon request and even provide a newspaper clipping service. Every morning they assemble and circulate *l'Argus*, a bound booklet of the day's leading political stories and editorials from newspapers throughout the country. In the Blue Room the "pages" scurry about to deliver messages or fill our water glasses, always bowing to the speaker if they pass in front of the chair. In-house messengers deliver envelopes or packages anywhere in the complex. Quebec treats its politicians so well that it is dangerously easy to fall into the trap of complacency and procrastination amid the abundance of perks. When you go to a restaurant, bar, hotel or theatre in Quebec City, you get special treatment and personal attention if you are recognized as an MNA. It is not surprising that politicians develop larger egos than the average citizen and become convinced that they are something more than ordinary mortals. The fire in the belly they show at election time can easily subside into a comfortable glow of self-satisfaction by midterm.

Politicians have developed a bad reputation in recent years for living high off the taxpayer hog, and while many deserve it, there must also be an enticement for quality individuals to be drawn into politics. Many of the politicians who have risen near the top have the charisma, the smarts and the erudition to make a lot more money in the private sector.

A certain bond develops between members of the legislature, which fosters a club-like atmosphere. Few people realize the extent to which you become a member of a very exclusive and private club of 125 select individuals. Political differences do not stop MNAs from different parties from talking and kidding around with each other outside the walls of the Assembly chamber. There could be a heated and emotional debate in the Assembly between two political enemies, but moments later you could see these same two warriors kidding around in the corridor or in the restaurant. When you are at a public function, no matter what party you are from, you feel as one with your fellow MNAs who are present, usually giving each other knowing glances if a speaker says something that you both may find peculiar.

It is not all play to be sure. Ministers and members of the opposition have to work hard and keep long hours if they hope to keep their jobs in the next election. Ministers are constantly busy, preparing legislation, sitting through parliamentary committees, overseeing their departments, putting out fires, fending off the media and preparing for question period. If an issue that falls within their domain is hot in the news one morning, you could be sure that the minister will be huddled with his staff all morning trying to correct the problem, preparing a response and working up a media spin. All the travel, and being constantly on call, puts tremendous pressure on family life.

Government back-benchers have the least to do. They quietly attend their committees and occasionally get to speak on a given piece of legislation if it specifically interests them, and the house leader and minister involved allows it. Members of the opposition are much busier as critics in their specific domains, formulating questions and preparing for debate on legislation touching on their areas of interest.

When the premier, or a minister, or a bureaucrat in a particular department wants a certain law to be passed, it goes to the full cabinet for preliminary approval. The draft text is then submitted to the Assembly's legal service, which puts the bill into legal text and cross references it with any other law that it might affect. Once cabinet gives it final approval to be tabled in the National Assembly, it goes through 5 stages before it becomes law. During les Affaires Courantes the Minister responsible introduces the bill by standing to read the explanatory notes. It is then handed to one of the pages who "tables" it by bringing it to the Secretary General and his two assistants who sit at the table on the Assembly floor between the government and opposition benches. It is now in the public domain and anyone can have a copy. This stage is usually a formality and when the speaker asks if the Assembly agrees to the tabling, it is very rarely refused.

Actual debate on the bill can begin the next day. This stage is called "adoption in principle" where any MNA can speak on the general thrust of the proposed legislation for up to 20 minutes. Usually just the Minister and the opposition critic take part in this phase, unless there is a special significance to the bill and another MNA wants to speak on it. Or, if the opposition is staunchly opposed to it, you may get a large number of opposition MNAs wading in to the debate, which in turn forces a larger number of government MNAs to take part.

What is most irritating about the British parliamentary system when there are only two major parties is that no matter what a given bill is all about, you will almost always have the MNAs on the government side emotionally defending its critical importance to Quebec society and the members of the Official Opposition brutally attacking it as a grave danger to society. The same goes for motions and amendments, and all votes are predictable to the extent that the government never loses. As MNAs gather to take their places before a vote, you often see a government back-bencher leaning over to a neighbour to ask how they will be voting on this one. On rare occasions, the official opposition supports the government on legislation. Our caucus voted according to what we felt were the merits of any particular bill, often with the government and on occasion with the opposition PQ.

After the vote on the "adoption in principle" phase, the Bill is sent to one of the eight parliamentary committees (commissions in French) which review the work of the different ministries. The Commission de la culture, for example, studies all legislation relating to the Cultural Affairs portfolio, including language matters, while la Commission de l'aménagement et équipement pores over all bills and matters dealing with the environment, transport, or public works. All ministries and government activity fall within the jurisdiction of one of the eight committees. All MNAs are assigned to sit on at least one of them. The government has a majority on all committees and therefore dictates the operations and wins all votes here as well. This stage is called "detailed consideration in committee". The Bill is debated article by article, and amendments can be proposed.

Parliamentary committees also study all spending by the different ministries. Every few months, the ministers have to sit before the respective committees and justify all the expenditures of their departments. In the weeks leading up to the May budget every year, the Finance Minister tables all the spending estimates for the coming year and opposition MNAs get to grill the various ministers on how they plan to spend the public's money.

Each stage of the passage of a bill is controlled by the government majority. In our system, the only way that the opposition can really change anything is if it manages, via the media, to direct enough attention to a bill's shortcomings and thereby shame or pressure the minister to back off or make changes. This is how the opposition does its job, and this is why the media are so influential in politics. Without the media, a government can do just about anything it wants without public checks and balances. If a terrible abuse of power takes place, or a proposed law has serious flaws, or a conflict of interest develops, or an outright blunder is made, no one would know about it if the media didn't raise a stink. Certainly the government wouldn't point the finger at itself. However, the media need a protagonist to draw attention to any given issue, and this is the opposition critic's job. If an opposition MNA can uncover an issue, or attack it in a way that entices the media to run with it, the critic has succeeded in putting the government on the defensive, which could lead to a minister making positive changes.

After a committee finishes detailed consideration of a bill it is sent back to the Assembly for debate on its details. This fourth stage is called the "consideration of the committee report" and the debate revolves around changes or amendments that may have been made in committee or concerns that the opposition may still have with certain elements that have not been changed.

After the debate and vote, there remains one final stage called "adoption" or third reading, where final debate takes place and the final draft of the Bill is voted on. After it passes, as it always does, the Lieutenant-Governor officially sanctions the bill at his lavish office, situated on the first floor of the Press Gallery building. A representative of each party is invited to this small ceremony which is traditionally preceded by a scotch.

This first National Assembly session was as much an orientation exercise for me as anything else. I worked doggedly at learning the rules of procedure and the unwritten rules, devouring National Assembly guides and reports and trying to speak out on as many pieces of legislation as possible. I had always been a bit of a workhorse, but never more so than in this situation because I was caught up in the belief that all eyes were on me. Many people had high expectations for the party, while many others were hoping for it to crumble. My constant concern about looking bad in such a highly visible job made me keep my nose hard to the grindstone.

I had many long dinners with Neil Cameron, who is a walking encyclopedia on the history of Quebec and Canada and political theory and practice in general. I spent a lot of time discussing the rules of procedure with Gérald Laliberté, the deputy Secretary-General of the National Assembly. It seemed on many occasions that he was more concerned with our caucus feeling comfortable than with his own job.

This first session would be a short one, having begun only at the end of November. For the first few weeks the media covered us closely, as we were embroiled in the procedural wrangling over our party's speaking time in Question Period and whether or not we should have a member of our party sit on the influential National Assembly Bureau, the body composed of 7 MNAs that makes most day-to-day administrative decisions. This body decides on snow removal contracts, for instance, or whether or not to change the sprinkler system; it determines changes in MNA salaries and severance packages for bureaucrats, and draws up the National Assembly's $80 million-a-year operating budget. It is chaired by the speaker and attended by the Secretary-General and other top bureaucrats. The key members of the bureau are the "whips" from the two major parties, the MNAs responsible for keeping the respective caucuses toeing the party line. There are rarely votes at the Bureau. All decisions are reached by consensus.

The PQ threatened to walk out and boycott the Bureau if the speaker ruled in our favour. Holden argued the case convincingly and the speaker granted us the spot. The PQ was pacified however when all parties concerned agreed on a compromise that would add 2 more members to the Bureau, thus creating a breakdown on the committee of 5 Liberals, 3 Péquistes and one Equality MNA, who turned out to be Holden.

We were also highly visible on the language front. We forced the National Assembly to debate and vote on a motion of censure of the government for its disrespect of the Canadian and Quebec Charters of Rights and Freedoms in passing Bill 178. The *Gazette* headline the day after the vote was, "PQ and Liberals unite to crush Equality motion of censure". We also made headlines urging Quebecers to defy the sign law, again quoting René Lévesque who once said that unjust laws should not be obeyed. Just before the first anniversary of Bill 178, the deadline for the federal government to "disallow" the provincial law—a power that had not been invoked in 45 years—we wrote to Brian Mulroney to ask him to consider using disallowance. It was a symbolic gesture, but it caused quite a stir in the press.

We also made headlines by calling anglo Liberals, like Nelligan MNA Russell Williams, wimps and doormats. His opening speech for example, was a textbook example of anglo apologist thinking in that it was wishy-washy and inarticulate. Williams, a former Alliance-Quebec functionary who had inherited Clifford Lincoln's former riding, had been one of the staunchest advocates of Lincoln's resignation over Bill 178 and the invocation of the notwithstanding clause. Not long after the way was clear for him to slip into Lincoln's seat, he suddenly found he could live with the Liberal language policy after all.

The novelty of our election had still not worn off. We were in great demand as guest speakers at community functions, churches and synagogues, and at all these appearances we heard nothing but encouragement and thanks. We were being extensively quoted by the media on a range of issues relating to the anglo community and the mail brought in a tide of letters praising our efforts.

There was a general consensus among Quebec's English speaking community that they had finally arrived in the National Assembly. Quebec's anglos were feeling vindicated and proud once again that their presence was being felt in a tangible way, and that their language was being heard loud and clear in Quebec City as issues of concern to the community were being raised regularly by our caucus during question period.

Toward the end of the session, *The Gazette*'s Don Macpherson even praised our efforts in a column entitled "Anglophones could use more sparring like this". He grudgingly wrote "There are signs that the vocal presence in the National Assembly of the Equality MNAs, and the pressure it exerts on the Liberals, may already be producing concrete results for the anglophone community. Last week in response to a planted question, Education Minister Claude Ryan announced long-overdue financial aid for badly underfunded English-language universities".

We felt that if another election could have been held at this point, we would probably have doubled our number of seats and increased our majorities substantially.

The year-end news shows all featured the Equality Party's election breakthrough as one of the top stories of the year. Bye-Bye '89, the hugely popular year end variety show on Radio Canada, even did a takeoff on the "Batman" movie music video in a satirical skit where the new anglo superhero was "Libman". The main character was dressed in a Batman suit with "Libman" emblazoned across the chest. He wore glasses on top of his mask and spoke French with a nasal tone and anglo accent. There were beautiful women dancing all around him, one of whom raised her skirt to reveal a tattoo on her leg that also said "Libman". It was strange watching myself in caricature, particularly on a show that normally draws 3 million francophone viewers across Quebec.

The public perception as 1989 came to a close was that the Equality Party was riding high. But the internal tensions which were to plague the party during the years to come were already beginning to simmer.

CHAPTER SEVEN
Party Problems

I can take care of my enemies all right.
But my friends, my goddam friends,
they're the ones that keep me walking the floor at night.
—*Warren G. Harding*

As it turned out, winning an election and going to the National Assembly was the easy part. The more daunting challenge now was to transform a spontaneous political movement, born of frustration over a single issue, into a real political party.

The language issue was so powerful and emotional a factor that many average people with no personal agenda were sufficiently motivated to work their butts off for the Equality Party just to stick it to the Liberal government. The election was a tangible enough goal in which to invest their energy. Once the election period had passed and their efforts were rewarded by the election results, many people felt they had made their contribution and could go on to other things. This was the first category of individuals actively involved in the Equality Party.

There was also a category that included many overzealous, hard-line language activists encouraged by our amazing success and the opportunity now available to shape the party in their own image. A young party must develop a fresh program and they were determined to imprint it with their own trademark. They abhor compromise, believing they have a monopoly on truth and political virtue.

There was also a group that believed very strongly in the importance of a genuine third-party option for the province and accepted that we would have to adjust our rhetoric and compromise on certain positions for the greater good of expanding the party's membership base. Certain principles could be moderated or given less prominence in order to cast as wide a net as possible, thereby improving our chances in the next election.

There are also many who get involved in a political party for reasons of ego. They like the personal attention that politics can bring and to see their names in print. Once the election passes, however, and if, as candidates, they failed to get elected, they either leave a little bit wounded or hang around for the eternal "next time". Others of this type see a political organization as an opportunity to nourish their egos by seeking positions of prominence in the hierarchy. Many of them develop personal agendas and ambitions which often arouse jealousy and put them at odds with others. This became a problem for some people in the party who had played a significant role from the start and were now greatly overshadowed by the newly-elected MNAs.

For example, there were problems brewing with Jean Pierre Isoré and Gerry Klein who resented the fact that Atkinson and Holden had arrived on the scene late in the game and were suddenly front and centre in the media spotlight. They felt the Equality Party in the eyes of the public had become only the four MNAs and many of those who had worked from the beginning were being ignored.

Another category of individuals consisted of the many committed volunteers who had no deep political conviction or political agenda, but liked to be around people and enjoyed politics for its own sake. They had to be continually motivated now that there was no longer the tangible objective of an imminent election. If the party remained in the news, which was perceived as the measure of its success and impact, volunteers continued to be "gung-ho". If we dropped out of the media for a while, therefore seeming less relevant, or if meetings became too long or acrimonious, many of these sincerely-minded volunteers would stay away until specifically called upon.

One way of keeping these various groups happy and motivated was for the leader to maintain regular contact with them and to take up their concerns whenever they arose. This was a problem, as I had less time and patience for all these things now that my Assembly duties took up a good portion of my working hours. Many trivialities, injustices, conspiracy theories and issues to raise in the National Assembly were brought to my attention. Very few of these suggestions were worth pursuing, but to keep party members devoted you have to give their ideas due attention. I was constantly being dragged in to mediate personal rivalries, knowing well that coming down on one side or the other was risky at the best of times.

A second problem was getting all these groups together to begin the task of defining the political orientation of the party and broadening its base. From the beginning there was disagreement on whether we even had to broaden the base. Some felt that what distinguished us from the Liberals was our commitment to minority rights and Canadian federalism, period. This was why we were elected in the first place and we did not have a moral mandate to go beyond it. I, on the other hand, felt that to be taken seriously and to gain broader credibility, particularly among francophone Quebecers, we had to venture beyond the language issue.

But where would we begin? How would we begin? How would we get such a disparate group of people to start with a blank page and develop a sophisticated program? The Equality Party, by virtue of having been built around a single issue, was in effect a coalition that assembled people from the left, people from the right, political ideologues, the morally righteous, the flexibly pragmatic, and a whole lot of "flakes". Especially now that the party had succeeded in carving itself a public profile, a strange bag of colorful (to say the least) individuals in search of a cause began attaching themselves to ours. How in the world could this amorphous crew possibly define social, environmental, and economic policy without tearing itself apart? Furthermore, a proper party constitution, bylaws, a fundraising campaign and a youth wing all had to be assembled, all under the watchful eye of the media who could be counted on to amplify any discord within the ranks.

Most new political parties establish this foundation first and cope with the inherent growing pains in relative obscurity before actually breaking ground in an election. Because of our near-instant success, we were forced to run before we could crawl. Another major difficulty, now that we had this wonderful new soapbox, was getting a handle on our growing number of spokesmen by establishing who was to speak on what. Considering some of the egos involved, I knew this was not going to be an easy exercise.

There were also problems over paid jobs. The party, by virtue of its percentage of the vote, was entitled to roughly $60,000 a year from the provincial government to help run our daily operations, which required full-time staff. The MNAs, who also had budgets to run an office, had to hire office help. Since there were only a few such jobs and many who felt they were deserving, there were the inevitable hard feelings among those who were passed over.

And then there was the caucus. I found myself the leader of three much older and very independent-minded characters. In addition, all considered themselves to be political authorities compared to their young leader, who never hid the fact that he was inexperienced and would have to rely on them. The problem of our age difference surfaced fairly early, especially with Holden. Whenever I would become a little too enthusiastic, or ask one of them to do something that they were not keen on doing, Holden would remind me that his son Arthur was my age.

At first there was actually a small measure of respect and appreciation for having pulled this thing off, resulting in these new jobs for all of us. But this was soon depleted. Before long, Holden and Atkinson became good buddies and barstool companions, a bit too comfortable with the perks of their newfound office, and seduced by the glamour of the job. They were much less eager to stick their necks out or get their hands dirty, and there was never any danger that too much hard work would make them dull boys. Therefore they became increasingly less tolerant of this energetic "pesky little kid" who was constantly hounding them to do this or that.

Tensions rose on occasion, and to make matters worse, they were also developing a sense of superiority over the "common folk," and those in the party to whom they referred to as the "crackpots". Their contempt for the party itself was growing, and the party in turn developed contempt for them. Holden began making noises anew about the Meech Lake Accord and the dire necessity of its passage to stave off the breakup of Canada. This set the party activists, many of whom were staunch opponents of the accord, into a mounting rage. I was told to keep Holden in line or else they would publicly denounce him.

Because I was irritated with the party myself to a certain degree for becoming too preoccupied with political issues and neglecting the bricks-and-mortar details of building a proper organization, I responded by challenging the party executive to recognize that its primary function was to administer the party's day-to-day operations and to harp less on the political end of things, which was primarily the responsibility of the caucus. This was difficult for them to swallow. Most people who joined the party did so for ideological reasons and not for love of administrative duties. Individuals like Klein and Isoré, who were the president and vice-president respectively, were less interested in the organizational labors of their executive positions and wanted to be political spokesmen. This left a gaping void in organization, and the party missed a golden opportunity to capitalize on its electoral success by following up with concerted membership and fundraising drives.

Riding associations were also demanding greater autonomy from party central. The treasurer of the party, Gerald Cooper, insisted that all money raised in the name of the party should pass through headquarters, and then a percentage would go to the ridings. The riding association executives were fighting for the reverse.

A meeting was called in late December to deal with these internal problems and to clear the air between the various factions, including the executive, the caucus, the riding association executives, a number of party activists and the defeated candidates. Despite much self-congratulation at the beginning of the meeting about our success three months earlier, the tension in the air was apparent and was not resolved. Many people who had played leading roles in the party or had been candidates claimed that the MNAs did not seem to care about the party any longer and were doing their own thing without proper consultation.

A few from the D'Arcy McGee riding were upset that I had the nerve to hire a Liberal for my riding office after so many people had worked so hard to "put me in office". I had to explain over and over again that I had needed someone who knew the ropes to ease the transition for me.

It was apparent from this meeting that the party would not be moving anywhere without a clear delineation between a political wing and an administrative wing. After the meeting I asked Klein privately if he would consider stepping down as president to make way for someone with a greater interest in administration. To mollify him, I suggested we would honour him with the title of Founding President of the party. Unfortunately, he saw this as an attempt on my part to usurp his authority and stormed off, thus straining our relationship even further. I tried to convince Isoré to relinquish the position of vice-president and become chairman of the party policy committee. He also saw this as a threat. He predicted the party's imminent demise if we did not address the problem with Holden and his support for Meech.

We approached the end of 1989 amid brewing storm clouds. My overall support was still strong among grass roots members thanks to the continued media attention. As that held up, I would have the authority that I might otherwise have lacked due to my age.

Pressure was building for something to be done about Klein. The administrative coherence a strong president would have provided was notably lacking. Since my standing in the party was solid, I decided that the only way to resolve the impasse was to call elections for executive positions in the hope this would invest a new executive with the moral authority now lacking in our currently unelected executive. I engineered a general council meeting where I disbanded the executive and named a provisional board of strong supporters to run the day-to-day operations for six months until executive elections would be held. While this was overwhelmingly backed by the rank and file, Klein stormed out of the meeting and quit the party; to this day we still have not spoken to each other. Isoré left shortly thereafter.

While all this was going on, I was also accompanying my wife to weekly pre-natal classes for the child we were expecting in mid-May.

In the period between Assembly sessions, the political scene is usually subdued and this gave me an opportunity to get my riding office in order, attack paper work and correspondence, and start thinking about my own initiatives to increase our base of support. The election numbers had shown that between 60% and 70% of the anglophones in all ridings where we ran candidates voted for our party. The first natural step therefore would be to establish links with the segment of the anglo community that did not support us, as well as with different cultural groups. This would require direct outreach, as well as indications that we were trying to build bridges with the francophone majority. I would have to develop a personal relationship with key community figures.

I therefore met with Eric Maldoff, the former president of Alliance Quebec, who was still a major force in the organization. I had lunch at the McGill Faculty Club with Storrs McCall, a McGill professor of philosophy, who was one of the original people involved with Alliance's precursor, the Positive Action Committee. I also met with Gord Sinclair from CJAD, who had been harshly critical of the party. I got together with former N.D.G. MNA Reed Scowen, who was in the process of writing a book about the anglo community. I courted the new president of Alliance Quebec, Robert Keaton, and other key community figures, like Peter Blaikie and Donald Johnston. Through June Weiss I also got to know constitutional lawyer Julius Grey, whose intellect and reasoned approach to all constitutional and language issues I had always followed and admired.

I was anxious to gain as much insight as I could from these individuals who had been involved in Quebec's political debates for years, and to soften some of the negative impressions of our party. With my new status as a spokesman for the anglophone community, which turned out to be more than I had originally bargained for, I had a sincere desire to learn from these people.

All of them held a measure of genuine respect for the party's accomplishments, but there was concern about certain unpredictable elements in the party, and whether their ability to grab the spotlight on occasion could inflame the language debate. If the party could be perceived as playing a constructive role in bringing key issues to the fore on behalf of the community without provoking a backlash, then we could greatly increase our basin of support and our level of credibility. It was crucial to reach out to the francophone community, and any sign that we were succeeding would go far with the anglo-establishment types we were trying to attract.

To that end I was accepting all the speaking invitations I could from francophone community groups, CEGEPS, and high schools. At the end of January I spoke to the political science faculty at the Université de Montreal. There were over 400 students in the large auditorium who, according to media reports, were not necessarily convinced, but saw more reason in what I had to say than they had expected. I was accompanied by Jacques Renaud, who also spoke. The speech and ensuing question period went smoothly and the coverage was encouraging; I was starting to be portrayed in the French press as a more reasonable and moderate individual than the anglo "enfant-terrible" caricature they had originally drawn of me. My message on these occasions was not very different from what I was saying to anglo audiences, but I quickly realized the choice of words and tone could make a big difference.

Many in the party were frustrated that *The Gazette* was covering hardly any of these activities. They felt the paper still had a bias against us and was determined not to depict the party in too positive a light. The media attention we had enjoyed since the election was beginning to wane, and the party activists were demanding that we become more outspoken. When I recounted at party meetings some of the steps that I had been taking to appeal to francophones and even members of the anglo establishment, I was criticized by a growing group of hard-liners for adulterating our party's stance and accused of beginning to "sell out". Being considered more moderate by the French press was clearly not their cup of tea.

This walking the fine line, between keeping the hard-core militants satisfied and trying to broaden the party's appeal, put me in a constant squeeze. Although some of the internal party tensions had been resolved by disbanding the executive and installing an interim board, the lag in media attention focused some of the discontent on me for the first time. Ironically, the events of the next few weeks would obliterate any discontent among the party members who wanted me to take a more outspoken and controversial stand. On the other hand, our efforts to break ground with the more moderate establishment of our community or the francophone majority were about to suffer a major setback.

CHAPTER EIGHT
Feeling the Heat

It's a strange world of language
in which skating on thin ice
can get you into hot water.
—Franklin P. Jones

Around the beginning of February 1990, the language debate began to heat up again. A handful of citizens of Brockville, Ontario, had deliberately stomped on a Quebec flag, a scene that was replayed dozens of times on French television. About the same time, *The Suburban* newspaper ran a column by Lionel Albert that was construed as having likened Quebec's language laws to edicts in Nazi Germany. Both incidents created a furore in the French press, and *The Suburban* was ultimately moved to issue an apology.

Then the Ontario municipality of Sault Ste. Marie, whose francophone community amounted to barely 3 per cent of its total population, felt the need to pass a resolution declaring English the town's sole official language on the grounds that bilingualism was costing the town too much money. This generated another media uproar as both English and French commentators condemned the action as bigoted and racist.

Our initial reaction was deliberately restrained. We deplored the resolution and called on the federal government to incite provinces to show their support for linguistic duality by opting into section 16 of the Canadian Charter of Rights and Freedoms. This provision allows any province to declare itself officially bilingual, as New Brunswick has done, thus guaranteeing provincial government services in both official languages. Our party had always promoted its belief that bilingualism is the glue that can best keep this country together, but our measured response to the Sault Ste. Marie controversy received scant attention.

At the time, much greater media attention was lavished on the messy departure of our francophone press attaché, who quit under a cloud of bitterness, claiming that we had not been paying her. Because her salary was split between the four MNAs, the paperwork got tangled up and her cheque was delayed. But she made a public spectacle of the whole thing, linking her departure to our opposition to the Meech Lake Accord and our alleged misunderstanding of francophones.

As the weeks wore on, the media—particularly the French press, which continually condoned the language restrictions in Quebec—relentlessly lambasted the Sault resolution as an intolerant attack on francophone communities outside Quebec. Despite our disagreement with the Sault resolution, we felt that the reaction was going a bit too far in light of some of the prevailing laws in Quebec. Richard Holden and I decided to fly to Quebec City to hold a press conference to comment on this, as well as Premier Bourassa's recent trip to Europe, where he had talked about a "superstructure" or "supranational parliament" as a potential constitutional framework if the Meech Lake deal came undone.

There was a large media turnout in the Hot Room, as there would be for any press conference dealing with the language debate, especially on a slow news day in Quebec City when the Assembly is not in session. The francophone journalists seemed ready to pounce, and we certainly gave them the opportunity.

I read a prepared statement reiterating my opposition to the Sault St. Marie resolution and those of other municipalities which had also voted for unilingual status. However, I created a link between the decisions of these Ontario municipalities to try to ban French and Quebec's language laws and their treatment of the anglophone minority. Our most salient point was to suggest that the hurt and insult that most francophones felt as a result of the Sault St. Marie resolution could inspire them to understand and empathize with the feeling of frustration and hurt of Quebec anglophones as a result of Bill 101. We made the point that Bill 101 forces the same unilingual status on a Quebec municipality if the population of anglophones drops below 50%, a far higher number than the 3% population of francophones in Sault St. Marie. Section 113f of Bill 101 not only revokes the bilingual status of any municipality if the non-francophone population drops below 50%, but of any institution as well. This means for example that if the clientele of the Royal Victoria Hospital becomes 51% francophone, this historic anglophone institution would lose its bilingual status. These restrictions are far more stringent than any language restrictions in the rest of Canada.

Holden also criticized the government's draft bill on the health care reform which would eliminate the boards of directors of individual health and social service institutions and replace them with territorial boards. When a journalist asked him if this was a plan by the government to exterminate the anglophone community, he said that it could "conceivably lead to that."

We also condemned Premier Bourassa's recent references to Quebec anglos being the best treated minority in Canada. He and other nationalist leaders are constantly saying that francophones outside Quebec would die to have what Quebec anglos have. Our point was that there is no basis of comparison for the allocation or removal of rights. The only yardstick against which rights are measured is the Universal Declaration of Human Rights. Any attempt to compare our community's status with that of francophones outside Quebec is gratuitous and should stop once and for all. There are over one million non-francophones in Quebec, 75% of whom live within a 25 mile radius of downtown Montreal. This population equals the total number of all francophones spread throughout the rest of Canada, and more than the population of 5 of the 10 provinces of Canada. It is only natural, therefore, that our community would build and maintain a comprehensive network of schools and institutions. We pay our fair share of taxes and deserve our fair share of government support. Any lamenting that the anglophones are spoiled because they benefit from their institutions, while francophones outside Quebec do not have anything comparable, is political wind. It is also time for the majority to recognize that all Quebecers benefit from the research and breakthroughs made at such anglophone institutions as McGill University, the Royal Victoria Hospital or Montreal Neurological Institute.

If anything, the anglo community wants most of all to be left alone. Provincial laws do not give anything to the anglo community so much as curtail and regulate what has already been created and developed by the community itself. This popular impression in some quarters that anglo institutions are a gift from a generous Quebec government is hogwash that should not go unchallenged.

The barrage of questions we provoked at the press conference and the chippy tone of some of them, left me feeling uneasy afterward about how our comments would be played by the media. Holden, however, insisted that what we said was truthful and if there is any honesty out there, we will have sparked a worthwhile debate.

The French newspapers went ballistic the next day. Large headlines blared that I claimed Quebec anglos were worse off than Ontario francophones: "Ici c'est pire qu'à Sault Ste. Marie, affirme Robert Libman."—*Le Soleil*; "Les anglo-Quebecois sont plus à plaindre, selon Libman"—*Le Journal de Quebec* ; "Selon Libman, les lois 101 et 178 sont bien pires que la résolution de Sault-Ste-Marie"—*Le Devoir*. There was an editorial page cartoon in *La Presse* entitled "La crucifixion de Mister Libman" that needs no further description to give you an idea of its vicious thrust. To make matters worse, the Holden quote about exterminating the anglophone community was attributed to me. The word "extermination" coming from a Jew and used in this context really got under the skin of many francophone nationalists. Lumped together with the Nazi story in *The Suburban*, it put us up to our necks in what George Bush quaintly termed "deep doggy-doo".

French radio talk show hosts like Pierre Pascau and Gilles Proulx spewed the most hysterical vitriol one could imagine, and incited their listeners to call my office and give me a piece of their mind. For the next few days, our riding office was assailed by an avalanche of racist and anti-semitic death threats, couched in vocabulary whose crudeness would have put the most articulately-virulent skinhead punk to shame. The digital readout on our answering machine displayed 157 messages over a three-day period, in addition to the calls we answered.

But apart from this telephone onslaught, I rarely encountered any anti-semitic sentiment whatsoever. Many people have asked me over the years what it was like being the only Jewish member of the National Assembly, having furthermore been elected on a controversial platform opposing Quebec nationalism. Fortunately, I can say that from my own personal experience, Quebec is not by any stretch anti-semitic in the way it may have been in the past. There were only two incidents that come to mind from my political career, both of them minor. In 1990, I was a guest on a French open line show in Sherbrooke and one caller suggested that I conduct my political experiments in Israel. The host of the show rose to my defense and jumped all over the caller. The only other incident involved PQ MNA Denis Perron. In June 1991, I refused to support the nomination of Claude Fillion to the Quebec Human Rights Commission. A former PQ MNA and language hardliner, I could not bring myself to vote in favour of naming him to a body that supposedly promotes and safeguards individual rights. The fact that such votes were normally formalities in the National Assembly didn't matter. Perron stormed over to me afterward and "informed" me, as he put it, that he had done business with Jews in the past, all of whom he considered honourable. I still wonder exactly what he was getting at.

The day after my now-famous press conference with Holden, a livid Claude Ryan, responding to the comments attributed to me about the government's desire to "exterminate" the anglophone community, held a special press conference to lace into me. The language minister's pungent advice, which made headlines all over the newspapers the next day, was that I should travel the province and "deniaiser" myself, which could be loosely translated as wising up through the process of losing my virginity. His attack was brutal. Bernie St. Laurent told me that evening that he had never seen Ryan so angry and shaken. The English media jumped on the bandwagon and relentlessly cut into me, despite acknowledging that what I said about the municipal status question was technically correct.

Also on this day after, Holden, unaware of Ryan's press conference, repeated his remark about the desire of the government to exterminate anglophone health care institutions, which brought an angry Health Minister Marc Yvan Côté into the fray. As a result of the fracas, Holden suggested that the National Assembly should move to Montreal so that the Quebec government and bureaucracy would have a greater understanding of Quebec's multicultural reality. Despite the relevant message in such a remark, it provoked further scorn and ridicule.

But this was only the tip of the iceberg. On this same day after the original press conference, I refused to take any media calls because I was preparing for a speech to the political science faculty at McGill University that afternoon. All the French networks and dailies therefore turned out at McGill to follow up on my Sault St. Marie comments. They got more than they bargained for, which again set them off. My speech focused on the potential implications of the Meech Lake accord if it were to be passed and a nationalist government subsequently elected in Quebec. It was a rhetorical speculation about how a government under "Premier Parizeau" could invoke the distinct society clause to justify passing nationalist-inspired legislation. I made reference to a brief that was presented in Ottawa by the National Association of Women and the Law to the joint parliamentary committee on Meech. The Meech accord said that the government of Quebec would be obligated to preserve and promote Quebec's distinct society. I quoted the portion of their brief that spoke about how an ultra-nationalist government, in order to counteract the effects of a declining birthrate among old stock francophones, might feel compelled by the distinct society clause to consider, for example, curtailing access to abortion.

As I approached this part of the speech I knew I was walking into a minefield and went out of my way to stress that I was quoting the National Association of Women and the Law in their brief to the House of Commons. Though I repeated this three times, the media had another field day at my expense. The following morning's headlines screamed about how I said that Quebec would use the distinct society clause to ban abortion. Once again, the hot-lines lit up with righteous indignation.

This time it was Parizeau's turn to hold a press conference to denounce my remarks. He was as angry and shaken as Ryan had been the day before, and was quoted in *The Gazette*'s front page headline accusing me of "arousing hate and racism" and telling me to keep my shirt on.

That afternoon, I was a speaker on the Meech Lake accord at Wagar High School as part of a panel of distinguished guests. The media was there in full force, which had the organizers of the event scrambling excitedly to place a school logo on the podium. Unfortunately, to the disappointment of the other panelists and school officials, the media wanted to know only one thing, and that was my reaction to Parizeau's remarks that morning. They tried to get me on record as having said that if Parizeau were Premier, he would ban abortions. In a scrum in the Wagar library afterwards, Irwin Block of *The Gazette* repeated the same question something like 19 times, despite my refusal to give the answer he was fishing for. He even tried to get me to compare Parizeau to deposed Romanian dictator Nicolae Ceausescu, but to no avail. I kept repeating over and over again that I was quoting the brief of the National Association of Women and the Law.

A few days later, Don Macpherson weighed in with what I thought was the most condescending column he has ever written, as though he was waiting for the chance to really hammer me. The title was, "Language Debate takes a Childish Turn: Too Many Kids are Playing with Fire." He started off in the most arrogant tone imaginable: "Well, I hate to say I told you so, five months after the election, but the good thing about a spoiled ballot is that it can't embarrass you by hanging around for the next four years saying foolish things on your behalf." He called me "boy leader" twice, "kid" once, and "boy spokesman" once, all in the same column.

The anglophone and Jewish community establishments ostracized me for a long time after this episode. Alliance Quebec took a swipe at me and was quoted in the French press as denouncing what I had said. Some anglophones who had warned against voting for our party, much like Macpherson, were now cackling, "I told you so". Nationalist groups denounced me and called on anglophone leaders to follow suit. Francophone groups outside Quebec did the same, and even the municipal council of Magog passed a motion of condemnation on the grounds that my remarks originally stemmed from a municipal resolution (in Sault St. Marie).

Lise Bissonette, writing in the Toronto *Globe and Mail*, said that I should resign over my statements, calling them the most damaging by a public figure since 1963 when CN chairman Donald Gordon declared French-Canadians unqualified for executive jobs. A few days later, he was burned in effigy over his remarks.

On both occasions my remarks were taken out of context, but there is no changing public perception in the short term once it is firmly established. It was convenient for the media to have me for dinner at this particular time, and no matter what you try to do in these situations, there is no way to slay the media mammoth or reverse its momentum once in full charge. Perception is reality in politics. You can only learn from experience and be more careful next time not to give them the rope with which they can try to hang you. Despite the embarrassment of bad press, time is a great healer. For a maligned politician, there is always the comfort of knowing that people line their birdcages and kitty-litter boxes with the newspaper the next day. In this respect, my youth and inexperience were an advantage for once. As you mature politically, past indiscretions are seen as less serious when they can be attributed to dampness behind the ears.

Despite an uncomfortable few days—I stayed indoors all that weekend because I was uneasy about meeting the public—what I discovered the following week was most telling. No one event in my political career provoked as much positive mail or feedback from ordinary anglophone Quebecers as this ordeal. I received hundreds of letters and phone calls from people thanking me for standing up and fighting for them. Once again, as on numerous other occasions, I was made aware of the attitudinal gap that sometimes exists between grassroots English-speaking Quebecers and the community's establishment and its media mouthpieces.

Wherever I went for days afterward, people would stop me in the streets to say how great it was to finally have someone honestly telling it like it is. Ordinary anglophones were still pretty steamed about what was going on in Quebec and felt that our controversial remarks were something they themselves were getting off their chests. Our community leadership, on the other hand, as well as many of our eminent journalists, terrified of being labelled anti-French, are generally too concerned about sparking controversy. They had a lot of trouble with this new kid on the block who had just thrown the francophone chattering class into a tizzy. This recent turmoil, coming from a community which is supposed to be quiet and accommodating, made them acutely uncomfortable.

Rejuvenated by the support of my constituents, I became increasingly bitter about the perpetual sniping from the establishment trenches.

The temptation to tell detractors to go to hell is sometimes overpowering. But losing your cool with the press or the public is suicidal in political life. I also believed that this whole affair was a positive development in the language debate. It is better to have one's cards on the table in a debate like this than to have people guess at what you might be thinking. Being more open and honest with each other ultimately helps the search for a compromise.

Unfortunately, there was another negative media eruption a few days later. Jacques Renaud called me and told me that he would be issuing a statement to the press announcing that he was leaving the Equality Party for good. He felt that my comments to the effect that Quebec's anglos were worse off than francophones outside Quebec, were more than he could stomach. Over the past year he had taken a lot of flak from too many sources for his association with the Equality Party. The past week had been unbearable for him, and he could no longer put up with the grief.

I took this as a serious blow to the party. It would graphically reinforce the widespread notion that our party had closed itself off from francophones. Though I repeated over and over to him on the phone that I never compared Quebec's anglophone community to francophones outside Quebec, but for all my pleading, he was dead set on getting out. He just wanted the load off his back.

As I thought, Renaud's announcement caused a media splash that gave rise to another round of speculation about the demise of the Equality Party; more negative editorials, columns and open line radio rants.

I agreed to be a guest—target might be a more appropriate word—on a number of French TV and radio talk shows that week in an attempt to diffuse some of the tension. For *Le Point*, Radio-Canada's flagship public affairs program, a confrontation was set up between myself and Guy Matte, the president of the Federation of Francophones Outside Quebec. During the interview I suggested that he and I travel the country together speaking up for minority rights. This extending of my hand changed the tone of the exchange considerably. We agreed on many things, to the point where after the interview, I overheard the host, Simon Durivage, tell his producer that to his chagrin, and contrary to what they had anticipated, there had not been a trace of animosity between us.

Ironically, this storm washed away any questions about my leadership within the party. Most of the party rank and file loved what was going on, and a unanimous motion of support for my leadership and condemnation of the media was passed at a general council meeting called specifically for that purpose.

The following week I did a feature interview with the Quebec City newspaper *Le Soleil*. The leadership race for the federal Liberals, following the resignation of John Turner, was in full swing, and when asked about it in passing, I mentioned my active support for Jean Chrétien, because of his commitment to the Canadian Charter of Rights and Freedoms and his disapproval, on that basis, of the Meech Lake accord. I had even joined the Federal Liberals earlier that year in order to vote for his slate of delegates for the leadership convention the following June. I also acknowledged in passing that part of the fallout of the controversial remarks that I had made the previous week was a spate of death threats.

We spent a long time discussing anglophone rights, Canadian unity, and the future of the party. Very little of any of this was reported. Instead, the next morning, across the front page of *Le Soleil* was my endorsement of Chrétien and the news about the death threats. These two items were subsequently carried by the wire services and splashed all over the rest of the media the following day.

The first call we received that morning was from the Chrétien camp, asking us to send out a release withdrawing our support for Chrétien. Fifteen minutes later, another call came in from the Chrétien camp asking us to ignore the first call. Any support was welcome the second caller said.

An interesting consequence of this public endorsement of Chrétien surfaced on the CBC national news a few days later. I was minding my own business, watching the news one evening, when a report came on about a swing by Prime Minister Brian Mulroney through Quebec, and his comments on the federal Liberal leadership race. Provincial Liberal heavyweight Marc Yvan Côté had recently come out in support of Sheila Copps, who was gaining popularity in Quebec even though Chrétien was expected to win. Mulroney seemed to go out of his way to highlight the fact that Côté, a very influential cabinet minister had endorsed Copps. He then asked rhetorically who in Quebec was supporting Chrétien. He paused and then said, "Robert Libman," followed by hearty laughter. I nearly fell out of my chair. This attempt to take a shot at Chrétien by capitalizing on my recent demon status in francophone Quebec was played on the national news in English and French and reported in many French newspapers the next day.

A few days later, as the dust finally began to settle, things turned sour again as Holden publicly broke ranks on Meech Lake and announced that he would be joining the "Friends of Meech Lake," a coalition of individuals dedicated to the passage of the accord. The chairman of the group was Montreal lawyer Alex Paterson and included columnist Gretta Chambers and other anglo notables. It didn't seem to bother Holden that only days earlier he had signed a joint position paper with the caucus, declaring our solidarity that the accord in its present form was unacceptable.

One of the group's initiatives was to travel to the holdout provinces and try to convince their premiers to soften their opposition to the accord. Ironically, their first stop was to be in Winnipeg the very weekend I was already scheduled to be in that city to give a speech to a group of Manitoba and Ontario francophones as part of a conference entitled "Development of Linguistic Rights in Perspective for the Year 2000".

The media played up the fact that I was delivering a speech in which I criticized the accord for its lack of protection of minority rights while my colleague, Holden was down the street, singing its praises. There he was on the news, saying how he wanted to do this for his grandchildren, so that he could tell them one day that he worked to save Canada when it was so close to being destroyed. It was a fitting testimonial, coming from someone who two years later would be sitting with the PQ as a separatist MNA.

My speech at the conference focused on the protection of minority rights throughout Canada and how the accord jeopardized some of those protections. Bill 178 or the specific concerns of the anglophone community of Quebec were not even mentioned. Once I finished and took questions, the francophone crowd immediately jumped on my "declarations" of a few weeks earlier that Quebec anglophones were worse off than francophones outside Quebec. Though I had never said this, they kept referring to my shocking "declarations" and were quite bitter that a Quebec anglo would have the indecency to complain about the treatment of his community.

The next day's coverage of my Winnipeg speech in *La Presse* accused me of devoting my entire speech to lamenting about Bill 178 and the way anglophones are treated in Quebec. This lead me to lodge a complaint with the Quebec Press Council. I had done the same for a separate editorial in *La Presse* that stated I had compared Quebec to Nazi Germany, obviously confusing my statements with *The Suburban* column by Lionel Albert. Two years later, the council finally ruled in my favour in both cases. The paper was urged by the council to correct the misinformation, but never did so. This is an indication of the uselessness of this body. There is no body in Quebec that properly monitors the press for accuracy. If someone lays a complaint with the Press Council, it generally takes more than a year for a decision to be rendered, and when it finally does come down, the council merely sends out a press release announcing the decision. Nothing compels a media outlet found in error to correct anything, and even if they decide to do so, it is usually buried somewhere in the paper in a far less prominent place than the original story.

Despite the barrage of bad press, I was managing to ride out this very turbulent and difficult period. To reinforce grassroots credibility, I scheduled a number of interviews with local and ethnic newspapers. We had also just wrapped up our negotiations with the Unity Party, and in hopes of getting some positive coverage for a change, we held a news conference to officially announce that the two parties would merge under the Equality Party name, and that we were now an organization with over 15,000 members and 35 organized riding associations.

Several weeks later the National Assembly finally reconvened. No longer the "new kid on the block," I was the newly-incarnated "anglo-extremist," feeling most insecure about how others seemed to be eyeing me, this being my first contact with the assembled company of my fellow MNAs since all the controversy. As I took my seat, Revenue Minister Raymond Savoie, who sat nearby, motioned to me. He whispered, "You've been a bad boy during the break".

I felt even more conspicuous when the session opened with a PQ motion condemning the wave of intolerance against francophones in the rest of Canada, targeting the anglophone leadership in Quebec and the Ontario municipalities as the two main culprits. The motion also reaffirmed the National Assembly's commitment to the notwithstanding clause as the last "rampart" of protection of the French language and culture in Quebec. It was moved by Jacques Brassard, the PQ critic for intergovernmental affairs, who specifically invoked my name several times in his diatribe, which did justice to his reputation as the most colorful orator in the National Assembly. Sitting there, I felt his wrath burn through my body like a high-voltage current.

Yet for all his fulsome theatrics in the Assembly, Brassard was quite a soft spoken, mild mannered man behind the scenes. No matter what he said about me any given day on camera, he was always courteous and very friendly with me in private. But I was not ready to take this swipe sitting down and when it was my turn to speak, I attacked the notion that the anglophone community was the best treated minority in the world. I also slammed the notwithstanding clause as anathema to any society claiming to respect minority rights. Ultimately, the PQ motion forced anglo Liberals to vote in favour of the notwithstanding clause, thereby alienating them even further from their own anglo constituents.

The session was dominated by the last-ditch effort to salvage the Meech Lake accord. There were numerous motions criticizing the rest of

Canada as well as motions condemning any attempts to amend the accord to make it more palatable to the holdouts. When a Canadian government commission studying ways to save the deal recommended a series of changes, the National Assembly passed a motion warning the rest of Canada that the five minimal conditions of Meech were innocuous enough and that no changes would be tolerated by Quebec. Our caucus broke the unanimity of the vote as we did with other motions aimed at turning up the heat on the rest of the country. These motions were all proposed by the PQ, but the Liberals were forced to go along in order to show their nationalist teeth to the rest of Canada. Because of our opposition, they lacked the resonance of what the media liked to trumpet as "a unanimous vote of the National Assembly," and therefore stirred fewer reverbrations in the rest of the country.

We also made big news by blocking a motion of censure against federal Liberal MP and leadership hopeful John Nunziata and Jean Chrétien. At a leadership debate, Nunziata called Quebec separatists traitors and Chrétien refused to denounce him. The PQ tried to pass a motion, condemning both of them, but we managed to block it entirely, since it was a motion without notice, requiring unanimous consent to be debated. Our election promise that we would not allow unanimous National Assembly motions detrimental to our community, such as the one condemming d'Iberville Fortier, was being respected.

This session was also marked by the controversy that erupted when the Montreal Catholic School Commission (MCSC) floated the idea of banning English in the playgrounds and schoolyards of French-language schools. I jumped into the debate, tabling a private member's bill that would prohibit such a discriminatory practise, and tabling a motion censuring the government, for not acting rapidly enough to condemn such an intolerant suggestion by the biggest school board in the province. I was also the centre of attention at the public hearings held by the MCSC where I called for the immediate resignation of chairman Michel Pallascio, while staring him right in the face.

Judging from comments I was getting, the average anglo on the street was delighted by this kind of outspoken representation. But while I was showered by ordinary anglos with warm wishes and thanks for standing up for our community wherever I went, *The Gazette*, and in particular columnists like Don Macpherson and Jack Todd, were still heaping ridicule on our efforts, constantly referring to me as "Little Bobby" and such. Apparently the dustup we had provoked a few months earlier would not be quickly forgiven by the mainstream media.

Amid all this, my wife's doctor decided in the first week of May that she should give birth the following week as the baby was in the breech position. On May 9 we checked into the hospital at 6:00 am. After four fruitless hours of induced labor, each one an eternity in itself, we decided to go for a caesarian. I had become an expert on breathing techniques through weeks of prenatal classes, but they were of no use at this point. I dressed up in surgical clothing and watched starry-eyed as the doctor picked up a beautiful 7 and-a-half-pound boy. I thought there could be nothing in the world to match this magnificent creation, whom we named Kevin Elliot. Political frustrations or concerns of any kind whatsoever were washed away by the sheer rapture of the moment.

Gordon Atkinson happened to be speaking in the National Assembly, ironically on a motion concerning daycare, when handed a note that I had just become a new father. In his inimitable style, he concluded his speech by making the announcement to the rest of the Assembly, prompting government and opposition house leaders, as well as the speaker, to congratulate me in words that are forever inscribed in the official record of National Assembly debates. When I returned to the House, I passed around chocolate cigars to my colleagues in the immediate vicinity of my seat.

Alas, life soon returned to normal.

With the June deadline approaching and Meech on the verge of collapse, the atmosphere around the Assembly was frenetic. All the warnings by Bourassa that the rest of Canada had better support Meech or face a serious separatist threat in Quebec, seemed to be developing into what could very well become a self-fulfilling prophesy. Despite the warnings, despite the threats, the deadline passed and Manitoba and Newfoundland had still not ratified the accord. Never had I seen the atmosphere in the National Assembly so dark and sombre as that day. I got a call from the Premier during the afternoon to tell me that I would have three minutes that evening to speak on the accord's rejection, while he and Parizeau would speak for five minutes each. The speeches would mark the closing of the session for the summer.

In his speech that night, Bourassa said that Quebec always was and always will be a distinct society. Parizeau extended his hand to Bourassa, calling him "mon Premier Ministre," and suggested that the two of them should join forces to lead Quebec down the path to sovereignty.

A nationalist tide surged across Quebec. I felt personally isolated and insecure, as if I, as an anglo Canadian, was now a target for angry francophones who, as their leaders put it, had just been humiliated by their fellow countrymen. That night, after the session adjourned, I felt that I would literally have to sneak out of Quebec City, so virulent was the reaction. I found myself avoiding eye contact with people at the airport, and breathing a sigh of relief as the plane lifted off.

CHAPTER NINE

Holding the Fort for Canada

We peer so suspiciously at one another
that we cannot see that we Canadians
are standing on the mountaintop
of human wealth, freedom and privilege.
—Pierre Elliott Trudeau

By way of turning up the heat on the holdout provinces during the futile Meech ratification scramble, Premier Bourassa had for months been predicting dire consequences if the deal fell through. Now that his bluff had been called, he had to reckon with a population that he himself had recklessly whipped into a nationalist froth with his doomsday rhetoric, to the point where the polling trend was running more than 60 per cent in favor of sovereignty. The St. Jean Baptiste Day parade two days after the Meech collapse was a massive nationalist extravaganza that turned Sherbrooke St. into a surging river of blue and white fleur-de-lys banners. The Canada Day parade along the same street a week later, and the first in which I participated, was a trickling stream in comparison. Political pundits were tying themselves into knots trying to figure out what would likely happen next. Talk of humiliation and how the rest of Canada had rejected Quebec was firing nationalist sentiment to a blistering heat.

In response, I assembled a group of constitutional experts for what we called the "Task Force on Canadian Federalism" to analyze and prepare for the next go-round of Quebec's constitutional carousel. Julius Grey and Stephen Scott, who was also a constitutional law professor at McGill University and had come to my defence publicly during the Sault St. Marie dustup, were becoming confidantes and good friends. Whenever I had a legal or constitutional question, they were willing to spend as much time as I needed to develop an understanding of the issue and to formulate a position. As well, John Humphrey, one of the signatories of the Universal Declaration of Human Rights, participated in our task force, as did economist Kimon Valaskakis, Morton Brownstein, and Roger Comtois, the former dean of law at the Université de Montréal. Alas, the only constitutional question that seemed to matter at the time was what premier Bourassa would do next. He clearly had his hands on the wheel of an accelerating bandwagon, and could well have succeeded in engineering a YES vote for sovereignty had he wanted to take the plunge at the time.

Many in our community had accused him over the years of being a closet sovereignist. Had this been the case, he had a golden opportunity to come out and state his true constitutional preference in the volatile Meech aftermath, and to pull off what the PQ had failed to accomplish in close to a quarter century. Even so, he never showed much of an emotional attachment or any great affinity for the rest of Canada that went beyond pocketbook considerations. First and foremost, he was a cautious economist who abhorred turbulence of any kind. He had always known deep down how irrational it would be from an economic point of view for Quebec to secede from Canada. He always preferred to avoid initiating anything dramatic in the hope that things would fall softly into place, convinced that the best way to go was always the path of least resistance. Add to that a consummate talent for seeming to be all things at once. Given the circumstances, he was probably the best person to be in charge at this time, though he was greatly responsible for the trouble in which he found himself. For starters, he would have to contain his influential youth wing, which had adopted a constitutional position almost identical to the PQ's sovereignty-association model.

It was a frustrating time for Equality Party members, who were staunch federalists and considered it the only true federalist party in the National Assembly. But in the grand scheme of things, we barely rated as bit players, and our constitutional arguments received scant attention amid the post-Meech clamor. Only occasionally would I be quoted in an article dealing with Quebec's future.

That July, Sûreté du Quebec officers stormed barricades that were set up by the Khanesetake Mohawks near Oka to protest the extension of a golf course on what they claimed as their traditional burial ground. An SQ officer was shot and killed during the brief exchange of gunfire in the pine forest at the edge of town. The police retreated, the Indians dug in behind their barricades and the festering crisis atmosphere provoked by the summer-long standoff, along with the lingering constitutional uncertainty, dominated Quebec politics all summer. Despite strong support by Equality Party members for Quebec native communities on many issues, we had trouble finding a niche in this debate.

Along with the natives, the members of the Equality Party were getting distinctly restless as well. When your name is not in the papers on a regular basis, the party members have less of a sense that you are out there hammering away at the issues that matter to them. You could be working 20 hours a day, meeting with constituents, going to ribbon cuttings, slicing through red tape for a constituent, representing your party at a community function or memorial service, giving a speech to promote your party at a church, synagogue, school or university. But if the media ignores you, it is like the proverbial tree falling in the forest with no one there to hear.

While the legislature was in session we would get regular coverage from our participation in Assembly debates and the media scrums that followed question period. But during the breaks between sessions we were deprived of these ready-made forums and had far more difficulty making the news. On issues as hot as the Oka crisis and the future of Quebec, the party naturally wanted us to be front and center. Our absence among the principal players during this summer, while Quebec was all over the news internationally, created tension in our party ranks and incited many members to get cranky with the MNAs.

The more restless the party got over the performance of the MNAs, the more hostile Holden and Atkinson became toward the membership. Holden, whose tolerance level for the party was already scraping rock bottom, showed up at a general council meeting one evening after a long afternoon's lunch that had overflowed into happy hour. He got into a boisterous shouting match with several of the members during the discussion of a motion calling for the resignation of his friend Brian Mulroney for allowing Canada to come this close to the brink. Holden called everyone stupid, and when asked to leave the meeting, he declared nothing would please him more and lurched off into the night. A few days later I convinced him to send a letter of apology to the executive and some other members, but it did little to smooth things over.

Bourassa's eventual response to the constitutional impasse was to create a special National Assembly commission with a mandate to consult Quebecers about the province's political and constitutional future. It was a typical Bourassa manoeuvre, putting off a hard decision until later. But it also had its obvious advantages. He quickly neutralized Lucien Bouchard, who had recently quit the federal cabinet in protest over the proposed changes to the Meech accord to form the pro-sovereignist Bloc Quebecois in Ottawa. The charismatically-touched Bouchard had been rapidly growing in stature since the Meech collapse. By naming him as the first member of the commission, Bourassa could keep a close eye on him.

Assuming that I would be named to the commission as well, we decided that I should tour the province in August and September with an unabashedly pro-Canada federalist message. We were anxious to see what kind of reception it would get out there, and to gauge the true feelings of ordinary people about the future of Quebec. We would go to all the major cities and many small towns to tap the local media, which were only too happy to have a crack at this "anglo bad boy" of Quebec politics in their own back yard.

For the first leg of the trip, my wife and I, accompanied by Chris Mostovac, spent a week driving along the coast of the Lower St. Lawrence, all the way to the Gaspé peninsula, passing through Rimouski, Matane, Mont-Joli, New Carlisle, and many other places along the way where I would stop for a hectic whirl of local print and radio interviews. The following weeks I was in Abitibi, followed by the Saguenay Lac St. Jean region, the Quebec City area, and Trois Rivières. After that came the Eastern Townships, followed by Ottawa-Hull. In many of the small towns, such as Rouyn-Noranda, Chicoutimi, or Jonquière, I dropped by the local MNA's office, usually a Péquiste, to say hello.

To my surprise, I was very well received wherever I went, and nowhere was there any overt sign of hostility. I got the feeling that francophone Quebecers enjoy meeting Quebec politicians despite any differences of opinion that might stand between them. In the regions, people are exceptionally warm one-on-one, and were only too happy to talk to an MNA on a friendly, informal basis. We spoke to farmers, pulp and paper plant workers, town councillors, and hospital staffers. The worst reaction I ever got was a little good-natured ribbing from sovereignists.

Toward the end of the summer I was off with Neil Cameron and Tony Kondaks to James Bay in Northern Quebec for two days. The first day would be spent on a tour of the Hydro-Quebec power generating facility, LG-2, on the La Grande River, followed by a day with the Cree in the nearby village of Waskaganish.

Hydro-Quebec puts on the full-court public relations press. Their representatives meet you at the airport, grab your bags and pile you into a plush air-conditioned touring van, which takes you directly to the town of Radisson, built just for Hydro workers at La Grande. At the town recreation centre a hearty lunch awaits.

The tour of the Hydro generating facilities was hugely impressive. They take you through a step-by-step demonstration of how electricity is manufactured, and even take you inside one of the giant turbines. Another highlight of the tour was a drive along the top of the giant dam overlooking the colossal spillway carved out of the Canadian shield. They also bring you to a lookout point where the massive dam appears to loom right there in front of your eyes, barely a stone's throw away. When they tell you that it is a kilometre away, you begin to grasp the full scale of its enormity. That evening after dinner we thanked our gracious hosts and got on the smallest plane I had ever seen for the one-hour flight to Waskaganish. Squeezing into it along with Neil Cameron, whose Falstaffian girth seemed to fill up the entire tail section, stretched my faith in aerodynamics to the limit.

We were greeted at the equally tiny airport by the town chief, Billy Diamond, the former grand chief of the Quebec Cree. He was also the key native negotiator of the landmark James Bay Northern Quebec Agreement signed in 1975. It established a framework for Hydro-Quebec's development plans for Northern Quebec with compensation for affected native groups, and however imperfect, it was historic in its recognition of native territorial rights and cultural values.

The next day, Diamond took us on a tour of the town, after which we piled into motor boats that took us to an island. It was pouring rain, and off to the side there were boiling rapids. For a lifelong urbanite, it was quite something to actually watch someone throw a net into a river and pull up 20 fish at a time.

The community was deeply concerned and greatly suspicious about Hydro-Quebec's plans to build more dams along the river. We left that evening with a genuine feeling for their anxieties.

Since the National Assembly would have to sit for a few days during September to officially create the new commission on the future of Quebec, we were in a strong bargaining position. Whenever the Assembly must sit under exceptional circumstances, unanimous consent is necessary to bypass some of the normal rules and regulations. The PQ was certainly manoeuvring to take advantage of the situation and we were determined to do the same in our own small way.

It was obvious that we would be allowed at least one member on the commission. Holden was greatly smitten by its historical significance and threatened to quit the party if he was not named as the Equality representative. Since the legislation creating the commission gave party leaders the authority to name their allotted representatives on the commission, I told Holden that I would agree to designate him on two conditions. First he would have to fight for an additional place on the commission for me as an ex-officio member, by virtue of the fact that I was a party leader. Second, he would have to go on the wagon for the duration of the commission's mandate. Holden was becoming ever more impossible to work with after his ritual liquid lunches. (It was around this time that his friend Mordecai Richler declared that anything Holden might say after two in the afternoon shouldn't be taken seriously.) He would constantly insult the Equality Party and petulantly resist the slightest push to do anything that involved hard work. Every request that would cut substantially into his extended cocktail hours would elicit a bitter and condescending retort.

He was so intent on getting a place on the commission that he agreed to the two conditions, going so far as to sign a paper saying that he would not drink for the duration of the hearings. Keenly aware that the commission deliberations would be a political and media spectacle of the first order, he went so far as to have a liposuction operation to reduce the growing plentitude of his chins.

We presented a series of conditions to the government in exchange for our procedural consent, along with my pitch for ex-officio status on the commission. We wanted extra representation for anglophones and cultural communities, English transcripts of the deliberations, and a say in the selection of commissioners who were not MNAs. All were set forth in a letter to the Premier, which we also released to the media. Bourassa got back to me on my car phone and we set up a meeting at The Bunker in Quebec City for later that week.

When I arrived at his office, I was ushered up to the rooftop terrace. There was a beautiful garden up there with a panoramic view of the old city. We sipped Perrier and discussed our party's conditions. In addition to our regular member on the commission, the Premier agreed to have me sit as an ex-officio member, fully able to participate, but without a vote. He agreed that all transcripts would be translated into English, and that we could recommend people for commission seats. Specifically, he asked us to find an anglophone business representative. None of our recommendations were ever accepted, but at least we were satisfied to have two of us—half the caucus actually—on the commission.

In all, 35 members were named to the commission. There were 10 Liberals, 7 Péquistes, Holden and myself, two municipal officials, four businessmen, four trade unionists, one representative from the co-operative sector, one each from the educational and cultural sectors, three federal MPs, plus the two chairmen, Michel Belanger and Jean Campeau. It was widely touted as the commission of the century, assembling the biggest names in Quebec for a full-dress road show devoted to the province's favourite pastime — discussing its political future.

The first meeting of the Belanger-Campeau commission took place in the Red Room, and it was my first opportunity to meet many of

Quebec's political, economic and cultural heavyweights. It was quite the extravaganza with all these notables gathered around the same table, ready to embark on a six-month odyssey that would take us around the province. It was an opportunity to get to know labour leaders Gérald Larose, the head of the CNTU, Louis Laberge of the FTQ, and Lorraine Pagé of the CEQ teacher's union, as well as Claude Béland, the head of the Caisse Desjardins, Ghislain Dufour of the Conseil du Patronat, as well as Lucien Bouchard and former federal Liberal cabinet minister André Ouellette.

Holden and I caused quite a stir at the outset about the lack of native participation, and I went so far as to hold a press conference with Konrad Sioui, the chief of the Assembly of First Nations of Quebec, where we announced that he would be my alternate on the commission in my absence. (This was eventually ruled out of order by the commission secretariat.) My threats to tie up the Assembly proceedings over better representation for native groups and members of cultural communities came to nothing when the three other MNAs refused to back me up on it.

A call for all interested parties to submit briefs on the future of Quebec was published in all newspapers, resulting in an avalanche of reading material for the commissioners.

The commission's public hearings began in Quebec City and switched to Montreal in mid-November, followed by a tour of the province's major regional centres. Most of the briefs were presented by groups in favor of Quebec sovereignty. When federalist spokesmen appeared, the more fervent sovereignist members of the commission bristled with hostility and condescending scorn. Things came to a head one evening when the task force on federalism that I had formed with Julius Grey presented its brief. The day before, a member of the same group, Don Donderi, a psychology professor at McGill University, allegedly compared Quebec to Nazi Germany in a speech on the West Island. This put the sovereignist commissioners into a boiling froth and they took it out on Julius Grey and the rest of the group. Even the supposedly pro-federalist co-chairman, Michel Belanger, barked at the presenters in a rare display of pique. André Ouellette was the only one to defend them, claiming that this was an example of the intolerance typical of Quebec's sovereignty movement when someone disagrees with them.

The next day the fur flew again as Holden accused Lucien Bouchard of being a traitor, saying that he would still be an unknown backwater lawyer had it not been for his friend Brian Mulroney, whom Bouchard had stabbed in the back. Bouchard blew his stack, launching into a furious tirade before being calmed down by the chair.

This was the kind of thing our voters loved to see. They had voted for us to speak out on issues of their concern, notably anglophone rights and Canadian federalism. Whenever we made big news like this that showed us shaking up the separatists, we would be flooded with congratulatory calls. Our presence on the commission, whose deliberations were televised live throughout Quebec, greatly raised our lately-sagging profile. Asking the occasional question in English often got us featured in the highlight reel on the English evening news.

There was a *Le Soleil*-CKAC poll that came out in late November showing Equality support up to an incredible 11%, the highest figure ever recorded for the party. Though the poll was ignored by *The Gazette*, it prompted Ghislain Dufour to mention to me that morning, as the commission caravan rolled into St. Hyacinthe, that our party could very well play a crucial role in the overall scheme of things during the coming months. Unfortunately, this run of good news was short lived.

The next day, *La Presse* featured a lengthy interview with Holden about the party's first year in the National Assembly. Despite his promise to me, Holden had been drinking again and a journalist from *La Presse* got to him late one afternoon when his tongue was loosened by extended lunching. The article was full of condescending Holden shots against me and the party, some of which Atkinson had backed up. He sneered at my youth and inexperience, and complained that I constantly pestered him like a little kid. In a scrum, I called Holden's remarks irresponsible, which generated a run of media comment over the next few days about how he and I were at war with each other.

Party members wanted him thrown out on the spot, especially after he referred to them as "rabble". But I opted for reconciliation, which was forthcoming the next day as Holden apologized in writing. I held a press conference announcing that we had given him another last chance to be a team player. This calmed things down, but only for the time being. The party had clearly suffered a major embarrassment. It was also a setback to my leadership authority at a time when we should have been capitalizing on a splendid opportunity.

In addition to our presence on the commission and in the Assembly, we had been holding a series of information meetings in the West Island on Bill 107, the government's education reform. The bill proposed a historic overhaul of Quebec's education system, replacing confessional school boards with language-based boards, a plan we felt would jeopardize the historic constitutional protection assuring our community's control of its own school boards. We were even given small credit when the government decided to scrap the original plan to consolidate the boards of minority community health and social services institutions into regional bodies. Unfortunately, whenever things seemed to be going well, something like this internal rift would invariably crop up and distract from our efforts. A single episode blows over after a few days, but as these things accumulate, it hardens negative perceptions in people's minds.

For a Jewish kid from anglo suburbia, the Belanger-Campeau experience, with its whirl of bus rides, dinners and hotel-hopping with Quebec's political elite, was an education in itself. While close affinities developed between like-minded members of the commission, all the francophone members, no matter what their political orientation, shared a certain kinship from which I felt apart. Certain jokes or cultural references often went right over my head. When we were not in session, I largely kept to myself, happy to bury myself in the piles of briefs we were given every morning for the next day's hearings. After a while I got the feeling that this whole thing was an elaborately choreographed travelling stage presentation with all the commissioners merely players, acting out their assigned parts. The sovereignist members were expected to be emotional and wax indignant, especially when a federalist group would present its brief, and federalists would carefully and methodically challenge the emotional hyperbole of the sovereignist briefs.

Every time we rolled into a small town the excitement among the local population made me realize just how seriously francophones take their provincial politics. For example, at Jonquière, which is in the nationalist heartland of Quebec, camera crews recorded the arrival of the commissioners at the airport. At the hearings, the entrance for the commissioners to the large hall where the hearings were to take place was cordoned off. On each side of the ropes, people waited four rows deep just to get a glimpse of the star politicians. As the commissioners began to file in, cheers went up for some as onlookers crowded more closely against the ropes. It was almost like being at the Academy Awards, I remarked to another commissioner, as I was being booed by a few hecklers on my way in.

Since most of the briefs submitted to the commission promoted sovereignty, as did most of the groups at the public hearings, the nationalist wave that arose after the failure of Meech was not only being sustained, but gaining momentum. Along with the other federalist members of the commission I soon got the insecure feeling that we were being outplayed by our sovereignist colleagues.

The Liberal party was expected to capitalize on this nationalist fervor, and there was much intense speculation about the constitutional stance it would adopt at its next all-party convention in early 1991. Jean Allaire, a hitherto obscure lawyer and Liberal back-room functionary, chaired the committee that was in the process of drafting the party's new policy. The convention eventually adopted most of the proposals in what became known as the "Allaire Report," a hard-line nationalist shopping list which demanded that Quebec be given jurisdiction over virtually everything previously in the hands of the federal government with the exception of the post office and armed forces. Adding insult to injury, it called for Quebec to continue receiving undiminished equalization payments from the federal government. For all intents and purposes, it called for Quebec to be a de-facto sovereign state while enjoying the benefits and privileges of Canadian nationhood.

The convention went so far down the sovereignist path that Claude Ryan walked out at one point, only to return the next day after Bourassa gave a somewhat more federalist closing speech than his opening number, emphasizing that the Allaire Report was a bargaining tool, not the government's constitutional bottom line. I attacked Liberal anglos for endorsing a party with such an aggressively nationalist program and called on them to show some backbone and conviction by quitting the party in protest.

For some reason, Alliance Quebec president Robert Keaton endorsed the Allaire Report with barely a whimper of protest, which further reinforced the impression that the Alliance was at the beck and call of the Liberal party. It provoked Peter Blaikie, for one, to quit the organization, angrily tearing up his membership card, while we made headlines by roasting Keaton for his lockstep compliance with the Liberal marching orders.

For the anglophone community, the language issue had by this time taken a back seat to renewed concern about Quebec separation. Having Bourassa and the Liberal Party strike out in this nationalist direction created yet another opportunity for us to reinforce and extend our support by jumping all over the Allaire report. Whenever the premier played a federalist card, our target clientele would scurry back to the Liberals. Our fortunes would continually hinge on the Liberal party's constitutional swing at any given time, making it difficult, if not impossible, to build a solid foundation for the party.

With the situation swinging in our favor, the four MNAs held a press conference announcing a major Canadian unity rally to be held in late February at the Dorval Airport Hilton. Anger in the community continued to build over the Liberal's flirtation with hard-line nationalism, and close to 1,000 federalists showed up that evening, jamming the hall and loudly proclaiming their Canadian patriotism. Money was literally thrown at our volunteers manning the membership tables.

The following month the party finally held its first policy convention, where 250 delegates from more than 30 riding associations spent the weekend hammering out a constitutional platform. We also discussed education policy, the environment, health and social affairs, native rights, immigration and the economy. A committee had been meeting regularly for several months drawing up a party constitution and bylaws, and our constitution committee, chaired by Vanier CEGEP English teacher Keith Henderson, had drawn up our alternative to the Allaire report.

The convention at the Monkland Community Centre in N.D.G. looked promising: rows of tables; colourful new posters and banners; handsome documents and a hefty turnout. Holden even introduced me graciously for my opening speech, singing my praises to the point where I thought I must be dreaming. My hope was that we could appeal to francophone Quebecers with this convention by coming up with a policy platform that would encourage them to give our party a serious look as the only true defender of Canadian federalism in Quebec.

But while the convention received national press coverage, most of it was unfortunately focused on the part of our constitutional policy endorsing the proposition that if Quebec were to separate from Canada, portions of Quebec—"enclaves" as the media called them—would be entitled to split from Quebec and remain part of Canada. It became the focus of attention, even though I had successfully downgraded this recommendation at the convention. The original proposal had been that promotion of this policy would be the party's top priority.

I did not disagree with the premise that territorial matters would be on the table if Quebec were to separate, an issue I had raised before. Don Macpherson of *The Gazette* had even commented approvingly, pointing out how the creation of the state of West Virginia was an interesting precedent. During the American Civil War, the legislators from the western part of the state of Virginia opposed the Confederate plan to secede from the union. This eventually led to the western part of the state breaking away and becoming a state unto itself, which to this day is the state of West Virginia. But even with the opening that had been afforded us to occupy a much larger federalist terrain as a result of the Allaire report, I felt that it was not a good idea to push for something with which many Quebec federalists are deeply uncomfortable. Even in its watered-down form, it got us blasted on the editorial pages for blowing this golden opportunity to assert ourselves as the only true federalist party in Quebec by advocating what the pundits characterized as this "Swiss cheese" formula for anglo enclaves in a separate Quebec.

The widespread media consensus was that my appeal for francophone support was hopelessly doomed.

Henderson's committee, however, was delighted. Their attitude was always to denounce those who disagree with us. Since we were clearly in the right, we should not be shy about shouting it from the rooftops. And despite the negative editorial comment, our high media profile in recent weeks and our strong language about Quebec's territorial integrity did not go unappreciated among ordinary anglophones.

The circumstances surrounding the conclusion of the Belanger-Campeau commission also worked wonderfully in our favour.

As Belanger-Campeau wound down, the Liberals badly wanted a consensus to emerge, which would give them a stronger hand in the negotiations with the rest of Canada for a new constitutional deal. The sovereignist members, meanwhile, were riding high on the nationalist momentum that the hearings had generated, and were confident they could call many of the shots at the marathon closed-door sessions where the final report would be assembled. These last few weeks of the commission unfolded at an old chateau near Quebec City, with the media usually camped outside its thick stone walls, like a besieging army.

One of the first closed-door meetings featured a slide presentation and economic analysis of a sovereign Quebec by Henri-Paul Rousseau, the government-appointed commission secretary, who also happened to be the chief economist for the YES campaign in the 1980 referendum. His study projected a sovereign Quebec that would be only slightly less economically viable than the Quebec of today. His hypothesis was based on the premise that an independent Quebec would be responsible for only 18% of the federal debt, despite its quarter-share of the Canadian population. The analysis was so ridiculously simplistic and so obviously tinted to paint a rosy picture of a sovereign Quebec that the federalist members of the commission couldn't help but roll their eyes at each other in disbelief. Disapproval was clearly expressed, but the study went unamended into the official commission record and would be cited time after time in coming years as the Belanger-Campeau Commission's bottom-line economic pronouncement.

Federalists were consulting on a regular basis. A number of us took a break one afternoon to go over to the Chateau Frontenac to hear Brian Mulroney deliver a speech to a bar association convention lunch. I was sitting at a table with Senator John Lynch Staunton, Holden, and the B-C commission's Tory representative, Outremont MP Jean Pierre Hogue, all of whom were staunch Mulroney supporters. The ornate ballroom was packed. I had never met Mulroney, and on the basis of his media persona was disposed to dislike him. The master of ceremonies announced the arrival of the head table procession, which made its way toward the front as everyone rose to their feet. The procession passed right by our table, and to my stunned surprise, Mulroney stopped momentarily when he saw me, extended his hand and said, "Hi Bob," and continued on. This small taste of his legendary charm dispelled a lot of the antagonism I had previously felt toward him. After lunch, I felt compelled almost to praise his strong pro-Canada speech in a media scrum.

Nearing the deadline for a final Belanger Campeau commission report, the co-chairmen and the commission secretary presented a "confidential" proposal. The word "consensus" was repeated ad nauseum throughout these deliberations, and we were given to understand that the absence of a consensus would condemn the commission to failure and hamstring Quebec in its quest for an honorable constitutional settlement. It was proposed that the National Assembly should call for an immediate referendum on sovereignty, with both the provincial Liberals and PQ on the YES side. The accession to sovereignty, however, would not come about until a year later, and only if the rest of Canada failed to come up with acceptable offers to keep Quebec in confederation.

This was the epitome of the knife-to-the-throat approach urged by Bourassa's nationalist advisers. The proposal, for obvious reasons, did not fly behind the commission's closed doors. All the federalists met that night in André Ouellette's hotel room and we determined that even if the provincial Liberals were to go along with the proposal, it would be a far too dangerous game to play. Ultimately the provincial Liberals themselves agreed that this would be taking brinkmanship to the point of folly.

After days of emotional wheeling and dealing, a modified version of the proposal gained the support of almost all the commissioners. It was proposed that the National Assembly would pass a law calling for a referendum on sovereignty, but only in another year or so. At the same time, the Assembly would declare itself open to constitutional offers from the rest of Canada. Two parliamentary commissions would be set up, one to study the offers upon arrival, and one to further examine the implications of Quebec sovereignty. If the offers were deemed unsatisfactory, the National Assembly would hold its referendum on sovereignty with the Liberals and the PQ presumably backing the YES side, and Quebec would become independent a year later. If the offers were found acceptable, the government could call off the referendum or put a renewed federalism package to a vote.

It was astounding how certain commissioners were being pressured to accept the proposal. The final meeting dragged late into the night. When a deal was finally struck, the media, still encamped outside the gates, were notified. When the doors were opened, they poured into the building like a barbarian horde storming a breach in a castle wall.

All the commissioners, save for Holden, myself, and André Ouellette, endorsed the proposal. We earned high marks from the English media for our defiance in not signing the final report, again somewhat diminishing the impact that full unanimity would have imparted. A few days later, on the last day of the Belanger-Campeau odyssey, all commissioners got to speak for five minutes in the National Assembly Red Room. Holden and I blasted the sovereignist movement and renewed our call for all true federalists to join forces to save Canada.

Holden chose this time to step on his tongue once again, carelessly telling a journalist about a private telephone chat he had with Mulroney the night before. They had discussed the commission's final report, and Mulroney had apparently compared it to a "hooker" trolling for the best offer on Montreal's Lower Main. Mulroney's remarks made for interesting headlines in the French press the next day, e.g. "Mulroney compares Quebec to a hooker". Needless to say, Holden received an angry (to say the least) call from the Prime Minister's office insisting that he take responsibility for the remarks, much as they sounded like the Brian Mulroney who had previously got himself in hot water by mouthing off about "old whores" during the 1984 election campaign. Holden nervously approached a number of press gallery journalists, claiming that he had actually made the hooker remark to Mulroney, and that the prime minister had only barely chuckled at the analogy. The news reports the next day gleefully reported how Holden had tried to cover his friend Mulroney's backside.

The final commission proposal was to be formalized in legislation passed by the National Assembly. This took the form of Bill 150, introduced by the Liberal government and passed a few months later, calling for a referendum on sovereignty in either June or October of 1992. The end result of the Belanger-Campeau exercise in March of 1991 further certified Equality as the only up-front federalist party on the Quebec political scene. Things were definitely looking up.

During the following month, the party would enjoy its finest hour, and I would be perceived by many, for the first time, as a mature politician. Ironically, it would be for reasons that had nothing to do with language or the constitution.

CHAPTER TEN

Hydro-Quebec Power Storm

I am persuaded that there is absolutely no limit to the absurdities that can, by
government action, come to be generally believed.
—Bertrand Russell

Since my visit to James Bay the previous year, I had been doing some reading about Hydro-Quebec's development plans in northern Quebec. The next big project was slated for Great Whale River, along which more dams would be built to generate more electricity. Upon completion of this multi-billion-dollar construction project, the final phase of the James Bay scheme would be undertaken. Known by its shorthand designation as N-B-R it called for additional dams to be built along the Nottaway, Broadback and Rupert rivers. Premier Bourassa was obsessed with the concept that Quebec's great northern rivers flowing into James Bay could be harnessed to manufacture electricity at low cost. This could then be exported to the United States at a highly profitable markup, but still be competitive with other energy sources.

In the National Assembly I had questioned Energy Minister Lise Bacon about how Quebec would be able to afford its ambitious plans for James Bay, considering that New York and Vermont were cancelling existing contracts to buy electricity from Quebec. With energy conservation being taken ever more seriously in the United States, much of the electricity these northeastern states had originally planned to buy from Quebec would no longer be needed. Quebec could, therefore, be spending billions to build generating plants in northern Quebec to produce electricity for a market that was rapidly diminishing. These evaporating export contracts had been counted on to eventually pay off the project's capital cost while making it possible to supply comparatively cheap electricity to domestic users in Quebec.

Bacon brushed me off, saying that despite these cancelled contracts, the development schedule would remain unchanged. She insisted that if the electricity was not sold to the Americans, then Quebecers would pay for it themselves, since we would need it for our own use eventually. She even went so far as to say that if the Great Whale project was not built according to schedule, Quebec would have to be lit by candlelight by the year 2000.

In March, the government suddenly had a court-ordered publication ban slapped on the details of a contract that Hydro-Quebec had signed in the late 1980s with Norsk Hydro, a Norwegian-owned magnesium manufacturer, to supply electricity for its recently-built plant in Becancour, Quebec. The Norsk contract was one of 13 "risk sharing" contracts that had been kept secret from the rate paying public. Radio-Canada and *La Presse* had got their hands on the Norsk contract, and when their reporters started making inquiries, the provincial authorities responded with the gag order. The details of this secret contract had already been published in Norway, Australia and the United States, yet the injunction made it illegal to publish them in Quebec, leaving Quebecers, who are after all Hydro-Quebec's shareholders, in the dark about what was going on.

It was suspected that a number of metals manufacturing companies were getting sweetheart electricity rates from Hydro-Quebec as incentive to establish their plants in the province. On the surface it did not seem unreasonable to give a foreign company an inducement to set up shop in Quebec and employ local workers. But there must have been a reason why the government was going to such extraordinary lengths to keep the contract secret. The media here reported that a publication ban had been imposed but were not willing to disobey it. They appealed to the Access to Information Commission to get the ban rescinded.

I had recently hired Dermod Travis on a contract basis to do special research for me on a variety of economic issues. Chris Mostovac's recent departure to pursue his legal career had left a void in my staff. Travis had called me out of the blue a few weeks earlier, having moved to Montreal from Alberta where he had been a researcher for the Alberta provincial Liberal caucus. I asked him if we could somehow get our hands on the Norsk contract, or at least on the details that were being published across the border. He spoke to a journalist friend of his in Boston who obtained the information from Boston energy consultants Goodman and Associates.

Over the phone, Travis got the key details, which proved not only that Hydro-Quebec was in fact selling our energy to Norsk Hydro at unbelievably low rates, but for less than it actually cost to produce. His friend would not be able to get a complete copy of the contract to us until late the following week, so we would have to go with the information we had if we wanted to get a jump on the issue. It was Friday, and the next Assembly question period was scheduled for the following Tuesday.

I sat on this information all weekend, and formulated a question for the Energy Minister. Since the law says that an MNA is immune to prosecution for anything he or she might say in the Assembly, we presumed I would be able to ask the question, which would expose the most damaging of the banned information, without violating the injunction by virtue of the fact that I was a member of the National Assembly and would be standing in the Assembly at the time.

I knew that the information that I had was significant, but I never expected the resounding impact it would have.

On Tuesday morning, I felt uncomfortable that I had not had a chance to speak to Neil Cameron about the question since he was our point man on energy issues and matters relating to Hydro-Quebec. I wanted to ask him if I could ask the question, or whether he would prefer to put it to the government. He did not show up for question period that day and was nowhere to be found, so I decided to go with it myself.

About halfway through question period, I jumped up twice hoping to be recognized by the speaker, but he looked the other way. He had let us ask several questions the week before, and probably figured he had given us our due for the time being. With about 10 minutes remaining, I decided to give it one last try. If the question was to go well, I would need at least ten minutes. A question with this kind of potential would be wasted with just a few minutes left, because there would be no time to slip in the appropriate supplementary questions. This time the speaker gave me the nod and I began my question to Lise Bacon. I first asked her to confirm for Quebecers what the people of Australia knew, what the people of Norway knew and what the people of the United States knew — that Hydro-Quebec had been selling power for years well below what it cost to produce.

She warned me to be cautious, for if the details of the contracts were known, other countries would offer the same deals to these companies and lure them away from Quebec. After a supplementary question doubting her true reasons for the secrecy, while she was answering, I turned to Holden and said I would reveal the numbers in my last supplementary. I was shielded by parliamentary immunity, and if I could get them out quickly enough, the speaker would not have time to cut me off. The rules say that any question currently before a quasi-judicial body, such as the Access to Information Commission, may be ruled out of order by the speaker. Holden said "Go, go for it".

I took a deep breath and asked Bacon to confirm that under the terms of the Norsk contract, Hydro-Quebec was actually selling this power at 1.5 cents a kilowatt-hour for the first two years, substantially less than the 2.4 cents per kilowatt-hour it costs to produce it, and for less than half the 4.5 cents a kilowatt-hour that Quebec households were being charged for their electricity. She refused to comment on the numbers I quoted, claiming the importance of maintaining confidentiality.

Outside the Assembly on my way down the corridor, I was corralled into a surging media scrum. Not only had I broken a highly controversial story, but I had challenged the injunction, which made me an instant media hero. Since the National Assembly debates are covered live on television, I had managed to get the essential figures on the air, and on the public record. It was illegal for the media to broadcast the details of the contract on their own initiative, but they were free to replay the clips of my question period initiative, and to quote what I had said in the Assembly.

In the scrum I charged that the only reason the government was keeping the rates secret was that it was too embarrassed to have the Quebec public know how dirt-cheap it was selling power to these foreign companies while ordinary Hydro rate payers were gouged at more than twice the super-discount corporate rate. Other large energy consumers in Quebec, like pulp and paper companies and greenhouse operators, were paying what is called the industrial "L" rate, lower than the top rate charged domestic consumers, but still much higher than the sweetheart deals these foreign companies were getting.

After the scrum I called Dermod Travis in Montreal several times to tell him that those numbers had better be right. He reassured me that he had cross-checked them with three separate sources that day: The Sierra Club, a leading American environmental lobby; an Albany New York political action group; and the Boston reporter, who had been digging deeper into the story in the meantime. I had promised in the scrum that I would produce the contract the next day, even though we still did not have a copy in hand.

My question period gambit unleashed a major uproar. I was even called that afternoon by Michel Morin, the renowned Radio-Canada reporter who had been ready to break the story a few weeks earlier, and whose probing had provoked the injunction. He called to congratulate me and said that it would be the lead story on the Radio-Canada broadcast that evening. All the media had received clearance from their lawyers that they could broadcast or quote the figures that I had revealed on the floor of the house, but they were also cautioned not to go much further.

It was the lead story that night not only on Radio Canada, but on all the networks, TV and radio, not to mention the banner headline in every Quebec newspaper. The next morning, I was awakened in my hotel room by an on-air phone call from a disc jockey on a Trois-Rivières radio station at 6:30 a.m., just to thank and congratulate me for spilling the beans.

Since I had promised to table the contract that day, we were now scrambling to get our hands on a copy. Travis' friend in Boston had obtained an English translation, but his fax machine had broken down that day. We arranged for a courier to pick it up at his house and bring it over to the energy consulting firm, which had a working fax machine. When they finally received it, it was only minutes before question period. They faxed the dozens of pages directly to my office in Quebec City. I grabbed it off the fax and ran upstairs just in time. It made for quite a photo-op when the cameramen asked me to brandish the contract on my way into the Assembly.

The entire Question Period that day was consumed by the fallout from the disclosure the day before. The PQ finally waded into the controversy, but even with their help, I was refused permission to table the contract, which would permit it to be distributed and quoted directly.

The government continued to stonewall for the rest of the week. Hydro-Quebec also held press conferences in a frantic attempt to put their own spin on the story. While refusing to confirm or deny the figures, Hydro claimed that the contracts would pay off in the long run.

Editorial comment in both French and English was unanimously in favor of making these contracts public since Quebecers had a right to know what was going on at their very own energy corporation. A desperate Lise Bacon tried to turn the tables on me by accusing me of being anti-Quebec, and attempting to undermine Quebec's economic well-being. This earned her a sound drubbing from the province's media heavyweights, including a number of nationalist journalists who grudgingly praised me for going out on a limb in the public interest.

From this day forward, some of my most unsparing detractors—notably Macpherson and Jack Todd of The Gazette—dropped their "Little Bobby" tag. MacPherson even predicted that this episode might allow the Equality Party to dispel its image as a narrowly-focused single-issue political movement.

Hydro-Quebec had been regarded as a sacred cow by most Quebec nationalists, who saw it as the bedrock of Quebec's economic independence. Yet to many Quebecers, Hydro's shining image had been tarnished in recent years by a run of major blackouts and chiselling rate increases. This made it easier for me to find support among francophone Quebecers. Also making it easier was the fact that the media had been stung by the injunction on their freedom to report important information. I had given them the opportunity to do so, and when Lise Bacon wrapped herself in the flag, it was not enough to cover her vulnerable backside.

An attempt a few days later by Hydro and most of the 13 companies to shut me up only enhanced my standing. Three days after asking the question, I received by fax a "mise en demeure," a legal warning from lawyers representing Hydro and its corporate cohorts threatening legal action if I continued to talk about the contracts. When we notified the media of this development, another uproar ensued. It was perceived as a direct attempt to intimidate a member of the National Assembly, and thus in violation of the National Assembly statutes. This was an even more hectic news day than the first. We held an impromptu press conference in my office and it made all the front pages the next day. Holden and Julius Grey were my legal advisers and they were widely quoted as ridiculing this attempt by the companies to silence me. I vowed that I would not back down under any circumstances.

The following Tuesday, I tabled a motion of parliamentary privilege, attempting to summon the companies which were threatening me for performing my duties as an MNA, before a National Assembly disciplinary committee. Though the speaker ruled the motion in order, the Liberals were determined to kill it, knowing it would turn into a hugely embarrassing media circus. They agreed to debate my motion, but only a few weeks later. They deliberately chose budget day to vote it down with their house majority, at a time when the media was in the budget lock-up, and the day's newscasts would be swamped with budget reports. The PQ was very much on our side as the Liberals made a mockery of the supposed rights of individual legislators.

Though the issue lingered in the Assembly and in the media for several more weeks, and Norsk Hydro eventually released the contract itself in the hope of putting an end to the controversy, there is more to the story than the media ever reported.

In the late 1980's, with an election on the horizon, the Liberal government in concert with Hydro-Quebec, signed a number of these so called "risk sharing contracts" with metals manufacturers. The manufacturing plants use massive amounts of electricity, so the price they pay for their electricity is an important consideration in deciding where to locate. If Hydro-Quebec offers cheaper rates than the competition, chances are good that such companies will build plants in Quebec. The

Quebec government could then claim to be creating employment in the small towns where these large plants would be built.

The eventual price the companies pay for electricity is pegged to the price of the metals they manufacture, and as such Hydro-Quebec shares part of the company's risk. For example, a magnesium smelter like Norsk Hydro signs a risk sharing deal with Hydro-Quebec. For the first several years, it will pay a certain guaranteed low rate for the electricity. After that, the electricity price depends on the world market price for magnesium. If the price of magnesium goes up, everybody benefits; the company gets higher prices for its magnesium, and Hydro-Quebec gets more money from the higher rates the company pays for its power. If the cost of magnesium goes down, the company is compensated by lower rates for its electricity, while Hydro-Quebec loses money, period. Lise Bacon and Robert Bourassa always claimed that since the price of magnesium would presumably increase over the duration of the Norsk contract, the government would eventually recoup its losses from the first few years of Norsk's guaranteed bargain-basement rates.

It was calculated that for the first several years of the contract, Hydro-Quebec, and ultimately Quebec taxpayers, would lose $160 million a year. Since the Norsk plant employed only about 600 people, it meant that Quebec taxpayers were paying a fortune for the creation of relatively few jobs. Nor was there any guarantee that the price of magnesium would rise enough to compensate these losses or assure an eventual profit from the deal. In addition, we discovered that Norsk was given an extra bonus of $23 million by the government's Société de Développement Industriel (SDI) and did not have to pay for its water for several years, a vital consideration since metals manufacturing requires vast quantities of water. On the whole, this was probably the most expensive job creation program in the history of western civilization.

But the real shocker was yet to come. Part of the fallout from the whole affair was that the U.S. Department of Commerce ruled that the cheap Norsk electrical rates, constituted an unfair subsidy that violated the Canada-U.S. Free Trade Agreement, and slapped duties on the made-in-Quebec magnesium exported to the U.S. (This could also be a major sticking point if an independent Quebec tries to negotiate its way into a North American free trade deal.) When we got our hands on the Commerce Department's confidential ruling, we discovered, to our disbelief, that Hydro had actually done a feasibility study on the Norsk contract before signing it, and that the study had predicted that magnesium prices would not rise enough to offset the losses projected in the contract over its lifespan. The government knew in advance that it would probably lose money on the deal, but went ahead with it nevertheless. The big picture was steadily becoming clearer.

It was obvious that in the late 1980s, with an election nearing, the government was anxious to show its ability to create jobs in the regions. It therefore signed numerous contracts with metals manufacturers, fully knowing that the province could well lose money on all these deals. They figured that by keeping the contracts secret, no one would ever know what rates were being paid and how much Hydro was losing. They could then point to all the jobs being created in these various regions, without the population ever knowing the full cost of these jobs to the province's taxpayers.

I jumped on this new information, and when I called Lise Bacon a liar in the National Assembly for having falsely maintained that the deal would ultimately be profitable, the speaker asked me to withdraw the remark on the grounds that it was un-parliamentary. (You get three warnings before being ejected for the day.) I was tempted to stick to my guns, but grudgingly relented and withdrew the allegation. I knew it would have got me a lot of media attention, but there is something intimidating about getting yourself thrown out of the National Assembly by the speaker, backed up by the sergeant-at-arms, that made me hesitate.

The Norsk Hydro deal was only one of 13 secret contracts signed during the same period. A Université de Laval study predicted that four of the secret deals alone will cost Quebecers more than $7.5 billion over the 25-year lifespan of the contracts. Aluminum was at one time thought to be the metal of the future, but it was becoming ever more doubtful that this would be the case, thus creating the potential for enormous revenue losses for Hydro-Quebec for years to come. But what makes the economic risk involved so highly dangerous is that these 13 plants consume such massive amounts of electricity—roughly the equivalent of all the power that would have been produced by the multi-billion dollar Great Whale development.

Lise Bacon had said that Quebec must keep building the giant hydro developments at James Bay to meet Quebec's own energy needs. But if so much of the electricity that we produce is going to companies that we are essentially subsidizing with below-cost rates, how could Quebecers possibly afford to spend billions more to build these mega-projects? The answer is, it can't. This energy policy is mortgaging the future of Quebec and will lead the province to economic bankruptcy if it is not scrapped.

If there was a market for the power, the cost of the projects would be potentially feasible. But with the trend toward energy efficiency and conservation in the United States, this seems increasingly unlikely. Therefore, if Quebec goes ahead with plans to produce power to be sold at a loss to these metals manufacturers, we risk choking the provincial economy. Quebec spent $1 billion dollars in 1976 to build a stadium. Almost 20 years later, we are still paying for it. Imagine asking Quebecers to shoulder the cost of a dozen more Olympic Stadiums with no guarantees that the investment will ever be profitable, and a far greater likelihood that it will be a perpetual money-loser.

At the time, the PQ called the Hydro-Quebec risk sharing contracts the economic scandal of the century. Now that they are in power, they must do something to get out of these contracts or renegotiate them. Because of the U.S. duties on its magnesium exports, Norsk eventually decided to renegotiate its contract with Hydro-Quebec, eliminating its fire-sale rate, much to the benefit of Quebec taxpayers. It is essential that the 12 other contracts, which still remain secret, be renegotiated as soon as possible. The PQ's decision to put the Great Whale project on ice is a commendable step in the right direction. Too bad this kind of economic common sense does not govern their thinking in other areas.

One of the crucial observations to be derived from the Hydro affair was how helpful a three party system could be in Quebec. With a soft nationalist Liberal government, and an even more nationalist PQ as the only other official party, many key issues never got a proper airing. Hydro-Quebec, because of its mythical lustre as a nationalist symbol, is an institution that the PQ was hesitant to attack. They jumped on this issue only after we took the lead, and when they saw where editorial opinion was headed. The Caisse de Dépôt et Placement is another public institution that with questionable investments was costing taxpayers a fortune. Yet the PQ would not attack it for the same nationalist reasons that made them reticent about going after Hydro-Quebec, since the Caisse is also considered a potentially powerful economic instrument expected to reinforce the economic foundations of an independent Quebec.

On minority rights issues, it is crucial for the National Assembly to have at least a handful of MNAs who can ask the important questions and keep pressuring the government. To hire more members of minority communities in the civil service; to monitor the implementation of greater English access to health care institutions; to push for increased access to English schools; or even to question the government on things like the ridiculous STOP sign rule, on which the government was finally forced to make a decision. It eventually allowed municipalities to decide if they want their signs to read "STOP," which is both good English and good French, or "ARRET," which sounds more French, but is actually

ungrammatical according to the Académie Française. (In France the
STOP signs say precisely that, yet the Québécois language purists had
been insisting that ARRET should be mandatory.) Whether the PQ or the
Liberals are in power, the representation and influence of minority
communities will be minimal within both the government and the
official opposition. The interests of the linguistic majority will predomi-
nate, leaving little room for minority community concerns.

As far as the defense of Canada is concerned, the Assembly lacked
real two-sided debate. In the absence of a federalist counterweight, the
Liberal government was constantly pulled in a nationalist direction by
the PQ. There is no reason for a Liberal politician to sound an ardent
defense of federalism, since for electoral purposes it suits the Liberals to
be as close to the PQ as possible in the hope of co-opting the crucial
soft-core nationalist vote.

This was obvious when Gordon Atkinson tabled a motion calling
for the placing of the Canadian flag in the National Assembly Blue Room.
Most legislatures in Canada have either no flag or the provincial flag
along with the Canadian flag. When the PQ came to power in 1976, the
Lévesque government decided to place only the Quebec flag next to the
speaker's chair. The day after the government's referendum defeat of
1980, Michel Pagé, then a Liberal opposition backbencher asked that the
Canadian flag be placed on the other side of the speaker's chair. His
request was refused. Now that Pagé was the Liberal Party house leader,
we phrased Atkinson's motion exactly in the same words as the previous
Liberal motion. The Liberals were clearly put on the spot. The flag was
greatly symbolic and placing it next to the speaker would be too overt a
federalist gesture for Bourassa's comfort. Yet, rejecting it could be inter-
preted as too nationalist a gesture and an insult to the rest of Canada.

Despite intense lobbying—notably by many female members of
the Liberal caucus—to coax Atkinson to withdraw his motion, he resisted and the Liberals were forced into the embarrassing situation
whereby the only way they could avoid voting either for or against the
Canadian flag was to shove it under the rug. Its parliamentary majority
amended the motion to refer the issue to the National Assembly Bureau,
which would decide on a case-by-case basis—as for the arrival of the
Lieutenant-Governor—when to bring out the Canadian flag and when
to keep it in the closet.

With the Allaire Report having been adopted as the constitutional
position of the Liberal party, wrapping ourselves in the Canadian flag
played very well to our constituency. Still riding high on the credibility
boost from the Hydro-Quebec affair, our party was looking stronger and

stronger, and our Canadian unity rallies were attracting encouraging crowds wherever we held them.

I was still making news on Hydro-Quebec, by uncovering little gems in confidential financial reports, leaked Wall Street documents about rate hikes, and company prospectuses. We uncovered bias and conflict of interest in a blue-ribbon panel of advisors selected by the utility. I was also involved in having a Hydro-Quebec worker fired for printing on an anglophone customer's bill, "Va chier en Ontario," after the customer had called Hydro to complain about something. The universe seemed to be unfolding as it should for the Equality Party.

I remember driving home after the Assembly had adjourned for the summer of 1991, saying to myself that things couldn't be going much better. The party was riding high, as was my personal popularity. I had a newfound political credibility, a wonderful son who had just celebrated his first birthday, and even a brand new car. I had also made a cameo appearance playing myself in a hilarious new film by Albert Neremberg called "Urban Anglo," a sendup of Quebec's language politics. The party had also planned a promising gala comedy evening and auction to celebrate Canada Day the following week, where radio personality Aaron Rand would be the emcee and auctioneer.

From these heights of enthusiasm, however, both the party and my marriage would begin their downward spiral that very summer.

CHAPTER ELEVEN

Up To Here With Holden

One of the evils of democracy
is that you have to put up with the man you elect
whether you want him or not.
—Will Rogers

My wife and I were in our mid-twenties when we married. But for all we had to offer each other, the gulf between the two very different worlds from which we came turned out to be more of an obstacle than we recognized during the heady whirl of courtship. We met within a year of my graduation from McGill, mere months after I had joined the work force. She is a very quiet and intensely private person who was led to believe that she had married someone who was going to be an architect for the rest of his working life. She had no interest in Quebec politics and would have preferred to keep it that way. Although she often accompanied me to official functions and political meetings, they made her uncomfortable, and she never recognized or accepted their significance. This made for tension whenever we had to appear somewhere.

Disagreements often flared over little things, mostly with regard to bringing up our son. Having a child can bring a couple closer together or drive a wedge between them. With us it was the latter. With our different cultural backgrounds we had a very different approach to child rearing. Hers was derived from the experience of growing up as one of 10 children in a working class household in Morocco that uprooted itself to Montreal when she was 15 years old, while mine was formed by a comfortably-settled middle class North American upbringing in a nuclear family that embodied the post-war suburban dream.

Eventually it became just a matter of time before it was over. My newfound political career, with its unrelenting demands that made for an unsettled family life, may have hastened the disintegration of our marriage. But our differences would most likely have caught up with us before much longer had I stuck to architecture, and at the end of 1991 we separated. A corrosively bitter custody battle ensued, lasting for two agonizing years, by far the most difficult time of my life. I also learned first-hand that the father of a young child is at a serious disadvantage from the word go in any divorce custody battle, no matter what the circumstances.

Just as my marriage was about to unravel during the summer of 1991, festering tensions in the caucus came to a head in a political family row from which the Equality Party emerged badly bruised.

Toward the end of the previous session I was often frustrated by Holden and Atkinson's cavalier approach to their house duties, and accused them of sheer laziness. They often did not show up for important votes, and their indulgent wallowing in the good life an MNA's perks assured in Quebec City was becoming obnoxious. They often missed question period, lingering in the parliamentary restaurant for a good part of the afternoon over post-prandials. They usually left in the late afternoon, never returning for the evening sitting, and rarely asked questions or made speeches in the Assembly. Whenever I questioned either of them about what they were working on, or suggested they might work a little harder, even in the subtlest of ways, I was rebuffed like a whining adolescent and told, usually by Holden, to take a hike.

I could not get Holden to do anything any more, especially for the party. He rarely attended committee hearings, unless they concerned the review of the new civil code, in which he had a professional interest that could be of personal benefit someday. In the various bars he frequented, he let everyone within earshot know about his contempt for the party in general and myself in particular. At least Atkinson was a dedicated riding man when not in Holden's company. He was very much a local fixture in N.D.G., and with his hustling riding assistant Liza Bouchard, he worked hard at staying in contact with as many community groups as possible. Holden didn't give a hoot about his constituents.

Holden had been a terrible influence on Atkinson, who was not at all the same forceful personage in the National Assembly as the hot-wired performer behind the radio microphone. He was very concerned about being on the good side of other politicians and constantly preoccupied with what people thought of him. His thunderous rhetoric, delivered with such brimming self-confidence before he was elected, had muted considerably. He also became nervous whenever he had to speak in the National Assembly, especially if he had to pronounce more than a phrase or two in French. The same guy who had vehemently denounced Robert Bourassa a "liar" and a "pipsqueak" not so long ago, turned to me in the elevator one day with a look of disbelief when I referred to the Premier as simply "Bourassa". "That's Mr. Bourassa, around here," he solemnly told me.

Once I was surprised to hear from his secretary that he would not be in Quebec City that week. I sent him a memo, asking him why he had not mentioned it to me before now. The fax he fired back started: "Hey asshole...." He went on to say that he had scheduled gum surgery for that week. Whatever he might have thought of me personally, this was hardly the attitude any MNA who respects his office would show toward his party leader.

Neil Cameron often backed me in my conflicts with Holden. Cameron is a confirmed night person, often reading and writing until the wee hours of the morning. He was rarely in the Assembly before noon, which meant that he generally missed question period during the intensive sessions when it takes place at 10:00 a.m. But Cameron picked up the slack as far as speeches in the Assembly were concerned. He could speak articulately on almost any subject, and he often addressed motions on behalf of the caucus. The dynamic in caucus generally had Holden and Atkinson pitted against Cameron and myself. To avoid conflicts I consulted the caucus less and less, to the point where Holden and I would communicate through acrid memos, always prompting Cameron to wade in with long missives of his own in an effort to smooth things over.

In mid-summer I was interviewed by Gilles Normand from *La Presse* who was doing a series of features on how some of the MNAs were spending their summer vacations. He came up north with a photographer to my parents' cottage on Petit Lac Long. The photographer took pictures of me waterskiing, playing with my son, and the like. The interview was very informal. We spoke casually for about two hours, going over my political career, the language debate, and the fact that my son was the progeny of a francophone mother and an anglophone father. I told the reporter how we were awaiting Kevin's first words to see if they would be English or French. Most of the talk was about how I spent my leisure time, anecdotes about the National Assembly, and various other casual topics. We did, however, touch on the constitutional issue.

I discussed a variety of possible scenarios and told him our party strategists were juggling a number of options in light of the Liberals' recent nationalist lurch.

One of those strategies under discussion was that we would threaten to place candidates in ridings where the Liberal majority was very slim, particularly in ridings where the Liberal candidate or MNA was a federalist. The idea was that this would give us leverage to force the Liberal to speak out more forcefully for federalism. We felt that this approach, albeit only a bluff, would perhaps push the Liberals to adopt a more overtly federalist stance for fear of losing the seat to a vote split. It was something we had talked about, but not something I had seriously envisaged actually doing.

The subsequent article, under a large front page photo of my waterskiing exploits, dealt mostly with how we were plotting to oust the Liberals by threatening to split the vote in ridings where they had only narrowly defeated the PQ. This caused considerable angst in the party when *The Gazette* picked it up and played it up in a major way. I was in Florida for a week that summer with my wife and son when the story came out and the first I heard of it was when I got a long-distance call from Elizabeth Thompson of *The Gazette*. Though I made it clear that this was one scenario among many being considered, *The Gazette* made it seem as though we were plotting to put the PQ in power.

In an effort to repair the damage, I wrote a letter to the editor of *The Gazette*, admitting I was wrong even to make the suggestion. But even at that, my longtime adviser Doug Robinson quit the party over the issue. Despite the provocation of Bill 150, he had been very much against threatening the Liberals. He thought I was playing with fire if our voters were led to believe that we would indirectly help the PQ. Worse yet, he felt, this would encourage some of the former Unity Party ridings into believing that they would have a candidate in the next election. He had wanted me to tell these riding association executives now that we could not risk splitting the Liberal vote, and that they should start working on other ridings we could safely contest. He had barked at me every time I raised the idea of trying to throw a scare into the Liberals.

Holden also threw a fit, taking advantage of the negative reaction to lace into me. He too had been very much against doing anything that could directly or indirectly help the PQ. Though he was in the hospital for eye surgery, he sent a vitriolic memo to the caucus about my comments in *La Presse*.

He wrote, "It certainly doesn't help us when Robert blithely announces that a PQ victory might chasten the Liberals. Our voters do not want a PQ government for any reason under any circumstances. They will not risk their future well-being on the flimsy notion that it would teach the Liberals a lesson." (As we all know, a year later the person who wrote this memo crossed the floor to sit as an MNA for the separatist PQ)

While my letter to the editor of *The Gazette* only mildly appeased Holden, it greatly upset and disappointed the Unity party ridings, which had been encouraged, as Robinson had predicted, to entertain false hopes when they read my original comments that we would run candidates throughout Quebec.

In late September, the feuding with Holden finally reached its climax. Holden released a document to the media entitled "Two Years Before the Mace," in which he assessed the performance of the Equality Party after two years in the National Assembly. It blew the rift in the caucus wide open and splattered it across the front pages of the newspapers. He was critical of my leadership, bemoaning the age difference in our caucus as a major cause of the party's problems, as well as my inexperience and inability to exert the necessary authority to bridge the gap between what he considered the eminently reasonable caucus and the "unsophisticated and downright redneck thinking of the party." This was the last straw. Though a few of his observations might have been considered valid by some, airing this kind of dirty laundry in public was beyond the pale. I had warned him after the previous flare-up a year earlier that he had one last chance. I now had no choice but to throw him out of the party.

I had always feared the impression it would create to have our party cut down to three members in the Assembly—a quarter of our representation hived off in one fell swoop. But keeping Holden on would have made us look even worse. Had I let him get away with it, I might just as well have issued a communique announcing that I would henceforth be a lame duck leader. I held a press conference in my office to announce his ouster, flanked by the president of our Westmount riding association, Betty O'Connell, and the president of the party, Martin Segal. I spoke of Holden's serious breach of caucus solidarity and how for the past two years I had attempted to accommodate his "gadfly tendencies". The quote that the media seized upon was my reference to Holden's friend Brian Mulroney's famous line, "You dance with the one that brung ya!" Holden, I said, "had been unwilling to dance with the one that brung him".

Holden's counterattack, which harped on the line that the Equality Party was anti-Quebec, unfortunately played well with much of the media. Some of the more susceptible pundits, notably in the French press, lapped it up like church ladies hearing the worst confirmed about a suspected house of ill repute. On the record, Holden said that he wouldn't join the Liberals unless they promised to change Bill 178. Behind the scenes, he practically begged them to take him into the caucus, but to no avail. Contrary to what he believed, they already knew him as a grandstanding loafer and a treacherous loose cannon. Spurned by the Liberals, who sniggered behind his back at the suggestion that they might want to take him into the cabinet, Holden sat as an independent.

Despite much favorable response for kicking Holden out, and unanimous support for my actions in the party, it was difficult for me having his condescending remarks about my age, inexperience, and lack of authority broadcast and quoted all over the place. It helped that on the night he was thrown out, he appeared on the news holding court in a bar, double scotch in hand, giving people a sampling of what he was really like. But I felt my efforts to build a solid base of credibility for myself and the party had been set back considerably.

When we were first elected, I had anticipated relying heavily on Holden to compensate for my lack of experience. As a lawyer with 35 years before the Bar, a veteran of the Conservative party back-rooms and a practiced political mover, I expected him to be a critical asset for our caucus.

As time went on, however, he became increasingly seduced by the cushy perks of an elected politician and too easily conned by political opponents. Whenever the Liberals needed something from us, Michel Pagé would have him over to his office for an intimate tipple. He missed at least half the votes in the Assembly and was rarely seen in the Blue Room after three in the afternoon.

It was also convenient for him to be part of a small caucus with a young leader who did not have the big stick that the major party leaders could wield to enforce their authority. I could not hold appointments over his head, or discipline him in any effective way. This suited Holden just fine, and he abused his leeway to the maximum. With Holden gone, there was a genuine sense of relief all around.

Because of his chummy relationship with Holden, it would now be important to handle Atkinson with kid gloves. He was also greatly fed up with the party, which had recently censured him in a General Council meeting for voting in favour of the new Quebec Cinema Law. It reduced to 45 from 60, the number of days within which a French version of a film must be ready, otherwise the English version must be pulled from the theatres. Atkinson wanted to make a gesture of reconciliation by showing francophones that we share their concern that they should be able to see films in their own language as readily as possible.

Atkinson was very uncomfortable about Holden's expulsion at first, and unsure of what to do. He was wary enough to figure that if he were to bolt the party his political career would be finished. Atkinson had to be stroked carefully to make sure he would resist any enticements from Holden to jump ship. The angry reaction to Holden in Westmount, as well as on *The Gazette*'s editorial page and on English language radio, was enough to convince Atkinson to keep his distance from Holden, at least for the time being. Their friendship, however, remained intact and they carried on as barstool buddies. One afternoon, shortly after one of their boozy lunches, a jovially-fortified Atkinson, while rising to vote against a motion that Holden had just supported, gave him the middle-finger salute. This was caught by the National Assembly TV cameras and broadcast across the province. The still-photo version was prominently displayed in all the papers the next day. Atkinson was made to apologize in the Assembly, which he did in the fulsome manner that only he can muster. He offered a "sincere, contrite, chastened, abject apology" for his "scatological gesture".

With my image bruised, the caucus diminished and the party discredited—however unfairly—in the eyes of the public, especially the francophone community we were trying to reach, what had started out as a banner year was turning into our time of greatest trial.

To address this I decided to send a letter to the party executive asking that a leadership review be held the following spring. I felt that a re-affirmation by the party was the only way to assert my credibility as leader. At the same time, however, I planned to approach a number of people about running for the leadership, and if I could find someone with the credibility and authority I could respect, and who could potentially broaden the party's base, I would gladly trade in all the aggravation and step aside. The recent Holden fiasco had made me yearn for the life of a simple MNA, able to focus on my riding and my special areas of concern without having to worry about all the duties and distractions of the party leadership. I was prepared to step down, but only if the right person could be found to take over.

I approached people like Peter Blaikie and Donald Johnston, both of whom I met one afternoon at their law firm. Johnston, who was the national president of the federal Liberals at the time, declined, as did Blaikie, who joked that with four kids in American universities he could not afford the job. Julius Grey also demurred, citing his law practice. Reed Scowen, the former Liberal MNA for N.D.G. who had recently published his book about Quebec's anglophone community entitled "A Different Vision," was equally untempted by an invitation to lead the party. As before, I found that maintaining friendly links with the government in power was more important for prominent members of the anglo community, than the so-called "thrill" of leading a movement like ours.

The outlook seemed bleak. However, as in the past when things seemed to be deteriorating, the best medicine was getting some news coverage on other issues to divert attention from the party's internal problems.

The two constitutional committees established by Bill 150 began their work that fall. The PQ boycotted the committee mandated to study offers from the rest of Canada on the grounds that there were as yet no formal offers on the table. This left the field open for me as the only opposition member on the committee, and I took full advantage of my unaccustomed status and the abundance of speaking time it afforded me.

When Ottawa's preliminary package of constitutional offers was issued in late September, I was widely quoted concluding that Quebec anglophones were caught between a rock and a hard place in this constitutional debate. If we felt the proposed reforms were not in the best interests of our community, what should we do? If we worked to sink any such deal, and were successful, the upshot would be a sovereignty referendum.

We also got good mileage out of our call to boycott a PQ task-force on anglophone community issues when it became known that the chairman of the committee, hard-line Chicoutimi MNA Jeanne Blackburn, had given a grant to a group of young language vigilantes to fund a province-wide witch hunt for English signs.

In December Jacques Parizeau went to Washington to speak to the U.S. State Department and other American officials. He returned triumphant, smugly giving the impression that he had convinced our neighbours south of the border that if Quebec votes for sovereignty, all outstanding details of Quebec-U.S. relations could be dealt with over a cup of tea. I seized on this by having the National Assembly library photocopy for me all standing treaties between the United States and Canada. When they arrived, I tied the two-foot high pile of documents in a red ribbon. At my session-ending press conference, I referred to it as my Christmas gift to Jacques Parizeau, as a reminder that all treaties between the U.S. and Canada would have to be reworked if the province were to separate.

I scoffed at Parizeau's suggestion that an independent Quebec would automatically become a full party to treaties like the Free Trade Agreement as patently false. I made the point that the mighty United States would be sitting down at a negotiating table with this new country of Quebec, with a population the size of metropolitan Chicago, hoping to illustrate Quebec's relative disadvantage in asserting itself with a trading partner that is so much more powerful. The photo with the pile of treaties was published across the country the following day. It was a nice change after the Holden fiasco only two months before.

Our recovery from the Holden setback was also helped by my refusal to allow our party to run a candidate in an upcoming byelection in Anjou riding in east-end Montreal, where a vote split could have delivered it to the PQ on a silver platter. I got good marks from The Gazette in a surprisingly glowing year-end editorial about my solid performance as an MNA and my growing political maturity. I was also thanked by dairy farmers for blocking a bill from being tabled in the National Assembly that would have penalized many milk producers.

With my image on the upswing once again as 1992 began, I became involved in organizing a tax protest for Montreal business owners, along with PQ MNA Michel Bourdon among others. It was an emotional issue that had angered the downtown business community to the point where otherwise respectable chamber of commerce types were prepared to storm city hall. The tax burden on commercial property owners was becoming unbearable as an indirect result of what was called the "Ryan reform." Claude Ryan, as Municipal Affairs Minister, cut annual provincial cash transfers to municipalities and revised municipal taxation powers, allowing the city of Montreal to impose a surtax on commercial property. This infuriated the owners of businesses already reeling from the recession.

It was also at this time that the Liberal party unveiled the Chambers Report, produced by a committee assigned to look into the future of English education in Quebec, headed by now-McGill chancellor Gretta Chambers. The report's first recommendation addressed the dramatic enrolment decline in Quebec's English schools. It suggested allowing all immigrants from English-speaking countries to attend English schools. We jumped right into the thick of the debate, pressuring the government in the National Assembly to act on the recommendation. Our party was also organizing a series of pro-Canada rallies at the time, and news stories began appearing about how we were picking up the slack and beginning to organize the federalist forces on our own for the looming referendum campaign.

I led a coalition of ethnic groups in denouncing remarks by Joe Clark, who claimed that if Quebec were to separate, the federal government would turn its back on Quebec's minorities. I also got involved in fighting the government's attempt to change the Westmount riding boundaries. The proposed changes would have reduced the percentage of anglophones in the riding, greatly diminishing our community's influence in that riding as well as our party's chances of winning it in the next election.

Things were looking up again. The Holden fracas had receded from peoples minds. Our profile was high, and our press was good. I was also getting along much better with Atkinson now that Holden's disruptive influence in caucus was gone. But I should have known by this time that such a run of good fortune could only mean one thing: trouble ahead.

My relationship with some of the more hardline members of the executive was sorely strained over my reluctance to forcefully advance the partition thesis adopted at the party's annual convention the year before. There were demands to announce the leadership review I had suggested in my letter a few months ago. I argued that since things were now going well, and with a referendum in the offing, the time was not right. Having been unable to recruit a serious successor, I was having second thoughts about the leadership review. Instead of affirming my leadership, it could just as easily spin out of control, causing bitter divisions in the party at a time when our only focus should be the referendum.

The majority of our riding associations were very supportive and had rallied around me from the outset of the Holden affair. At a general council meeting to discuss the leadership issue, I expressed reservations about the leadership announcement because of the timing and lack of credible candidates, and the General Council subsequently quashed the leadership review proposal. This incensed the members of the executive committee who were pushing hard for a review and further poisoned relations at the party's senior level.

Sure enough, the confidential letter I had sent to the executive about the leadership review was leaked and the leadership issue blew up in the media, with myself cast as a ditherer who couldn't decide if I was coming or going. There was a lead front page story in *The Gazette* with the banner headline: "Libman might quit Equality leadership." Don Macpherson wrote a column on how my indecision was paralysing the party. Once again the party's demise was declared imminent, even though the rank and file were strongly behind me, as the General Council vote had amply shown. The trouble was being stirred up by two or three people, some of whom were thinking about running for the leadership themselves. But the media gleefully portrayed the affair as a concerted revolt against the leadership.

I made it clear several days later that I would be staying on as leader, willing and able to fight the referendum battle. But even while putting on my brave face, I knew this latest episode had damaged the party's credibility once again. The perception that the party was always rife with infighting was woefully reinforced. Morale was sagging and some quality people we couldn't afford to lose were washing their hands of the party.

According to our pattern thus far, alternating from good times to bad times, we should have been due for some sunshine at this point. Instead, an even more serious conflict was brewing. It would put the party to its most difficult test to date—one from which it never quite recovered.

CHAPTER TWELVE

The Constitutional Divide

United we stand, divided we fall.
—Aesop

A ll this infighting and the bad press it generated was guaranteed to alienate anyone with a measure of political know-how. Any pragmatic individual interested in getting involved with a viable political party would no longer look to the Equality Party as a serious option. Instead, many of the members who had stuck with us this far had it up to here by now and were leaving the party. Others in the community, whom I had taken to consulting on a personal basis, let me know of their disappointment and frustration. Just showing up for a meeting was enough to drive the sturdiest soul to abject despair. Those who were staying tended to be ideologues who clung to hard-line positions with the unyielding ferocity of underfed pit-bulls.

Ideological hard-liners of any persuasion are guided by obsessive conviction and a dogged reluctance to compromise on issues, in the unshakeable certainty that their dogma is the absolute truth. The constitutional issue was a heaven-sent opportunity for them to draw battle lines; hardliners on language issues are also hardliners on constitutional issues. They believe that the only acceptable constitutional changes are ones that strengthen the federal government. Any compromise is regarded as a sellout that could leave anglo Quebecers at the mercy of a provincial government with no compunctions about riding roughshod over their language rights. They are undeterred by confrontation; if anything they relish the opportunity to smite the misguided with their righteously-inflamed rhetoric. Every time they carried the day, more of the moderates would defect.

As constitutional discussions in the country were heating up in response to Bill 150's call for offers from the rest of Canada, I was concerned that any deal that would be acceptable to Quebec and hence avert a referendum on sovereignty would not be acceptable to most of our party's active membership. This, I knew, would really put us between that rock and the hard place. Most members were concerned about the distinct society clause showing up again in a new deal. They also feared that too much power would be handed over to the provinces by a federal government desperate to get the Quebec government's signature on a constitutional pact.

Should Quebec agree to a new deal, and if a referendum were held on the new constitutional package, the PQ would be heading the NO side. No matter what the deal, they were bound to reject it as a betrayal of Quebec's aspirations and its people's destiny. The Liberals would be seen by francophone federalists and the overwhelming majority of anglophones as the Canadian unity alternative to the PQ. If we were to reject the package for catering excessively to Quebec nationalist demands, we would have to join the ranks of the NO side, and would be perceived as being in bed with the PQ. Most of our federalist rank and file would be alienated and our party would be squeezed out of the action, and out of the picture.

A referendum on sovereignty would be comparatively easy. The party would unite with the Liberals and other federalists on the NO side and fight the referendum good fight with a vigorous federalist message.

I therefore urged Bourassa to call a referendum on sovereignty, which surprised a lot of people. In addition to keeping our party together, it would put the true question to the people once and for all, a question I was convinced would be defeated. I suggested that if the federal offers were acceptable to Quebec, they should come into force if Quebecers reject sovereignty. There would be no referendum on the offers themselves, but it would be understood that if sovereignty were rejected in a referendum, then the package of offers would stand as accepted. This would have thrown the PQ on the defensive, by forcing them to defend their option instead of giving them a free pass to tee off on the federal offers for the duration of the campaign.

We also decided to initiate a court challenge in an attempt to nullify the sections of the referendum law that force all participants in a referendum to work under either the YES or NO umbrella organization. Under the existing law, virtually all spending during a referendum campaign must be approved by either the YES or NO committee. The government typically controls one and the official opposition the other. This forces a third party like ours to seek permission to spend money from a political adversary. For example, if the referendum were on the federal offers and we were on the NO side, we would need the PQ's consent for virtually everything, from holding a rally to printing fliers. We maintained that this was clearly in violation of our freedom of expression and association.

Our court challenge to the referendum law was widely condemned as a mischievous attempt to delay or sabotage the referendum, even though a favorable verdict would only nullify certain sections dealing with restraints on spending. It would require the government to amend only those specific sections of the referendum law to allow us to spend our due share of the NO side budget as we saw fit. The challenge was rejected by the courts three months later, as was the subsequent appeal.

It would take the 1992 referendum itself, and the strange alliances it engendered, to convince some of our harshest critics at the time, notably *The Gazette*'s editorial board and Lysiane Gagnon of *La Presse*, that our challenge to these ridiculous sections of the law was not altogether without merit.

Tensions were already building in the party between myself and the constitutional purists, who had formed a circle around our constitutional committee chairman, Keith Henderson. Many of the moderate members of the party had become inactive, tired of battling the more zealous and morally overbearing hardliners who were tightening their grip on the party and increasingly dominating its meetings. Under no circumstances would this group accept a new constitutional deal with any reference to a distinct society, even innocuously placed in a preamble. They suspected that the caucus and I would be less inclined to oppose a deal that had the support of the other provinces, and started to prime their artillery for a showdown as we approached our policy convention in June.

They had been generally supportive of my leadership up to now, but in this constitutional crunch, any softening on my part, real or perceived, would be unforgivable in their blinkered view.

An explosive situation was also building in the party's youth wing, which was already developing its own independent spirit, though it was not yet formally recognized by the party. Its structure and bylaws were to be enshrined in the party constitution at the upcoming convention. The group was headed by a pair of brash self-styled young political wannabes, Giuliano D'Andrea and Erik Reich, who were far more willing than the mainstream party membership to soften the party's position on language rights and the constitution.

When I had called for a boycott of the PQ's anglophone commission, which I felt was merely a public relations exercise and a superficial attempt to stroke the anglo community, our youth wing leaders nevertheless took it upon themselves to present a brief. They had also come out in favor of a distinct society clause in a new constitutional deal, despite the party's clearly stated reservations.

Since Henderson and the constitutional hardliners saw the youth wing as a threat to their entrenched positions at the convention, they moved to cut them off at the knees. The older group tried to limit the number of voting youth delegates at conventions and sought to lower the age limit for youth wing members to keep its overall numbers down. In meetings leading up to the convention, where riding associations were asked to propose resolutions, there were often bitter shouting matches between the youth wing and senior members. At a meeting in Cowansville, where I was not present, it was alleged that a chair had been thrown in the heat of debate. Legend also has it that someone threatened to call 911 after a shoving match had to be broken up.

To head off a potential catastrophe at the convention, I invited D'Andrea, Henderson, and a few other members of the executive to Quebec City a few days prior to the big event. In a marathon meeting with the caucus, we hammered out a youth wing structure that tenuously held the party together for the time being.

On the eve of the convention, Phil Authier, *The Gazette*'s cynically-inclined bureau chief in Quebec City, wrote a viciously unfair scene-setter about how the Equality Party was a festering mess, comparing our members to "feuding ozark hillbillies." I could picture him drooling on his keyboard as he railed about the party's leadership, policies, and performance.

At the convention, Henderson and his cohorts on the constitutional committee succeeded in pushing through all their hardline motions, rejecting the distinct society clause and just about anything else that might lead to a constitutional compromise. To make matters worse, the most ardent hardliners were elected to key positions in the party.

For all the youth wing's dissatisfaction with these developments, there was no explosion that weekend , thanks to the agreement in Quebec City the week before. Nor was there any discussion whatsoever about the leadership. The party had dodged a potential disaster, albeit in a fragile state, despite the hardline constitutional resolutions. I could cushion their impact for the time being by claiming that they were not fully binding. I promised that if the alternative to the federal offers meant lining up with the PQ in a referendum campaign, the membership would be consulted once more.

We were therefore stunned to read Authier's report in *The Gazette* the next day that the youth wing had walked out in protest and that my leadership had come under fire. I wondered if he could have been at the same convention as we were. Many of our angry members called *Gazette* ombudsman Robert Walker to complain. By then he was already on familiar terms with the party. In his next column, he wrote: "Editors, reporters, switchboard operators, and the ombudsman's office probably receive more complaints from Equality Party members than from members of all the other parties combined—provincial, federal and municipal."

We had navigated the convention shoals, but trouble still lurked beneath the surface. Our constitutional position remained unsettled, and could not be resolved until Ottawa and the provinces agreed on a new deal. The youth wing constitution also needed more work, and had been turned over to a special committee. At the time I thought it was just a matter of ironing out a few minor details.

It turned out to be much more than that. In the end, the fight over the maximum age for membership in the youth wing brought the whole thing crashing down. Most believed that age 25 should be the ceiling. But D'Andrea, who was 29, wanted to keep his power and stubbornly held out for extending the age limit to 30. The committee insisted on 25.

Instead of trying to negotiate a compromise, D'Andrea decided this was his chance for a moment in the sun and staged a noisy press conference where the youth executive and 20 youth wing members made an elaborate show of tearing up their membership cards. The Equality Party had become an easy target and D'Andrea milked his opportunity for grandstanding for all it was worth. He charged that by rejecting the concept of a distinct society, the party had reduced itself to a retrograde anglo-rights rump, composed largely of rednecks and political nostalgics.

It had always been convenient for opponents to brand the party this way, but by now there was no question that the predominant group of party activists was a small, cranky group that would be unwilling to accept any progressive notion of renewed federalism. The constitutional purists, led by Henderson, were clearly in control of the party apparatus, and the youth wing fiasco had inflicted yet another embarrassing black eye. But there was still more impending doom in the possibility that the eventual constitutional package from Ottawa would be acceptable to myself and the caucus. This would surely mean the decisive split in the party.

Early August brought gross insult and grievous embarrassment to Westmount as Richard Holden joined the PQ, to the apoplectic ire of his constituents. He had been flirting with the party for weeks. He had invited Jacques Parizeau to lunch at the Ritz Carleton Hotel and formally offered his services to the separatist cause—on the same premises where he once caroused with Brian Mulroney, who still slept upstairs on occasion when in town on prime-ministerial business. A delighted Parizeau accepted on the spot, no doubt smiling his Cheshire-cat smile at the thought of being served canary-on-a-platter, at the Ritz of all places.

Holden claimed that his flip-flop off the high board was inspired by his deep conviction that anglophones needed a voice within the sovereignty movement. Few believed him. Some laughed, some cried. It was clear to anyone that the only reason why Richard Holden joined the Parti Québécois was to salvage his sinking political ship.

Having been rousted from the Equality Party and spurned by the Parti Libéral caucus, his only hope of being re-elected was for the PQ to run him in a riding where the PQ was at least in contention; somewhere in the Laurentians maybe, or in Verdun. That the PQ even took him on was a sign that they were either hopelessly out of touch with the anglo community or blindly desperate if they believed for a minute that Holden would be a glowing testimonial of their new-found openness, and that he would be able to rally anglos to their cause. The move backfired loudly as both the French and English media roundly portrayed him as an opportunistic buffoon. I felt a little bit guilty for springing him on Westmount in the first place, but in its own small way this little saga indirectly worked in our favor.

It revealed him as the unreliable character he really was, thereby spiking his criticism of the party the year before. This time it was my turn to have a field day in the sound-bite department. I suggested that if Holden would be as much of a pain in the neck to Jacques Parizeau as he had been to me, this was the best news federalists have had in months. I also released a number of past statements and memos from Holden in which he had railed vigorously against the PQ.

For example, just a year earlier, in a scathing memo blasting my trial balloon about threatening to run candidates against Liberals in close ridings, Holden wrote: "What will happen . . . is that the Parti Québécois will pick up twelve to fifteen seats in districts which normally return Liberals. Thus will the EP abet in putting into power a government diametrically opposed to everything I stand for, i.e. Canada, individual rights, and bilingualism."

The new PQ MNA also wrote the previous September in his "Two Years Before the Mace": "Our stance must be one of never playing footsie with the PQ. We cannot put strategy ahead of principle. To do so, is to undermine the confidence of our electorate..."

In Holden's closing speech to the Belanger-Campeau Commission he said, "Those who are opposed to Canada believe that it cannot be salvaged. I say to you, Mr. Chairman and to all Canadians — in Quebec and across the country — WE WILL SAVE CANADA; WE WILL OVER-COME."

When Canada's nine other premiers and the Federal government finally concluded a proposal to be presented to Quebec, it looked as though some of the concerns about a split between the caucus and the rest of the party were unfounded. The proposal fell short of what I believed to be in the best interests of Quebec's anglophone community. Once again the sticking point was the level of protection for minority communities needed to provide a sufficient counterweight to the distinct society clause. On the constitutional table now was a "Canada Clause" whereby Quebec would be recognized as a distinct society. The clause declared that Canadians and their governments are committed to the vitality of the minority communities, thus implying that governments were only required to "preserve" their rights as opposed to the requirement for governments to "preserve and promote" the distinct society of Quebec.

As in the Meech Lake accord, this was a concern for those of us who believed our community should not be subjected to a double standard in terms of minority rights. According to the wording of the clause, it was reasonable to conclude that the courts might allow a Quebec government greater latitude to promote collective rights by enacting legislation that might otherwise violate the Charter of Rights. It was clear that I could not go along with it as it was.

I therefore organized a group of ethnic community leaders for a press conference in Ottawa on Parliament Hill. We warned that if the final agreement was not modified to improve minority community protection, Quebec's minority communities might join the NO side to fight the new accord. We suggested that the wording dealing with minority rights must be as strong as the wording for the distinct society. The press conference made headlines throughout the country, though Don Macpherson wrote in *The Gazette* that we were dreaming in technicolor, and suggested that Quebec federalists should be happy enough that a deal—any deal—had reached the table before the Bill 150 deadline for an October referendum.

As it turned out, Bourassa would take a conciliatory step backward and accepted a modified wording of the distinct society clause that put official language minorities on a more equitable footing. When a final agreement, ratified at a last-ditch conference in Charlottetown, was deemed acceptable to the Quebec government, even many staunch and normally hard-line federalists spoke of a national unity miracle. William Johnson of *The Gazette* and Julius Grey were initially effusive in their praise. But with the party holding fast to the hard line, its heels dug in as deeply as ever, I saw dire consequences ahead.

Atkinson and Cameron told me right away that they would be supporting the Charlottetown accord. At the same time, I knew that there was no way that Henderson's clique would go for it.

I was torn down the middle. I was deeply worried about a potentially fatal rupture within the party, as well as my own lingering problems with the deal. But since I knew that most of our community would be in favor, it was clear to me that the only way to save the party was to convince the membership that we had no choice but to go along with the Charlottetown package.

With Bourassa's concession on the wording of the minority rights clause, which calmed my principal concerns, the caucus was poised to rally to the YES side. We delayed going public as long as we could, knowing the decision would surely split the party if we announced it too abruptly. We held press conferences urging the government to reassure the anglophone community that in return for a resounding YES vote, the government would be willing to address the community's major concerns, either by striking down Bill 178 or adopting the Chambers report's first recommendation on greater access to English schools.

The provincial government tabled legislation in September to amend Bill 150 and call for a referendum to be held on October 26, not on sovereignty, but on the new constitutional proposals in the Charlottetown accord. The federal government would hold a national referendum on the proposal in the other provinces on the same date.

Cameron, Atkinson, and myself had by now firmly decided to come down on the YES side. We felt that despite the package's inadequacies, federalists in Quebec had no better option. It is, after all, not so much the actual wording of a constitution that ultimately determines the course of any society as the political, social, and economic realities of the day. If the accord were defeated, the Quebec sovereignist movement would have the wind in its sails, and its leaders would stridently proclaim that the pursuit of renewed federalism had reached a dead end, and that sovereignty is the only way out of the Canadian constitutional impasse.

The MNAs held a press conference on Labour Day where we announced that with some reservations, we would campaign on the YES side along with the Liberal party, and that we would do everything possible to convince the Equality rank and file at a General Assembly later that month to do likewise.

Tony Kondaks, who had worked with me since my election three years earlier, felt he had to quit his job on principle and became a key organiser for the marginal "Federalists for the NO" committee. Replacing Kondaks would not be easy. He was a workhorse whose extraordinary output equalled that of three people. At one point I had to let my first secretary go, and during the period before hiring another he would even do her job along with all his other duties. We had our disagreements, but he rarely let his dogmatically-held beliefs get in the way of our working relationship. He had been by my side virtually every day from the beginning and we had become close friends. We played golf together and during the summer he would often come up north to visit with my family. I still believed that after the referendum, we would be able to patch up our differences and work together again.

I did a lot of speaking and campaigning for the YES side in my riding of D'Arcy McGee. Not so much on the accord's merits but on the opportunity to stall the sovereignist momentum and finally get Quebec's signature on the 1982 Canadian constitution. I urged skeptics that the political implications for Canada of a strengthened PQ, buoyed by a referendum win, outweighed the residual concerns about some of the details of the accord.

This was the reasoning I used in a debate I had with Stephen Scott in the "Moot Court" of the law faculty at McGill. After the debate a young man approached me and said that he and his dad were very disappointed that I did not stick to my guns and oppose the accord. He told me his name was Justin Trudeau. This caused me a great deal of personal turmoil. Pierre Elliott Trudeau's political vision of the primacy of the Charter of Rights, bilingualism, and a strong central Canadian government to ensure a national will, was always a beacon for myself and the party. His disappointment hurt.

During the first part of the referendum campaign I arranged meetings with the different riding associations, trying to convince them of the importance of our party working together in support of the YES side. The three MNAs' offices did extensive polling of Equality Party card carrying members and found that an overwhelming majority were disposed to support the accord. Unfortunately, the party bylaws would not let all members vote at General Assembly meetings. Only delegates chosen at local meetings could vote, and inevitably the hard-line zealots would fight hardest to be chosen.

Sure enough, at the party assembly in late September, the vote was in favour of rejecting the accord, thereby driving a huge wedge between myself and the party executive, not to mention its most active members. I stood by the caucus position and suggested the party had made a mistake.

The referendum campaign was my first chance to work closely with the anglo establishment and Liberal party organization. Since our challenge to the referendum law had been struck down that summer, the three Equality MNAs were forced to work under the YES umbrella with the Liberals maintaining a firm grip on the handle. The Liberal YES committee for D'Arcy McGee had its headquarters in the Cavendish Mall's shopping concourse, so it was convenient for me to spend a lot of time there. At first it was awkward, since the committee chairman was my former Liberal opponent, Gary Waxman. As well, most of the office volunteers and staffers had worked against me in the last election. It did not take long to fit in, however. Waxman was not there often, and I quickly clicked with the office staff.

My relentless campaigning made for bitter feelings in the Equality Party. There were times when I was heckled by Equality Party members working on the NO side. Tony Kondaks was often seen outside the meeting halls where I gave speeches, distributing pamphlets for the NO side.

I was also included on the anglo steering committee for the YES campaign, and I found myself speaking on the same platform as the Premier one evening to launch the YES campaign in the West Island ridings.

This was due in part to a National Assembly procedural technicality. There was talk about the two principal leaders, Bourassa and Parizeau, engaging in a face-to-face debate on the Charlottetown proposal. Initially, the preferred format was a debate in the National Assembly, in which case I would have the right to participate, if only to a limited extent, by virtue of the Assembly's standing rules. Bourassa's chief of staff, John Parisella, had asked if I would waive my right to speak, and I told him only on condition that I participate more actively in the campaign to sell the YES option to anglos. He was readily obliging, and I was given opportunities to speak at key public meetings. When it was decided that the debate would take place in a TV studio, not in the National Assembly as expected, I was no longer invited to share the main stage.

I was also very uneasy about the YES committee's overall strategy, which I felt was far too nationalist. It made much of the new powers the government of Quebec would be getting and very little of the benefits of being part of Canada. Anglos, I argued, were uncomfortable with this kind of rhetoric and wanted to hear more about how ratification of the accord would bring greater hope for Canadian unity. I also found myself constantly clamoring for more material in English and the presence of at least a maple leaf on some of the literature.

When referendum day finally arrived, the result showed over-whelming support for the accord from anglophones and constituents in the ridings we represented. At 92 per cent the riding of D'Arcy McGee recorded the highest percentage of YES votes, not only of any riding in Quebec, but of all ridings in Canada. The overall result in Quebec was 55% to 45% against the accord, consistent with the result in the rest of Canada, though for greatly different reasons. The majority of Quebecers felt it did not go far enough, while most Canadians thought it went too far. I was not terribly disappointed by the accord's rejection, but I was proud of the result in D'Arcy McGee. I also felt vindicated in my battle with the Equality Party executive after the anglophone community had so emphatically supported the position that we the MNAs had endorsed.

After the result was in on referendum night, the YES camp gathered for its final bash at the Spectrum, a downtown showbar that normally caters to rockers not pols. I arrived at the packed hall just prior to the much-anticipated arrival of Robert Bourassa. I did a few interviews before being called onstage along with all other MNAs and Members of Parliament from the YES side.

As I stood there, I could not help but get a sick feeling in the pit of my stomach, fully aware of the bitter reckoning that awaited me at the next meeting of our sorely divided party. When Bourassa began speak-ing, it occurred to me that I was close enough to him to be in camera range. Not wishing to aggravate things any further, I began edging discreetly toward the side of the stage.

CHAPTER THIRTEEN
Letting Go of the Leadership

As to the presidency,
the two happiest days of my life
were those of my entry upon the office
and my surrender of it.
—Martin Van Buren

A few days after the referendum, an executive meeting was called by the party's new president, Howard Greenfield. The only positive thing to come out of the recent General Assembly was the election of Greenfield. A reasonable and pragmatic lawyer who was determined to bring the party together, he had the trust of both the caucus as well as the hard-liners. His plan was to begin the healing process by fostering a reconciliation between the MNAs and the rest of the party executive.

The meeting at the party's central office began as a sombre affair. Too much time was initially spent clearing away inane administrative details while the ill will in the room simmered like a noxious stew on the back burner. When we finally got around to the referendum campaign, I asked that we get right down to the nitty-gritty. Speaking on behalf of the caucus, I mentioned that the referendum result had given us a moral mandate to ask for a new party executive, since the incumbent executive had clearly shown themselves to be on a different political wavelength than our own electorate.

The executive committee members, notably Henderson and Gilles Pepin, a new party vice-president, were beside themselves. In their deeply-held view, the leader and caucus had shown that they were out of step with the majority of Canadians, who had voted against the accord. Tempers were close to a boil, but everyone kept taking deep breaths to keep things from getting out of hand. The impasse was as impenetrable as ever. The executive insisted on an emergency general council meeting the following week where it could be decided whether the executive or the leader should come under review. I made it clear that I had no interest in subjecting myself to such a kangaroo court and that I would be out of town in any case. I went home that night assuming that no such meeting would be scheduled.

The following week, my son and I flew to Seattle to visit my brother, Warren. Ironically enough, we returned one afternoon from the Washington State Zoo and there were two messages on my brother's answering machine, one from Bob Benedetti of PULSE News and the other from Geoff Baker of *The Gazette*. The executive committee had gone ahead in my absence and called an emergency general council meeting where a faction led by Henderson tried to have me ousted as party leader, citing my "flagrant disregard for the party in supporting the YES side in the referendum." This attempt failed, as many who may have disagreed with me on the referendum, still felt that this was too drastic a step for the party to take. The hard-liners did, however, succeed in having the general council call for a leadership convention, to be held the following February.

At this point, the only active members who were able to stomach the party were the purest of the constitutional pure who seem to think of nothing else all day but the Canadian constitution. In most of their eyes, Henderson would faithfully represent their beliefs as leader, immune to the diabolical temptations of reasonable compromise.

Upon my return from Seattle, I had to start fresh in my riding office. It was now impossible for Kondaks to come back to work for me after he had worked so vigorously against me during the referendum campaign, to the point where tempers had flared. So I hired Terrence Levine, a journalist with *The Suburban*, as political attaché, as well as Glenn Nashen, a Côte St. Luc city councillor, to run my local riding affairs. I had first thought of eventually hiring Levine during the referendum campaign after he wrote a column explaining why, as a Quebec anglo and despite his dislike for the Charlottetown accord, he was still backing the YES side. In the piece, he had touched on the same reasons that had prompted my reluctant support.

The deadline to submit candidacies for the party leadership was mid-January. It was obvious that Henderson would be a candidate. Also sure to run was Pepin, a former tennis instructor who liked nothing more than to see his name in print. He always spoke of how important it was for the party to enhance its image by having a francophone leader. Since he was one of the only francophones left in the ranks, he concluded that maybe he was the man of the hour, recounting how on a trip down the

Saint Lawrence on his sailboat he realized out of the blue one day that politics was his true calling.

I had very little desire to run for the leadership at this point unless all card carrying Equality Party members were given a vote. The executive committee was pushing for representational voting, whereby only delegates chosen at riding association meetings would elect the leader. They had engineered this into the party bylaws over the past few months, knowing that my chances of keeping the leadership were far greater if the entire membership could vote, as opposed to the limited circle of hard-line activists who now dominated most of the riding associations.

At an acrimonious general council meeting in December, my appeal for a universal party vote was rejected in favor of the delegate system.

I already felt that any further attempt by the party to broaden its appeal to the larger federalist community had been doomed by its rejection of the Charlottetown accord. Rightly or wrongly, the anglophone community overwhelmingly disagreed with the party's stance. Even if I were to run and win, the prospect of cleaning house and starting to build the party all over again was hardly an inviting prospect. I would inherit a divided and bitter executive and a fractious party whose strongest supporters felt I had betrayed them on the constitutional issue. Just thinking about it made me shudder.

If I ran and lost, to either Henderson or Pepin, my credibility would be shot by losing to someone the media would likely consider a marginal extremist. On the other hand, whenever I thought of shedding the burden of the leadership of the Equality Party altogether, I felt tremendously relieved and serenely at peace with myself.

My entire staff, both in Montreal and Quebec City, felt it was time for me to just cross the floor and join the Liberal caucus. I had just worked very closely with them on the referendum campaign and a number of MNAs had been making persistent joking suggestions that I was due for a new political home. When I was onstage with all the Montreal-area Liberal MNAs on the night of the referendum defeat for Bourassa's concession speech, a number of them asked me that evening what I would be doing. All I could say was that I really didn't know.

Many people around me agreed that the political dynamic was now vastly different than during the last election, and over the next year or two the provincial electorate would polarize around the question of Quebec sovereignty. There would be no room in the middle for the Equality Party.

Despite the attraction of guaranteed re-election that running for the Liberals would offer, the Liberal language policy was still intact. Unless Bill 178 was changed, which was after all the very raison d'être for my plunge into politics, I felt I could not make such a switch and still use a mirror to shave in the mornings.

When the National Assembly reconvened in December after the referendum break, Cameron, Atkinson and I held a press conference to force the language issue back on the political agenda. The notwithstanding clause has only a five-year life span and the government would have to decide next year whether or not to renew it to keep Bill 178 on the books. As far as I was concerned, switching to the Liberals was not out of the question, but only if they did not re-invoke the notwithstanding clause.

For now, however, I would have to confront the hard decision about the leadership of the Equality Party. Convincing someone of credible stature to run would be impossible at this point.

Fighting the delegate system itself would make me look like a crippled leader trying to cling to power. Running for the leadership under the delegate system would be inviting humiliation. All the hardline zealots would work like the devil to make sure their delegates were chosen. I did not have the energy or desire to dirty my hands in that kind of scrap. Even if I did pull it off, the party would split down the middle, and I would have to rebuild from the scattered wreckage.

To appease those around me who were pushing me to cross the floor to the Liberals, I set up a lunch meeting for early January with John Parisella. I had come to know Parisella around the National Assembly and we often collaborated during the referendum campaign. He was a hard-nosed partisan and a cagey political pro, and I knew I would have to tread carefully. I would raise the language issue with him and ask if the Liberals had serious plans to change the sign law. If so, I would broach the question whether I could be invited to join the Liberal caucus as a sign of reconciliation with the anglophone community. I felt that with an assurance that Bill 178 would be scrapped, my political credibility and private conscience would remain intact since I would have directly affected the change to the law that triggered my decision to enter politics.

I could thus offer our community the service of being an outspoken advocate within the Liberal caucus, constantly pressing for more changes. If he informed me that they would not be changing their language policy, then I would have to dismiss any interest in the Liberals and wage a much more aggressive campaign in the National Assembly, in anticipation of the outraged backlash that refusal to change the law would surely provoke.

Unfortunately, Parisella's office called to cancel on the morning the meeting was scheduled. The Premier had a relapse of his skin cancer, which touched off a media frenzy and caused considerable concern for all those around him. The meeting would never be rescheduled.

Another solution to the leadership conflict was suggested by the members of the D'Arcy McGee riding association, who had supported me on the YES side in the referendum. They wanted me to go so far as to change the locks at the party's central office, believing that the referendum result had given me the moral authority to lock out members of the executive. It was a messy scenario, and not one I craved.

With all these alternatives sitting in front of me, the most reasonable and the most comforting was the thought of taking a step back, graciously foregoing the party leadership and continuing on as the MNA for D'Arcy McGee. The prospect of being able to devote my undivided attention to the riding and to my duties in the National Assembly gave me an inner peace I had not felt for a long time.

I decided to resign from the leadership, but stay on as the Equality Party MNA for D'Arcy McGee. I would give the new leader a chance to pull the party together. The constitutional hard-liners would surely seize full control, but I still had a certain respect for Keith Henderson's intelligence. Assuming he would win, I expected that he would rally the respect of those remaining in the party and keep it on a narrow, yet cohesive track until the election that would come within the next two years. I also quietly hoped that once exposed to the demands of leadership he too would learn to compromise in areas where compromise was necessary.

I announced that on January 15, 1993, which was the deadline to submit candidacies for the leadership, I would be holding a press conference. Since it was assumed by many that I would be announcing my intention to run in the leadership race, some of the media might not show up. Therefore, the day before, I called Pierre O'Neill of *Le Devoir* to give him the scoop that I would be stepping down. O'Neill is one of the most respected veteran journalists in Quebec and had always been very fair and professional in writing about me and the party. If *Le Devoir* reported the story the morning of the press conference, the English media would surely be out in force. *Le Devoir* did in fact help by splashing my leak on its front page.

Four years after assuming the leadership of the Equality Party, I stepped down after making the most difficult political decision of my life. I praised the party's achievements, first and foremost its success in bringing to light, as no one else had ever done, the injustice of Quebec's language laws toward anglophone Quebecers. I also announced that I would be staying on to work with the new leader.

The consensus among the pundits the next day was that I would be a Liberal candidate in the next election, a prospect I had refused to rule out at the press conference and in a number of interviews.

At the Equality Party leadership convention the following month I received a standing ovation before and after my speech. Joining in were many I had considered back-stabbers only weeks before. One of the strange things about politics is that your bitter enemies can suddenly revere you for having led them, once you are no longer their leader.

In my speech, I stressed the critical importance of defending our principles, but warned that we should not let them" encrust us." Henderson was elected by a surprisingly narrow margin, and at his press conference afterward he seemed notably unmoved by my advice, staking out a defiant hard-line position, and boldly announcing that the Equality Party would be running in dozens of ridings, vote splits be damned.

It goes without saying that for the next few days I was portrayed in the French media as the very picture of a reasonable anglo, compared to the new party leadership, which was widely ridiculed as a collection of extremist anglo dinosaurs. By now I understood that in politics everything is relative.

CHAPTER XIV
Signs of Progress

I conceive you may use any language
you choose to indulge in, without impropriety.
—W. S. Gilbert

With the Charlottetown accord gone down to defeat, the chance for any changes to the language laws seemed slim to nonexistent. The PQ had the wind in its sails after the referendum victory and all polls indicated that they would handily win the next election. The language issue had simmered down, and with a provincial election on the horizon, there was no percentage for the Liberals in reopening this can of worms.

On the other hand, the notwithstanding clause would have to be renewed within a year to sustain Bill 178 for another five years. The sign law had always been an embarrassment to the Liberals, compounded by the success of the Equality Party in the '89 election and our steadfast campaign to highlight its infringement on individual liberties. Bill 178 had also been blamed by many for the Meech failure, having soured opinion in the rest of the country on the distinct society clause. The signal Bill 178 sent to the rest of Canada was that in the eyes of the provincial government, "distinct society" would mean in practice that it could actively repress English in Quebec without having to resort to the notwithstanding clause. But it also was clear from a number of public opinion polls that francophone Quebecers were willing to accept bilingual signs. One way or another, the government would have to do something. If Claude Ryan, the minister responsible for the French Language Charter, had any plans to quietly renew the notwithstanding clause to maintain the ban on English signs, we were determined not to let him get away with it.

In my National Assembly speech on the Charlottetown accord, I had suggested that Quebec anglos were willing to make a leap of faith by accepting the accord. But in exchange for their support, I rhetorically suggested that our community expected its "booty"—appropriating the term Bourassa himself had used a few years earlier to remind the federal Tories that they owed him for helping them out in the last election. I felt that our community deserved to have its rights restored, and that Bourassa would owe us at least this for our support on the constitutional front. This exchange in the National Assembly prompted Gord Sinclair of CJAD to call me a "political whore" in so many words for attaching conditions to the anglo community's support for the accord.

One of the first questions I asked during question period when the Assembly resumed sitting after the referendum was to Claude Ryan, inquiring what his plans were with respect to the sign law. I reminded him that his government had a history of delaying delicate decisions on language until the situation had built to a crisis point, after which a hastily improvised and generally unsatisfactory decision would be reached. He promised me that the government would shortly put the sign law under review, and agreed that it would be in everyone's best interest to not wait until the last minute.

Ryan's response provoked a flurry of speculation. A new opportunity was suddenly developing for our party to reposition itself on the issue that had always been our strong suit. A few weeks later, Ryan held a press conference where he announced that the government's advisory body on language, the Conseil de la Langue Française(CLF), would be preparing a report in response to five questions from Ryan. The first of these dealt with the language of commercial signs and how to avoid reinvoking the notwithstanding clause. The Conseil was also asked to tackle the issue of access to English-language education, the question of bilingual status for municipalities and administrative bodies, rules for public safety signs, and laws governing francisation in the workplace.

I felt that it was important in the meantime for the anglophone community leadership to prepare itself this coming year for a concerted campaign to change the language laws. I wanted to organize a one-day, non-partisan summit of anglo community leaders to discuss the future of the community, key issues of concern and joint strategy. The forum would address the same five questions that Ryan had submitted to the Conseil, but from the perspective of the anglophone community.

The first thing I did was to meet with Alliance Quebec officials. Despite initial positive reaction, Alliance Quebec decided not to participate officially because they felt that any such initiative should be under their auspices, and they were unwilling at this time to undertake such a project. They suggested, however, that they would have no objection if I were to proceed on my own.

I invited Peter Blaikie, Michael Goldbloom, Eric Maldoff, Alex
Paterson, Graeme Decarie, Julius Grey, lawyer Casper Bloom, Stephen
Scott, and Maurice King. I also approached Alan Butler, the chairman of
the Protestant School Board of Greater Montreal; Peter Riordon, head of
the Quebec Association of Protestant School Boards; Joe Rabinovitch,
head of the Association of Jewish Day Schools, and Joel Hartt. I stressed
that this was not an Equality Party initiative, but something I was doing
on my own. Almost all of them initially welcomed the idea and agreed
to participate.

It was only after the hall had been booked, the literature printed
and most of the logistics worked out that I heard from some of the
participants that they had received a call from Len Macdonald of Alliance Quebec, urging them to refuse our invitation. A number of them,
in particular those who were closely affiliated with Alliance, notably
Goldbloom, Rabinovitch, Bloom and Paterson, backed out immediately
with profuse apologies. Alliance Quebec's attitude was that for any such
initiative, they should be the only ones carrying the ball, even though
they had nothing planned themselves. Their defensive concern that
someone else would steal their thunder on an anglophone issue of such
importance was yet another example of our community's consistent
inability to get its act together.

The meeting was held nevertheless with a respectable turnout of
participants. There was a solid consensus that the sign law had to be
changed and probably would be, in light of the embarrassment it had
caused the government. But many also felt that it was no longer the
primary issue for our community. They argued that Quebec's anglos
should be pushing first and foremost for greater access to English
schools.

The numbers, as we all knew, were becoming increasingly disturb-
ing. From 1971 to the present the number of pupils in Quebec's English
schools had declined from 250,000 to 100,000, a 60% drop in 20 years.
More than a third of all English schools in Quebec had closed during this
same period. Many young anglophone families were leaving the province, and since newcomers were barred from the English school system,
the community was denied any chance to replenish itself through immigration. It is a situation that persists to this day, with no solution in sight
or any sign of political will to address it.

With the devastating decline of enrolment in our schools, the
government must be somehow compelled to allow at least a percentage
of immigrants into English schools. Recognizing that complete freedom
of choice would not be taken seriously as an option by Claude Ryan, we
urged adoption of the Chambers Report, which would allow immigrants

from English-speaking countries to send their children to English schools. In addition, we suggested that all Canadian citizens of English mother tongue should be allowed to have their children educated in English. The mother tongue rule for access to minority-language schools applies to French-speakers elsewhere in Canada, but as a compromise to Quebec during the 1982 constitutional negotiations, English schools in Quebec were restricted to the children of Canadian citizens who had attended English grade schools in Canada.

The argument would be made that these two changes would amount to a maximum drain of 10,000 students from Quebec's French school system, less than 1 per cent of its total school population of more than 1 million. The total enrolment in English schools would increase by a life-sustaining 10 per cent of its present 100,000 school population. The consensus at the meeting was that the schools question should top the anglophone community's political agenda in the coming year.

The Conseil de la langue française report was issued shortly thereafter, and its recommendations fell far short of anything acceptable to our community. On the sign law, it suggested that only stores owned by individuals—as opposed to corporate entities—should be permitted to post bilingual signs. There would also be a host of restrictions, including the obligation that the French on bilingual signs must be at least twice as prominent as the English. In all other key areas, including access to English schools and the bilingual status of municipalities and institutions, it recommended the status quo. The CLF even declined to allow English on safety signs, even if a pictogram was insufficient to get the message across. The proposals were widely criticized by anglophone spokesmen as far too timid, and it was now up to Claude Ryan to grasp the nettle.

It was also around this time that Maurice King called to inform me that the United Nations Human Rights Committee, which had been studying Bill 178, had declared it in violation of the UN's International Covenant on Civil and Political Rights. King had engineered the challenge to the UN on behalf of Gordon McIntyre, a funeral home director in Huntington, Quebec, and both the Canadian and Quebec governments had pleaded before the UN body in favour of Bill 178.

I had the decision faxed to me by Julius Grey, who had handled the legal end of the UN challenge, and distributed it to the media the next day. If Ryan or Bourassa needed an extra push to go beyond the Conseil report, the UN decision gave them the justification they needed.

Ryan did indeed decide to go the extra mile. He unveiled Bill 86 in the National Assembly and called for public hearings by the Culture Committee of which I was a member. Bill 86 allowed all merchants to post bilingual commercial signs, inside and out, as long as the French words are at least twice as prominent as the English equivalent. The only exception would be large public billboards, where English would continue to be banned. The cabinet would retain the power to regulate the circumstances under which these bilingual signs would be permitted without having to resort to legislation or National Assembly approval.

Ryan went a lot farther than I had expected, especially since he had allegedly threatened to resign back in 1988 had Bourassa not invoked the notwithstanding clause and introduced Bill 178 in response to the Supreme Court sign ruling.

In addition to changing the sign law, Ryan also opted to do away with La Commission de la Protection de la Langue Française, colloquially known as the "language police" or the "tongue troopers" to Quebec anglophones. He also took the power to revoke bilingual status for municipalities and public institutions out of the hands of the Office de la langue française(OLF), leaving it up to the municipality or institution involved to decide. In the controversial Rosemere case, for example, the OLF proceeded to revoke the town's bilingual status after its anglo population fell below 50 per cent, even though the mayor and council wanted to maintain its bilingual status, as did a majority of residents who voted for bilingualism in a referendum.

Unfortunately, the key question of greater access to English schools was not addressed by Ryan's legislation. I continued to raise the issue in question period, but neither Ryan nor the Education Minister, Lucienne Robillard, was prepared to countenance any such change. Ryan even insisted that statistics showed English school enrolment in Quebec had increased during the past few years and that the trend would continue.

The Culture Committee held several weeks of public hearings which were covered by the media. The issue barely caused a ripple in the general population despite attempts by the PQ and nationalist groups to foment a backlash by depicting the reform as an assault against the French language that would inexorably lead to its extinction in Quebec. It was clear that on the issue of commercial signs, francophone Quebecers were far more tolerant of bilingualism than their nationalist vanguard.

On second reading, the adoption-in-principle stage, I voted against Bill 86 for its failure to broaden access to English schools. During the clause-by-clause study in the committee stage, I tabled a number of amendments. I tried to have the bill changed to eliminate the cabinet's power to regulate the conditions or exceptions to the sign law. Giving cabinet such a power could allow significant changes to be made behind closed doors, without even the benefit of public debate in the National Assembly.

For symbolic reasons, I tabled an amendment that would allow full freedom of choice in language of education. But I also attempted to find a reasonable compromise. I proposed another amendment that would allow any parent educated in an English school system anywhere in the world to send their children to English school in Quebec. All of these amendments were shot down by Ryan after scant consideration. Another amendment, which Ryan considered far more seriously, proposed a change to the rules governing bilingual status of municipalities and institutions. The present threshold of 50 per cent was too high, I argued, and urged him to consider lowering it to 25 per cent. I also submitted an amendment proposing that any community institution that had bilingual status should always maintain that status, even if its anglo clientele declined below the statutory benchmark.

If there was an issue on which it was imperative for the Equality Party to maintain a united front and have its act together it was language. Yet the party almost tore itself apart once again at a general council meeting called to discuss the new language bill. With the hard-liners now firmly in control, it was proposed that we harden our position on signs by insisting that merchants should have the right to post English-only signs. It was the same debate we had gone through before the 1989 election when it was decided that we should take a more reasonable approach, in keeping with the Supreme Court sign decision. The motion was only barely defeated.

Henderson informed the MNA caucus that we must vote against the legislation or the party would scream bloody murder. Since the law maintained a ban on billboards and allowed cabinet to arbitrarily change the conditions of allowance, while failing to extend access to English schools, he insisted we were honor-bound to resist it.

While we agreed with this in principle, Cameron, Atkinson and I felt that consideration should be given to other factors. Once again we were torn between moral righteousness and reasoned pragmatism. The change to the largely symbolic sign law represented a step forward by the Liberal party, and a gesture of reconciliation toward the anglo community. And while it was based not so much on a genuine desire to help the anglo community as the realization that the sign law had become an international embarrassment, it was the first major change for the better to Bill 101 as far as the anglophone community was concerned. I felt that the new outlook on the sign law was largely induced by our party's success in the last election. I felt that by voting in favour of Bill 86, we could claim a significant victory since the sign law, which had provoked the formation of the Equality Party in the first place, had been changed to the satisfaction of the great majority of our community. With an election on the horizon, this would be a powerful message; that our election impact and our continuing presence, had generated the impetus that pushed the Liberals to make this critical change. We could go to the community with the promise that if re-elected, we could continue the push for even more changes. I also felt that by voting in favour of Bill 86, we would be making a conciliatory gesture toward the francophone majority. Acknowledging their willingness to seek common ground in the language debate would pave the way for further changes.

Politics, on so many occasions, boils down to the dilemma of choosing between what is morally right and what is politically expedient. Even as the day for the final vote on Bill 86 arrived, I was unsure how to approach it. In the earlier stages, I had voted against it, but it is the "adoption" phase where the significance of a vote is greatest.

In our final speeches, I praised Ryan for going beyond the Conseil recommendation and allowing bilingualism back on signs in Quebec for the first time since 1977. I explained the soul searching I had put into my decision, and the moral dilemma I faced. Claude Ryan even came up to me afterwards and congratulated me. But when the final vote was called, I could not bring myself to vote for it. I rose in my seat and voted nay. In the end, I felt it just did not go far enough to dispel the alienation that had caused so many Quebec anglos to leave the province during the past two decades.

After the vote, I remained in my chair for a good 15 minutes after most MNAs had left the chamber. I realized that this was another watershed in my life. Because of my anger over the government's decision to uphold the ban on my language almost five years before, I had worked hard to protest this injustice to the point of becoming a professional politician. I could now take some satisfaction in the knowledge that my efforts had helped to redress it. It was all done democratically, I thought, as I sat there in the same room where d'Iberville Fortier was censured, where Bill 178 was passed, where Marx, Lincoln, and French had made their stand and resigned.

When I finally got out of my chair, I remember muttering to myself about how it was all so incredible . . . and so bizarre.

CHAPTER FIFTEEN
Leaving the Party

One should always have one's boots on, and be ready to leave.
—Montaigne

As the summer of 1993 approached, all was calm. After all the talk and expense there was no new constitutional arrangement in place, nor any further discussions on the horizon. The language debate was also dormant. The Liberals had amended the language law, taking the sting out of the Bill 178 insult to the anglo community. It was becoming clear that Robert Bourassa would soon be stepping down as Premier and leader of the Liberal party. Potential successors were all considered strong federalists, including cabinet ministers like Gerald Tremblay, Lucienne Robillard and Daniel Johnson.

I realized it would be extremely difficult for the Equality Party to position itself within this new political context. The polling trend had been showing for some time that the PQ would probably win the next election, expected within a year. In the last election, even with their intense anger against the Liberal party, and knowing that the PQ would not win, many anglophones were still nervous about splitting the federalist vote by voting Equality. This time, with the sign law de-fanged; with the greatly unpopular Bourassa no longer on the scene; with the succession of embarrassing misfortunes that had undermined the Equality Party over the years, and with the Liberals as the only party that could possibly beat the PQ in an election, Equality's chances ranged from dismal to nonexistent.

Even one of the party's foremost objective allies in the last election had turned on us. CFCF's PULSE news, the number one television news show for Quebec anglos, had always given the party good coverage and a fair shake. This had changed when a young hotshot director named Daniel Friedman became news director in 1992. One of his first acts was

to replace Ralph Noseworthy, who had been the Quebec City correspon-
dent for 17 years, with Barry Wilson from the Montreal newsroom.
Noseworthy had a low tolerance for Quebec nationalism and appreciated the Equality Party's feisty attitude, and it came across in his regular
coverage of our caucus activities. Wilson, on the other hand, was less
respectful of the party's efforts and paid us considerably less attention.
But then he was also under orders from the top.

I had recently been slipped a shocking and grossly unprofessional
in-house memo, sent by an angry Friedman to all PULSE reporters,
complaining that the Equality Party had lately been getting too much
coverage. He wrote: "First. A warning. This is a howl of outrage ...
written in the heat of anger.

"The subject is our continued irresponsible and unprofessional
coverage of the Equality Party. The Equality Party is a fringe movement
with no future. Beset by internal problems, it is supported by 6% of the
population. But to watch PULSE News you would have a very different
impression. Time and time again we have discussed the need to take a
more balanced approach by covering the Equality Party in some kind of
proportion to its importance. Time and time again we fail. Why this
bizarre and inexplicable blind spot? Are we pathologically incapable of
exercising routine editorial judgement when it comes to the Equality
Party? . . . Let's discuss it at Tuesday's newsroom meeting. And let's get
it right this time . . . GODAMMIT! And lets's come up with some
common sense answers. (In the meantime, let's KILL the (Equality) story
for PULSE TONIGHT).

"Exasperatedly yours—dfr"

Despite his complaints, the party had felt that its visibility on
PULSE had already suffered greatly. This memo dashed any hope we
may of had of getting the kind of sustaining coverage on PULSE in the
upcoming election as we had been accorded in 1989.

My personal popularity in D'Arcy McGee was still reassuringly
high, and my best chance of being re-elected, other than by running as
the Liberal candidate, would be to focus my campaign more on my
individual performance during the past four years rather than my party
affiliation, especially the tarnished image of the Equality Party.

It was time to get a re-election team together. The Liberals had not
yet chosen a candidate for D'Arcy McGee, and their riding association
had virtually collapsed during the past four years. Once a happy hunting
ground for Liberal bagmen, D'Arcy McGee had kicked in less money to
the Liberal coffers than any other riding in the province during the
party's last fundraising campaign.

Many constituents and supporters had been urging me to run for the Liberals now that the language law had been changed. Many also stressed the importance of all federalists working together to fight the PQ. Even my parents, who had become fed up with seeing me constantly harangued in the Equality Party over the past year, wanted me to cross the floor. As well, most of the volunteers I had worked with during the referendum campaign offered to work for me should I decide to make the change.

One member of the Liberal executive, Barbara Mintzberg, who had run the committee room for my opponent in 1989 as well as the D'Arcy McGee Liberal YES committee during the referendum, was willing to work for me if I were to run for the Liberal nomination. Gerry Weinstein, the president of the local federal Conservative association, and also a key figure on the D'Arcy McGee YES committee for the Charlottetown referendum, had volunteered to be my fundraising chairman. Irwin Steinberg, who had run many of the ground-level operations for the D'Arcy McGee YES committee, had offered to be the campaign manager for my nomination bid. A nominating convention would eventually be called, and whoever signed up the most members of the party and got them out to vote at the convention, would win the nomination. Steinberg had spoken to some of the top Liberal brass and reassured me that while they would not be thrilled if I decided to go for the nomination, they would not stop me from running.

Steinberg was told that there would probably be a concerted attempt to have me defeated. If I were to lose this way, I would not be able to justify running in the upcoming election as an independent or otherwise. If I were to win at the nominating convention, the Liberal leader would still have the last word, though it would be difficult for him to thwart the democratic choice of the D'Arcy McGee delegates.

It seemed a little odd to me that they would allow me to run for their nomination so easily, considering how outspoken and critical I had been of the Liberal party for the past four years. Still, they must have thought I had done a reasonably good job as an MNA. At the annual St. Jean Baptiste Day party thrown by the Premier at the Botanical Gardens a few weeks before, Bourassa had mentioned to me that I was a good, hardworking MNA. So I figured they would at least allow me to run, despite their discomfort.

Robert Bourassa did retire a few months later, and was replaced by an uncontested Daniel Johnson who played up his federalist stripes as no Quebec Premier had done in recent memory. His statement when he officially announced that he would seek the leadership of the Liberal Party was that he was "a Canadian first and foremost." This was warmly welcomed by the anglophone community as an unbelievably positive development. Some anglophone political analysts even felt uneasy that Johnson might have gone too far. After all, to defeat the PQ, courting the soft nationalist vote was more crucial than stroking committed federalists. It was now clearer than ever that the next election would be a showdown between the "separatist" PQ, led by Parizeau, and the "federalist" Liberals, led by Johnson.

Keith Henderson was nevertheless still unwilling to make a commitment that the party would not field candidates in marginal ridings where they could split the Liberal vote and thus help the PQ leapfrog to victory. Instead, he promised me that he would do what he could to rein in the riding associations. Already the burden of conflicting demands that came with the party leadership was catching up to him. The riding associations in the Eastern Townships, where the vote split threat was greatest, had not joined the party to sit out an election, and it would be difficult to convince them to do so.

The solid core of party hard-liners claimed that despite the relaxation of the language law and Johnson's heartfelt endorsement of federalism, there was still little difference between the PQ and Liberals. Whatever truth there might have been to this, it was not what the average voter believed. In the upcoming election campaign, it would be Parizeau versus Johnson every evening on the newscasts. It would reinforce the prevailing impression that the only way to beat Parizeau would be to vote for Johnson's party.

"The only way to overcome this reflex would be to have our voters fully understand two things. First, by voting for an Equality Party candidate in a federalist stronghold where the PQ had only marginal support, the anglo vote could split down the middle and the PQ would still finish third. Second, if an Equality Party candidate were elected, that seat would still be a federalist seat. If the Equality Party were to wind up with enough seats to hold the balance of power, it would obviously forge a coalition with the Liberals to keep the PQ out of government.

If Equality was caught running in any riding where a Liberal vote split could in fact help the PQ, the party would be dead meat. Federalists and anglophones would shun the party even in other, safer ridings on the grounds that we were undermining the federalist cause at this critical time. Nevertheless, the party decided to field a candidate in the Portneuf byelection, where we had no chance of winning, but where our candidate could conceivably siphon off enough of the federalist vote to give the PQ a leg up. The candidate, Gilles Pépin, eventually finished 11th of 12.

The caucus was also upset with Henderson's endorsement of a federal Equality Party initiative, a project doomed to failure from the outset. Quebec anglos have a natural affinity for the federal Liberal party, the party of former Prime Minister Pierre Trudeau who incarnated their federalist ideal. Nor do they consider the House of Commons as the place to make their stand on language rights. A poor result would reflect badly on the provincial Equality Party, which is exactly what eventually happened. We tried to dissuade Henderson on both these initiatives, but he was adamant that we had to take advantage of every possible opportunity.

A jump to the Liberal party at this point looked like an enticing prospect, and it was definitely something I was contemplating. But before going any further it was important to do something to help improve the image of the Equality Party to lessen the impression that I was just jumping off a sinking ship.

I convinced the executive committee to make economic issues the focus of our next annual convention. There was nothing to be gained on the constitutional front at this point, and despite the inadequacies of Bill 86, language had become all but a dead issue for most of our community. The Liberal government was, however, still highly vulnerable on economic matters. By stressing the argument that the straitjacket of Quebec nationalist economic policy had been choking our economy for the past 30 years, we felt we would cut a distinctive profile.

The size, appetite and power of Hydro-Quebec; the nationalist Quebec Inc. policies of both Liberal and PQ governments; the Caisse de dépôt et placement and Quebec's labour unions would be targets of criticism. So would Quebec's bloated provincial bureaucracy, by far the fattest in the land. I worked hard with Neil Cameron and Roger Jones, who chaired a committee of party members, elaborating and fleshing out economic principles for our election platform.

A week before the convention, we held a press conference to unveil the economic platform. Much to my dismay, Henderson went off on a tangent when asked about the party's chances in the coming election. He predicted that the party would be running in dozens of ridings and that the Liberals were no different from the PQ. I was shocked that he would go off like this, with me sitting right next to him and knowing how I felt about the vote-split issue. Such a pronouncement was tantamount to telling our potential supporters that we were resolved to guarantee that the PQ would win the election.

After this press conference, I told my key organizers that this was it. I was going to leave the Equality Party. I did not want to spend the entire campaign trying to explain why my party was running candidates in ridings where all we could do was help elect the PQ. I would also have to worry at all times about what the leader might say any given day, or any of the other candidates, most of whom were bound to be belligerent hard-liners.

I decided that I would make the announcement of my departure from the Equality Party at a press conference in Quebec City the following week.

The night before the announcement, I visited Neil Cameron in his office to break the news to him. Cameron had been with me since the earliest days. He had stood by me and supported me through thick and thin. Though disappointed, he was fully understanding and respectful of my decision. He gave me a bear-hug afterward in a rare display of emotion.

The morning of my press conference, I officially informed the speaker of the National Assembly by letter that I would henceforth be sitting as an independent. At the press conference, I announced with a lump in my throat that I was leaving the party I had founded five years before. There was an attempt by the media to draw me into admitting that I intended to run for the Liberals. I refused to say so, but did not rule it out.

Before I would make any such statement, I would have to get official clearance, notably an assurance from Daniel Johnson that he would accept my candidacy. I knew that he would never hand me the nomination on a platter. I would have to win it fair and square by selling more memberships than anyone else and getting my backers out for the nominating convention.

By this time there were two serious candidates in the running. Jack Jedwab, an official at Canadian Jewish Congress, and Joe Rabinovitch, who was the director-general of the Association of Jewish Day Schools. Two other candidates, one of whom was an unknown notary named Lawrence Bergman, were not regarded as serious contenders.

Having been on very friendly terms with both, I was taken aback that Jedwab and Rabinovitch were taking a shot at my job, which is what the winner at the nominating convention would eventually wind up with. Much as it was their perfect right, it hurts when people you know start working to unseat you, and it becomes hard to keep bitterness and resentment at bay. You have to tell yourself that this is not personal, but simply politics. At times like this you understand what the veterans mean when they say politics is a blood sport.

Rumours started to fly that I would be running for the Liberal nomination, which prompted some members of the Liberal riding association executive, including the diminutive president, Herb Cohen, to start plotting ways to head me off at the pass. Relying on Steinberg's assurances, I decided to start selling memberships discreetly. Many of my personal supporters were already Liberal party members and they easily procured blank forms. Several board members of the Mount Royal federal Liberal riding association, of which I was still a member, pitched in to advance my candidacy.

Having committed myself to run, I sent a letter to Daniel Johnson informing him of my intention to seek the D'Arcy McGee nomination. I stressed that I intended to be a team player, hoping he would understand that as a member of the opposition for the past four years, I was compelled to play my assigned role as a government critic to the best of my abilities. Whatever I might have said about the Liberal party in the past could be viewed in that context.

Our campaign team rented a storefront at the Cavendish Mall and had a huge banner printed proclaiming: "Liberals for Libman". We established committees to recruit members, raise funds, and to staff the office. A core steering committee began to meet regularly. We decided to officially launch my nomination campaign at a wine and cheese ribbon-cutting ceremony on a Sunday evening a few weeks hence.

During the first week of the unofficial campaign we had already sold more than 200 memberships. In addition, Joe Rabinovitch called to tell me that since I had decided to run, he would withdraw and hand over the 250 memberships he had sold. My campaign team was fired with enthusiasm. They knew that winning the nomination was the real challenge in D'Arcy McGee. The election itself would be a romp if I was the Liberal candidate.

Since I had still not heard from Daniel Johnson, I approached some of the key Liberal MNAs. Marcel Parent, the MNA for Sauvé and Liberal caucus chairman, whose Assembly seat was close to mine, said that if I were to win the nomination, I could join the Liberal caucus in the National Assembly prior to the next election.

At the National Assembly, I also spoke to André Bourbeau, the finance Minister and Johnson's right hand man in cabinet, to ask about official protocol in these circumstances. He suggested it would be a good idea to confirm my intentions with Pierre Anctil, the director-general of the Liberal party. I called Anctil, and a meeting was arranged for the following week at Liberal headquarters in Montreal.

I came to the meeting alone and was asked by the receptionist to wait as Mr. Anctil was still out for lunch. I sat there in the waiting area, my mind churning with mixed feelings, with all the leaders of the Liberal party since its inception gazing down at me from framed portraits on the walls. When Anctil arrived he politely ushered me into the elevator, which took us up to the eighth floor. A few people got in and out of the elevator as it made its way up. On our way to his office, we passed a number of people working at their desks. Many of them could not help but do a double-take at the sight of me in their midst.

My objective that afternoon was not to ask for permission to run for the Liberal party, but to officially inform the party that I would be announcing my intention the following week to run for the nomination in D'Arcy McGee. Anctil and I chatted for close to an hour about different political issues. He expressed concern about how I would justify my positions on Hydro-Quebec, Meech Lake and my vote against Bill 86, in an election campaign. Then he dropped the bomb.

He told me that after discussing my candidacy at an executive meeting the day before, the party had decided to ask me to sit this election out. They would be happy to have me as a member of the party, and welcomed my participation. But before I could run, I would have to earn my stripes in the ranks. Under those conditions, I might be a candidate in four years.

I was taken aback. At first I was not sure if this wasn't just a test. I told him that I had already put my profession on hold for four years. To go back now and try to rebuild my career, with only a vague possibility of coming back to politics later, and in that event having to put my career on hold again, was just too much to ask. I told him that I had already sold several hundred memberships and fully intended to continue. I would understand if the party wanted to work against me to defeat me at the nomination convention. If this was their intention, so be it. Even under those circumstances I was confident I could win.

But then he warned me that regardless of what I did, and no matter how many memberships I sold, my name would not be on the ballot at the nominating convention. This really caught me by surprise. Never had I expected that they would pull anything like this. Working to defeat me at the convention was one thing. If I won at the convention, Johnson could still refuse my candidacy, but at that point he would be hard-pressed to turn me down. Not even permitting me to run for the nomination seemed too blatantly undemocratic for the Liberal party to even consider. This had never been done by the party in its modern history. The last time anything similar had happened was when Bourassa refused to accept Harry Blank's candidacy in St. Louis in 1985 because he wanted the seat for an up-and-coming Jacques Chagnon. In a pre-emptive coup, Blank had staged a nomination convention where he was acclaimed the Liberal candidate, after which Bourassa refused to sign his papers.

Struggling to keep my composure, I told Anctil that I would like to think about it. He asked if I would sign a membership form, which I did, only to take it back shortly afterward, suggesting that I would prefer to reflect on it and then mail it in. I was still unsure of what I would do and did not want to compromise my remaining option to run as an independent. In that case, I couldn't very well slam the Liberals with any credibility after having taken out a party membership just a few weeks previously. I took the form with me, but it never made it into the mail.

I left Liberal headquarters feeling stunned. As I was driving away, who should call me in my car, but Phil Authier of *The Gazette*. Feigning sincerity and curiosity, he asked me if anything was new regarding my Liberal nomination bid. He had obviously been tipped off, yet pretended that he was in the dark. I refused to comment despite his insistent prodding. I drove over to Irwin Steinberg's office and found him with Dermod Travis. They were both shocked at the news. We decided that no comment should be made until a meeting with our election team the next evening.

I was to meet Joe Rabinovitch that afternoon to collect his membership forms. When I informed him of what had transpired, he suggested that this was probably illegal under the party rules, and if I continued to sell memberships, the party brass would probably back down.

That evening I went to the Alliance Quebec Christmas party, which was also a sendoff for outgoing president Robert Keaton. I bumped right into Bill Cosgrove, who was now the Liberal party's anglo vice-president. The uncomfortable look on his face led me to believe that he was aware of the headquarters decision. The next day's front page story under Authier's byline in *The Gazette* reported that the Liberal party had refused my candidacy in D'Arcy McGee.

At an intense meeting with my campaign team that evening, we decided that all was not lost. We would continue to sell memberships and try to provoke a grassroots reaction in favour of local democracy. The following weekend, the meeting that had been planned to announce my bid for the Liberal candidacy would proceed as planned, but without me. "Liberals for Libman" was officially launched with an additional mandate. Apart from selling memberships, we would pressure the Liberal party to let the people of D'Arcy McGee choose their own candidate without interference from headquarters. The meeting drew over 400 people, including almost all local city councillors and the mayor of Côte St. Luc, Bernard Lang, who made a strong speech on my behalf.

Once the storefront was officially opened, volunteers were able to sell close to 800 memberships in only a few weeks. The meeting got front page coverage in *The Gazette* and *Le Devoir*. It appeared that the strategy was working, until Daniel Johnson finally responded publicly, declaring that he would refuse my candidacy come what may. His official reason was that I had continually undermined a key plank in the Liberal party's economic platform. I assumed he was talking about Hydro-Quebec. If this was the true reason, it was ironic that one of my greatest political successes, and the issue that finally earned me some measure of recognition as an effective and mature politician, was the reason that I was unacceptable to the Liberal party.

To keep trying to force myself on an unwilling bride at this stage seemed fruitless. It also seemed pointless to ask our volunteers to sell memberships after the party leader had categorically said that I would not be the candidate. We had to throw out hundreds of "Liberals for Libman" letterhead, envelopes, flyers and brochures. We decided to send a letter of explanation to all the members we had signed up. We returned the $5.00 membership fee to those who requested it and donated the rest to the annual Telethon of Stars.

My options now were to run as an independent, or not run at all.

I knew that slamming the Liberals would be more difficult after having tried to join them. I realized that I should have followed my gut instinct, which had told me all along that there was no way whatsoever that the Liberal party would just let me to waltz in and be their candidate in a plum riding. I had been a source of great discomfort and embarrassment for the party in the last election. I had denounced their indiscretions over the years and caused serious problems for them with regard to Hydro-Quebec. The Liberals also knew that in this coming election, anglos would vote Liberal en masse and D'Arcy McGee would likely follow suit no matter who carried the banner. Their main concern was to win seats in francophone ridings, where soft nationalists would have to be convinced to spurn the PQ. If I were to be a Liberal candidate, many candidates in those ridings would have a difficult time justifying the presence in their ranks of an ultra-federalist and anglo-rights activist like Robert Libman.

I was also not the typical anglo with which the Liberal Party is comfortable. Liberal anglos have a history of being far more accommodating, and they probably considered me too unpredictable in a situation where party solidarity could conflict with the best interests of the anglophone community. This was the angle I would take if I decided to run as an independent, that the Liberals were not yet ready to have such an outspoken anglo advocate in their ranks. I decided to take a few weeks during the Christmas holidays to really contemplate what I would do. I was scheduled to give a speech in late January to the Côte St. Luc Senior Men's Social Club, whose many members had been very supportive over the years. I decided that this would be a good venue for my official announcement.

As it turned out, the decision was not all that difficult. If I decided not to run, the rejection by the Liberal Party would have ended my political career on a sour note, though I would go out never having lost an election and having accomplished something worthy. But I would always wonder if I might just have been re-elected had I decided to go for it.

I felt that I still had broad support among my constituents, having given my all during the past four years from the moment I was elected. It is also very difficult for a politician to just let go. Despite the aggravation, the sacrifice and the ups and downs, when an election is near, the adrenalin surges. Part of the motivation for every effort on behalf of a constituent, every appearance at a community event, every letter of congratulation or condolence, every grant, every smile, every speech and every vote in the National Assembly, is that it will count for something when the next election comes around. Everything a politician does while in office, consciously or otherwise, is linked to getting re-elected.

After all the tension of the past five years, the insults and the sacrifices, I felt that I had to assure myself that my hard work was at least appreciated. Even if I did not win, the people I had represented should be given the opportunity to judge me, and those who thought I did a good job should have the opportunity to show their approval. I needed to know.

I decided, therefore, that I had no choice but to run as an independent. Too many people who had worked with me over the years and who believed in me did not deserve to be let down by a no-show.

Though I would run as an independent, my supporters who had been selling "Liberals for Libman" memberships stuck by me. Virtually all the key organizers for the D'Arcy McGee Liberal YES committee in 1992, some of whom had worked for my opponent the last time, remained on board. On January 20, I announced that I would be seeking re-election as an independent candidate in D'Arcy McGee, undeterred by the fact that no independent candidate had won a seat in a provincial election in 28 years. A few weeks later, Gordon Atkinson would also announce his departure from the Equality Party to run as an independent. Neil Cameron was the only one of the original four who remained.

My official status in the National Assembly had not changed. I was still asking questions and felt much freer to speak on any topic without having to consult anyone.

My campaign would focus on three main political issues, all of which were of particular importance to D'Arcy McGee voters. One was the commitment to fight any encroachment on the universality of health care and the implementation of user fees, a fundamental issue in a riding like D'Arcy McGee, with the highest percentage of senior citizens of any riding in Quebec.

The second issue on which I zeroed in was the youth exodus. The Jewish community is particularly sensitive to this issue as so many of its younger generation have transplanted their roots to Toronto. I had been meeting with a group of young people for several months to develop a blueprint proposal entitled "Creating Optimism for the Future: A program to keep the anglophone community youth in Quebec". The plan got much positive news coverage when we unveiled it at a press conference where I was flanked by about two dozen young Quebec anglos. Certain representatives from Alliance Quebec complained I was poaching on their domain again, especially with the suggestion of a youth employment resource bureau, something they were apparently planning as well.

The third issue on which we focused was the importance of having a forceful representative, with a free hand to speak out on behalf of Canadian unity and his community in the Quebec legislature. Our plan was to hammer away at these issues throughout the campaign, and with no official opponent thus far, I had free rein for several weeks.

By this time, Lawrence Bergman, who was also the president of a local synagogue, had signed up most of the members of his synagogue in his bid for the Liberal nomination and his numbers were growing faster than expected. Even two members of my campaign organization who had refused to buy memberships from Bergman nevertheless received Liberal party cards in the mail a few weeks later.

This was creating considerable anxiety for Jack Jedwab, who began agitating for an earlier nomination meeting. Herb Cohen, who was still the riding association president, was concerned about Jedwab's candidacy, convinced that Jedwab would eventually want to replace the existing executive with his own people. Cohen therefore had the deadline for signing up new members extended a week, allowing Bergman to outstrip Jedwab in the card-selling sweepstakes. Jedwab subsequently pulled out of the race, leaving Bergman the only candidate for the nomination. He was duly acclaimed, leaving a number of local Liberals and members of the Jewish community feeling somehow cheated. They had felt that both Jedwab and Rabinovitch had cabinet potential, while Bergman would surely be consigned to the back benches.

While our camp was pleased with this turn of events, we found ourselves behind the eight ball from the start as the Liberals launched a scare campaign to stampede local voters into believing that they needed every seat they could get to defeat the PQ. Their literature carried the slogan: "Every seat counts."

Given the deep fear of the PQ, particularly among senior citizens who make up over 25 per cent of the riding, this tactic was almost impossible to counter. I nevertheless tried, arguing that if I were elected, and my seat was the one seat out of 125 needed to give the Liberal party a majority in the National Assembly, I would surely align myself with the Liberals to tip the balance against the PQ. As for the riding itself, the vote in D'Arcy McGee could be split evenly between a dozen candidates, and the PQ would still not win the seat.

Yet fear, however unfounded, is a powerful incentive, and in D'Arcy McGee it dominated the campaign. It would most likely have tipped the election in the Liberals' favor even without the bolt from the blue that was about to deal my re-election prospects another crippling blow.

CHAPTER SIXTEEN
The Price You Pay

Experience is the best teacher, only the school-fees are heavy.
—Friederich Hegel

Thursday April 7 was to be a very busy day. In the morning I had a feature interview scheduled with the *Journal de Montreal* in my office. Afterward, an interview with the Dawson College radio station, followed by lunch with Don Macpherson of *The Gazette*. Later that afternoon I was to meet with a constituent who complained about inadequate Urgences-Santé service in English. In the early evening I had a meeting at the B'nai Brith offices followed by a Holocaust memorial service at a synagogue in the riding.

I was looking forward to the opportunity of sitting down with Macpherson for the first time to have a heart-to-heart discussion. I had originally owed much of my limited political awareness to reading his daily column, and mistakenly even mentioned this to him once at the Alliance Quebec convention where I spoke before the 1989 election. He sarcastically used this admission against me in a later column.

Over the years Macpherson had repeatedly savaged the party and written a number of condescending columns about me, referring to me on countless occasions as "Little Bobby". He was more instrumental than anyone else in forcing me to develop a thick skin. Originally, his negative columns really bothered me, yet I still read him every day and agreed with him at times. Eventually he even wrote favourably about me on some occasions, notably for my criticism of Hydro-Quebec's risk sharing contracts. When I stepped down as party leader he gave me credit where it was due with an eminently fair analysis of the strengths and weaknesses of my leadership performance.

Years before, when I was complaining to the caucus about Macpherson, I suggested that I should have lunch with him to try and clear the air. When you are on friendly terms with journalists, it often takes the edge off their negativity toward you. Neil Cameron vigorously discouraged it, claiming that Macpherson is one of those journalists with a bone to pick, and any attempt on my part to build a bridge would likely be greeted with cynicism and ridicule. Macpherson somehow got wind of this discussion and chided us for it in a subsequent column. When he called me to discuss an issue relating to the current campaign, I suggested that since Cameron and I were no longer in the same caucus, perhaps we could finally have that lunch. He readily agreed.

We met at Chilli's restaurant in the Cavendish Mall and talked for about two hours. For all the bones I had to pick with him, it turned out that I felt very relaxed and comfortable in his company. It was actually quite fun discussing the Equality Party, my political career, or the life of an MNA behind the scenes in Quebec City with someone so intimately familiar with the terrain. We talked about constitutional issues as well as the race in D'Arcy McGee. I hoped he was being more than kind when he suggested I had a good chance of winning as an independent. But then kindness had never been Macpherson's strong suit, so I felt reassured.

After lunch I went up to my office. About an hour later, my life veered off into what can best be described as a waking nightmare. Geoff Baker, *The Gazette* court reporter whom I had known for many years, called to say that he had some extremely bad news and wanted to know if it was true. The media was all over a story that I had been charged with assaulting my ex-wife. Reporters had been waiting around the courthouse for the verdict in another high-profile case when someone got wind of the charge against me. From there the story spread like quicksilver spilling across a marble floor.

My divorce and two-year custody battle had been finalized just over a month ago. The final judgement specified that I could pick up my son at school every Friday to spend the weekend with me. Summers would be split between myself and my ex-wife, as well as all Jewish and other school holidays.

The Jewish Passover holiday had been two weeks ago. I had dropped my son off early Sunday evening at my ex-wife's apartment after my regular weekend visit. According to our agreement, I was to pick him up the next morning for my half of the Passover holiday. In the hallway of her apartment building I said good-bye to my son and told him that I would see him the next day. She then informed me that she had changed her mind about my extra time with him over the weekend, and that I would not have him as previously agreed and as was specified in the agreement. She grabbed his hand and started walking away. I argued with her about how she continually ignored the judgement and that if she persisted, we would end up right back in court. She whirled around and whacked me in the face, sending my glasses flying and cutting me under my left eye.

Instead of turning around and walking away as I should have, I reacted impulsively, kicking her once in the rear end as she was turning away. I stormed away furious. I had never struck her in any way in the past, even on the occasions when she would vent her anger on me with a slap or a shove.

I went to the police station to file a report for the record on the violation of our court agreement, but was talked out of it by a sergeant-detective whose name was Binette. He suggested that involving the police in a divorce wrangle was in no one's best interest. I took his advice and left the station without laying a charge.

The detective had then tried to reach me later in the day, but we never connected. After a week of telephone tag, when we finally spoke, he told me that after I had left the station, my ex-wife had filed a charge against me for the kick. I had no choice at that time but to file the charge I had originally intended to lay against her.

I was thunderstruck when I got the call from Baker a few days later, never having expected such a relatively minor altercation, in the context of a long and bitter custody battle, to blow up this way into a media circus. All my years of clean living, and all the hard work I had put into establishing some credibility for myself as a politician seemed to be going up in smoke in a matter of seconds. Merely having it reported that I was charged with assault was enough to make many people presume the worst about me, never mind what actually happened. Even if the courts eventually clear your name beyond any reasonable doubt, the stigma of an episode like this can endure for the rest of your life.

The reports the next day, all of them replete with unfounded insinuations, were absolutely devastating. Listening to the eight o'clock morning news on CJAD, I nearly choked on my coffee as my wife was quoted as saying that I had hit her in the past, and that she wanted to send a message out to all men who beat their wives. She repeated this in several interviews that day. There was no attempt to balance her allegations with my side of the story. I watched helplessly as my name was dragged through the mud and my reputation smeared. In the process, my fighting chance for re-election went down for the count.

I will never forget the torture of walking the streets for weeks, not being able to make eye contact with anyone, because I was sure they were all thinking the worst about me. I felt like screaming from the rooftops that it just wan't true. But I also knew that this would only intensify the media feeding frenzy. I could only hope that people would recognize that the picture of me that this story painted was too outrageously ridiculous to be true.

Because of this experience I can no longer tolerate complaints about politicians having it easy, knowing first-hand the misery a fishbowl existence can inflict. Stories like this make for "sexy" news. For the media, this outweighs the consideration that a person's name and reputation is being hauled through the sewer. When the case was eventually dropped by the crown, it received only a fraction of the coverage lavished on the original charge. At the height of the hullabaloo I sat down with a *Gazette* reporter for over an hour to give my side of the story, after a follow-up story to the original report presented a grossly distorted picture of the situation. Yet *The Gazette* decided not to go with it. Nor was it written or mentioned anywhere that I had been cut under my eye, which was clearly stated in the police report.

It is perhaps asking too much of the media to be more careful in such instances, but serious consideration must be given to withholding the names of the accused in criminal cases until a court finds them guilty. This applies to young offenders at present, and should be extended to everyone to prevent the negative impact on innocent lives by the broadcasting of unfounded charges.

The unstinting commitment of almost all my campaign workers and volunteers was deeply gratifying and helped greatly in getting me through this most difficult period of my life. Raphaël Schachter, who took the case in my defense, kept my thinking on an even keel. There were also many letters of encouragement, including a very kind poem from Sid Stevens of Sun Youth, whose message was that I should keep my chin up.

I appeared calm and collected when I was around other people, and did my best to reassure them that this was not by any means the end of the world or the campaign. But it was eating me up inside. Nevertheless, I was determined to ride out this storm and more resolved than ever to win re-election. Having my constituents show their faith in me in the voting booth would be my ultimate vindication. Difficult as it was, I continued to attend scheduled functions and give speeches wherever I was invited. One of these was a breakfast speech I was asked to deliver only a few days after the story broke, at Lawrence Bergman's synagogue.

Daniel Johnson called the election on Sunday, July 24, for a September 12 vote.

The campaign in D'Arcy McGee was unpleasant, to say the least. My opponent's camp did not shy away from exploiting the assault allegation against me. In their door-to-door campaign, some of their canvassers often raised the issue. When I was on radio phone-in shows, they had callers bring it up. Someone in the Liberal backroom even photocopied the newspaper articles and had them piled up in the committee room until a more level-headed organizer ordered them discarded.

Both the Liberals and myself had rented large storefront committee rooms in the Cavendish Mall, which heightened the animosity between our two camps. It was a down-and-dirty campaign; locks were glued, posters were torn down, and furious accusations flew back and forth from start to finish. In one episode, partisan politics sunk to a new low at the expense of Jewish education, over the issue of subsidies to private Jewish day schools. Joe Rabinovitch had been lobbying the Liberal government for years to grant Jewish day schools associate status with the Montreal Catholic School Commission, thereby allowing the Jewish schools a higher level of government funding. Suddenly, at the height of the campaign, the Liberals decided to approve the associate status and to announce it at a press conference in D'Arcy McGee. Since I had often raised the issue in the National Assembly over the years, Rabinovitch invited me to attend the press conference and I accepted. Word spread quickly, and before long a frantic Jonathan Goldbloom, a Liberal communications staffer, was on the phone to Rabinovitch, warning him that the press conference would be cancelled if I insisted on showing up.

A chastened Rabinovitch called me to rescind the invitation, and I promised him that I would stay away. My campaign team was furious, however, and I was pressured to stop by while the press conference was in progress. One of the hyper Liberal youth volunteers posted outside saw me coming and ran in to tell the organizers that I was on my way up the steps. At that point I just shrugged my shoulders and left.

The next few days proved that this announcement was an empty political manoeuvre as the Catholic School Commission, the teachers union and other interested parties expressed surprise that they had not even been consulted, never mind given approval to the Jewish schools proposal. Unfortunately, this episode reflected the general level of the campaign.

It lacked both the spark and sophistication of the last election. This time tactics counted far more than policy considerations. The only issues the D'Arcy McGee Liberals seemed to raise were accusations that we put up posters too early, or that we picked red and white as our campaign colours to confuse voters into believing that I was a Liberal candidate. They told voters that a vote for me would aid and abet the PQ, and warned senior citizens that by voting for Libman they stood to lose their pensions in a separate Quebec.

I was especially dismayed when federal MP Sheila Finestone publicly endorsed my Liberal opponent. I had become friends with Sheila over the years and my mother had worked for her during the federal election campaign the year before. She had even told me once that she would have to remain neutral in this campaign. I was pleased that the media reports picked up on the dissension her endorsement caused within her riding executive, but also I felt hurt and betrayed by someone I had supported and respected.

The Equality Party, out of deference to me as party founder, decided not to run a candidate in the riding. Nonetheless, it was a long march of frustration. No matter what line of argument we tried, we were unable to convince people that the overall outcome of this election did not hinge on D'Arcy McGee electing a Liberal to the National Assembly.

Toward the end, with the PQ seemingly cruising to an easy victory and the media honing in on my opponent for ducking debates and avoiding issues of substance, it seemed as though people were starting to come around. But a few days before the election, a major poll showed that the Liberals had moved to only a few percentage points of the PQ. That pretty well sealed my fate. Those who had recently started feeling comfortable with the idea of voting for me, figuring that the PQ had the election in the bag anyway, promptly scurried back to the Liberals. I knew then that it was game over.

On the evening of September 12, I watched the election results in the basement at Gerry Weinstein's house. When the D'Arcy McGee numbers flashed across the screen showing I had been defeated, I felt completely drained. When I stood up, my legs felt a little wobbly. Gerry and I embraced each other, and I thanked him for all his support and devotion. He told me I did not deserve to lose, but I philosophically suggested that maybe it was all for the best, that going back to private life might be just what I need. I had gained a great deal from this experience, but I had also paid a steep price. I figured it might be a good thing in the long run to get my personal life back in order and possibly return to politics one day, a little older, a little wiser and with the dignity a few grey hairs impart. We switched off the TV and left for the committee room to thank my supporters.

Many of my campaign workers were in a very emotional state, and some were crying. Seeing my mother with tears in her eyes gave me a lump in my throat, but I remained calm and tried to cheer people up, joking that after five years in architecture and five years as a politician, it was back to the drawing board for me. I thanked my supporters and then went to congratulate my opponent. I was gratified that 10,000 people had voted for me, the highest number recorded by any independent candidate in Quebec during the past quarter century. But in the final standings I would still be lumped in with the losers.

In 1989 I rode a wave of protest that swept me to victory. This time, I was swamped by a wave of fear that washed me away. From the fullness of victory to the emptiness of defeat, I had done a lot of growing during the past five years, which seemed to have passed in a flash. I had gone from aspiring MNA to former MNA. From party leader to party pariah. For the media, which had hailed me as a fresh new face five years ago, I was now old hat.

Numbed as I was by the shock of finality that every losing candidate feels on election night, the few steps to Lawrence Bergman's committee room just across the mall felt like the longest walk of my life. My future was a blur of uncertainty, but at that moment there were two things at least that I knew for sure.

Winning feels a hell of a lot better than losing. And no one would be calling me a kid any more.

CHAPTER SEVENTEEN
Looking Forward

I like the dreams of the future better than the history of the past.
—Thomas Jefferson

For a young anglo Quebecer with a typically sheltered upbringing in a world largely removed from francophone Quebec, my six-year political odyssey was an eye-opening voyage of discovery. I experienced first hand what makes Quebec tick. I was right in the thick of it all during a crucial period in the province's history. So what have I learned? And what might the future hold for English-speaking Quebecers?

On the one hand, I now recognize the sustaining fraternity of francophone Quebecers and the importance they place on their connection to their language and culture. I also accept that protecting and promoting the vitality of this language and culture should be a concern for all Quebecers, no matter what their mother tongue. But I also believe that the extent of concern expressed by some, as well as many of the measures invoked to further this eminently desirable objective, are greatly exaggerated. No one who has spent much time in or around the National Assembly, could seriously think for a moment that French is not the clearly predominant language in the province, or that it is in imminent danger. Everything I have seen and every situation I have encountered on my political journey for six years has reinforced this.

Quebec is now more French than it ever was. Politically, socially, culturally, and economically; at all levels of enterprise and society, Quebec's heart beats primarily in French. This stems from a number of significant developments during the past quarter century, notably the secularization of Quebec society, the affirmation and modernization brought on by the Quiet Revolution, as well as a concerted initiative by francophone Quebecers to assume a commanding presence in all areas of Quebec's economic life. Francophones can no longer claim to be victims of the same injustices that may have prevailed a generation ago. Those who do are purveyors of political demagoguery intended to divide Quebecers. Quebec has changed drastically during the past 30 years. Anglophones are by no means the baronial taskmasters they are accused of having been in the past. Quite the contrary.

Quebec nationalists claim that this "new reality" in Quebec is largely dependent on Bill 101. It has indeed forced immigrants to better learn French by channelling them into the French school system. It has made large companies operate more fully in French and created openings for francophones in upper management positions. Yet with all the other changes that have naturally come about in Quebec society during the past three decades, the new reality would probably have evolved in much the same way without the restrictions or impositions of Bill 101.

As a result of certain sections of Bill 101, the pendulum has swung so far that the effect on the anglophone community has been highly detrimental. It has incited anglos to leave the province by the thousands, and fostered the perception that anglophones will no longer have the job opportunities they once had. While the stated intention of Bill 101 to protect and promote the French language in its North American heartland is a laudable objective, the means it prescribed were not. Viewed by many Quebecers as the ultimate tool to help French-speaking Quebecers achieve new levels of self-assurance and prosperity, it had the opposite effect on English-speaking Quebecers. It would not be exaggerating to say that Bill 101 has devastated the anglophone community in this province. It has resulted in the shutdown of many schools and other community institutions. It has split families and alienated many anglophones who consider themselves Quebecers as much as any "vieille-souche" francophone.

Bill 101 was simply overkill. So much so that Pierre Etienne Laporte, the former head of the government's language watchdog body, the Conseil de la langue française, recently concluded that reverse discrimination against Quebec's English speaking community has become a problem worthy of consideration. Camille Laurin, the father of Bill 101 even conceded that this may be true. These are startlingly frank admissions—particularly by Laurin—and this acknowledgement lends hope for the future of the community in that some key players may finally be recognizing the most important lesson of Bills 101 and 178 — that just ends demand just methods.

But our community needs more than lip service. In the short term there must be concrete gestures by the government that directly address two crucial and immediate concerns:

—The desire of many young anglophones to pick up and leave Quebec;

—The need for the anglophone community to renew itself through broader access to its school system.

Only a concerted effort by both the Quebec government and the anglo community itself can succeed in addressing these concerns. But it requires the government to make the first move. Whether Liberal or PQ, the government must accept that these two primary concerns are inextricably linked to Bill 101.

To begin with, the psychological impact on the community of a law that stifles or denies the use of its language is significant. The negative attitudes of many anglophones toward Quebec, and the alienation that causes so many young people to leave, are a direct result of Bill 101's excesses. Many will insist that young people leave the province primarily for economic reasons. But while this may be true to some extent, for many young anglos the additional burden of the language laws atop all the other obstacles and pressures in a young person's life, is often enough to swing the final decision to abandon their home province.

The second concern could be addressed by changing Bill 101 to make it possible for the community to replenish itself by allowing a share of the immigrant population access to English schools.

In the best of all worlds, from an anglo point of view, article 1 of Bill 101, designating French as the official language of Quebec, would be eliminated. It would also be ideal if all Quebecers would have the freedom of choice to be educated in either of the two official languages of Canada. But this is not going to happen in the near future. The anglo community has already accepted this reality and has made a considerable effort to learn French.

Calling for the outright repeal of Bill 101, or the elimination of any of its key provisions, would invite a storm of indignation. Yet Bill 101 could still achieve its purpose if some of its more repressive sections were modified.

Adopting the first recommendation of The Chambers report, or implementing section 23(1)a of the Canadian Charter of Rights, would be a step in the right direction. But in the long run it would not mean very much for the anglo community in terms of numbers. The government will also claim, as it has in the past, that both proposals are fraught with problems. Implementing the Chambers Report, they say, would create two classes of immigrants, those from English-speaking countries and those from elsewhere, who would not have the same right to send their children to English schools. Section 23(1)a, permitting those of English mother tongue to go to English schools, would require the kind of language testing that proved to be highly problematic in the past.

The only solution that would sufficiently enlarge the basin of students eligible for English schooling, and not detract substantially from the objectives of Bill 101, would be to maintain the requirement for immigrants to send their children to French schools in Quebec, but only for a limited number of years or until they become Canadian citizens. At this point they would have the right to send their children to English schools if they wish. This way it would be made clear that they are part of a society whose defining common language is French, and stress the fundamental importance of learning and speaking the language. But once they become Canadian citizens, they should have the freedom to choose. In addition, there is no reason why Quebec francophones who are also Canadian citizens should not have the right to send their children to an English school to gain the benefit of speaking both languages.

The law should also allow any municipality or institution to obtain bilingual status if its population or clientele is 20% English. This would mean that these institutions or municipalities would provide services in English to those who require them, which does not diminish in any way the guarantee and delivery of services in French. As for signs, the law should stipulate that French must be present and predominant on all commercial signs, but that any other language can also be used with equal or less prominence.

The government must also get serious about recruiting members of the anglophone and other minority communities for key upper management and hiring positions in all sectors of Quebec's civil service to ensure a more proportional representation of non-francophones. At present, anglophone Quebecers hold less than one per cent of the jobs in the provincial bureaucracy.

These few changes to Bill 101, which would affect the francophone majority only negligibly, would immensely benefit the anglophone community and fully reconcile it with the contemporary Quebec reality.

It would not only give the community a tangible way to re-establish and reinforce its presence in Quebec, but it would be a signal to young anglophones that the governing majority wants them to remain in a province where their language is not taboo. If young people have more confidence and a sense of permanence here, this continuity would ensure that health care and educational institutions will in turn be sustained and remain viable.

The anglophone community itself must also assume responsibility for instilling a greater commitment in our young people to remain here. If the government shows a willingness to make the first move, our young people must be encouraged to stay here to maintain the vibrancy of our institutions and to ensure the future of our community. This can be done by reshaping attitudes through schools, through our community organizations and through the media. Parents must encourage their children to remain in Quebec, and our institutions, community infrastructures and business networks must focus on finding jobs for our young people. English-speaking employers must be willing participants in any initiative to provide hope to our community's coming generation. One of the surest ways of doing so is to offer them the realistic prospect of finding full-time employment. To this end, Alliance Quebec has established an employment centre for young anglophones. Anglophone professionals and business people should make it a reflex to contact this bureau whenever they have a job opening.

But this will only work if the community feels that its efforts will not be stymied by the government's restrictive language laws and exclusionary attitudes. This is why it is crucial for the government to make these necessary changes to Bill 101.

It could make for a powerful new French-English partnership that would build a much stronger Quebec as we move toward a new century and a new millennium. If Quebec wants to survive economically and be competitive with the rest of the world, it will have to become an integral, co-operative part of the greater North American common market.

Global economics will force Quebec to open up to this North American reality in which the language of trade, commerce, communications and high-tech is English. Young, educated and bilingual anglophones in this province could play a major role in the Quebec of tomorrow as a window to this reality for our francophone compatriots. If the government creates an atmosphere wherein anglophone distrust has dissipated and the community has a solidly positive outlook for the future, we could be critical allies in forging a more prosperous future while working together to preserve and promote the vitality of the majority language and culture in the province.

For this, our community must get its act together. One problem is how to speak to the government. Another is to find people who can herald this new relationship on behalf of the community.

At present, the issue of community cohesion and direction is in a state of flux. The leadership and structural components of the anglophone community are widely scattered. It is like the days before the 1976 election of the PQ when anglo Quebec did not really define itself as a

distinct minority community, or see the real need for concerted community leadership on the political level. Alliance Quebec is a very important
resource as far as research and materials for the anglophone community
is concerned. However, few anglos today feel that any one group, in
particular Alliance Quebec, speaks for them. Nor do they recognize the
Equality Party as a credible vehicle any more. The Equality Party served
an important purpose in its time, though in many ways it was destined
to be a one-term phenomenon. Anglos are unaccustomed to breaking
out of their individual shells too often to take bold collective stands in a
French majority society.

Prominent members of the community are always hesitant to do
anything that would be construed as rocking the boat or being confrontational. The community at large is far more aggressive in its thinking and
personal conviction, but will rarely participate in any concerted effort.

The one time we broke out of our shell and took a firm stand was
in the 1989 election, and it resulted in the majority community finally
sitting up and taking notice. The surprise 1989 election result shook up
the nationalist elite and changed forever the way language laws are
perceived by the majority. Unfortunately, the party became bogged
down over differences of approach.

For those who believe that the community is monolithic, the Equality Party proved otherwise. The party showed that despite widespread
agreement on the substance of issues, be it Bill 101 or Quebec independence, strategies and tactics for dealing with these issues vary drastically within the anglo community, to the point where we tend to be
more vicious in our family quarrels than in any confrontation with
Quebec separatists.

When it comes to language politics, there are three distinct groups
in the anglo community: anglo "hard-liners," anglo "appeasers," and
those in the middle. The "appeasers," as they are unaffectionately called
by the "hardliners," will publicly say that they accept the goals, objectives, and "necessity" of Bill 101. They frown upon any outspoken
rhetoric from our community; they disliked the Equality Party from the
start; they constantly speak of building bridges with the francophone
majority; they support the concept of working within the proper mainstream political channels, and therefore support the Quebec Liberal
Party. Most prominent members of the anglo establishment—chairmen
of the boards of most institutions, organizations, and big businesses—tend to fall into this category. They have a sustaining need for
relations with the powers that be, and will therefore speak in appropriately conciliatory tones and try to stay out of hot water for fear of being
seen as pariahs in the eyes of the francophone elite.

The third and largest group, those in the middle, are mostly similar to the hardliners in being dead-set against any language legislation and will gripe about it on radio talk shows and among friends at the water cooler. But they are unlikely to get involved in political activism unless seriously provoked. They are more willing to compromise and are more forgiving of the Quebec Liberal Party.

All three groups have one thing in common — they despise and mistrust the PQ and they fear Quebec separation. This is why the middle group will join the appeasers and flock to the Liberals to fight separation if it seems as though the PQ is gaining strength. The hardliners, on the other hand, will instead speak of partitioning Quebec or denying the legality of the vote, before relying on the provincial Liberal party to defend Canada. This is what happened in the last election and will continue to be the political dynamic in the anglophone community as long as a separatist party is one of two parties with a chance to win a Quebec election.

Thus, after voting Equality in 1989 under dire provocation by the Liberal Party, Quebec's anglo community has now reinvested its trust in the Liberals and Daniel Johnson's federalist leadership. But it has not done so out of any great affection for the party. For as long as the present-two-party system persists, our community will always be caught short in this political mug's game. On one side is the PQ, whose program calls for toughening language legislation and breaking up Canada. On the other are the Liberals, who also support language legislation in principle, but have been more circumstantially committed to it than the PQ. But more important, they do not support Quebec independence. The anglo community, therefore, whose major concern at present is maintaining a united Canada, finds itself stuck with the lesser of two evils. Under these circumstances, there is no room for a party devoted primarily to advancing the interests of the anglophone community.

But if sovereignty is defeated in the upcoming referendum and the Liberals return to power with the separation threat dispelled, they should by now know better than to take the anglo vote for granted again if they are ever tempted to play the nationalist card by passing discriminatory language legislation. The lesson they learned in 1989, and the resultant changes in attitudes make this unlikely. The prevailing sentiment and emotional pitch on the language front is vastly different than it was back in 1988 and 1989. The francophone majority is steadily losing its enthusiasm for repressive language legislation, and growing increasingly tired of the embarrassment it engenders.

Ironically, any changes to Quebec's language laws to the extent outlined in this chapter could probably be initiated only by a PQ government, the anglo community's traditional enemy. The Liberals, who already have the anglos as a captive clientele, would be more likely to stand pat on language, since tampering with Bill 101 would expose them on their vulnerable nationalist flank. If the PQ wins its referendum and Quebec becomes a sovereign nation, Quebec anglophones would give up on Quebec en masse. If, on the other hand, the PQ loses the referendum as widely expected, and independence is no longer its raison d'être, it will have to change its approach on language. There may be a period of residual vindictiveness, but it will become clear even to the PQ that in the new reality of the global market, suppressing English would be courting economic suicide.

Politicians and political analysts claim that the language issue has found a happy medium and should not be reopened. But for the anglophone community, the viability of its future depends on some further changes.

It would be wonderful for our community to have the luxury of a party committed to speaking out on its behalf and specific concerns. External pressure is of critical importance in politics. A handful of representatives exerting pressure from the outside, along with some anglo MNAs working within the mainstream parties, would be the ideal combination for our community. But at present there is no credible or coherent political vehicle for exerting such pressure.

Since the community, in the past election, chose to forego any independent representation capable of bringing its concerns directly to the floor of the National Assembly, it must make the best of what it has at its disposal. This means—as it did before 1976—that the heads of our educational, health-care and cultural institutions and our media must carry the load in their respective domains. But the lesson we learned during the past decade was that it cannot be done in a timid way, or by seeking accommodation through capitulation. We must remember how we got results the last time — when we finally showed that we were capable of speaking out forcefully and flexing our political muscle. It is not an easy thing to do, but it has to be done.

I can say from my own experience, that it is much like riding rapids in a birch-bark canoe. It is never less than risky; more dangerous than the rocks straight ahead are the ones below the surface around the next bend. You have to trust your instinct to read the current, and your reflexes to keep you on top of the flow. It takes commitment to push off from the safety of the shore, and unswerving determination to go the distance.

INDEX

Actualité, L' 93
Adamakakis, Adam 20
Aislin 69,
Albert, Lionel 36, 37, 40, 57, 118, 127
Allaire, Jean 139
Allaire Report 140, 141, 154
Alliance-Quebec 13, 26, 28, 33, 34, 36, 37, 39, 43, 48, 66, 67, 71, 109, 116, 123, 140, 185, 186, 199, 202, 204, 215, 216
Allouettes 11, 17, 61
Anctil, Pierre 197, 198
Apartheid 29, 68
Archduke Ferdinand 25
Argus, L' 105
Assembly of First Nations of Quebec 137
Association of Jewish Day Schools 186, 196
Atkinson, Gordon 25, 51-55, 57, 58, 69, 76, 77, 82, 85-87, 89, 91, 92, 95-98, 112, 114, 130, 133, 138, 154, 157, 158, 161, 162, 165, 174, 181, 189, 201
Auf der Maur, Nick 50, 51, 90
Authier, Phil 170, 199
Azeroual, Malia 21

Bacon, Lise 96, 145-152
Baker, Geoff 179, 205, 206
Barbucci, Jean Paul 65
Bauch, Hubert 40
Beïque, Jacques et Associes 22
Beland, Claude 137
Belanger, Michel 136, 137
Belanger-Campeau Commission 136, 139, 142-144, 172
Belisle, Jean-Pierre 102
Bennedetti, Bob 66, 179
Berger, David 61
Berger, Sam 61
Bergman, Lawrence 196, 202, 207, 210
Bernstein, Nat 73
Bill 22 12, 17, 28
Bill 86 187-190, 195, 198
Bill 101 29-31, 35, 63, 119, 121, 189, 212-216, 218
Bill 107 138
Bill 142 50, 72
Bill 150 144, 159, 163, 167, 173, 174

Bill 178 11-13, 32, 34-37, 39-41, 44, 48, 51, 62, 67, 69, 73, 81, 85, 109, 121, 127, 161, 174, 181, 184, 186, 188, 190, 191, 212
Binette, Sergeant Detective 206
Biondi, Yvette 86,
Bissonette, Lise 124
Black Coalition of Quebec 29
Blackburn, Jeanne 163
Blaikie, Peter 14, 39, 46, 48, 49, 67, 116, 140, 162, 186
Blais, Yves 103
Blank, Harry 11, 198
Bloc Québecois 133
Block, Irwin 123
Bloom, Casper 186
B'nai Brith 38, 204
B'nai Brith, Camp 18, 22
Bouchard, Liza 91, 157
Bouchard, Lucien 133, 137
Boulerice, André 103
Bourassa, Premier Robert 11-14, 24, 25, 27, 31, 32, 35, 38-40, 45-47, 49-51, 55, 56, 59, 62, 66, 71, 73, 76, 77, 81, 84, 85, 90, 96, 98, 99, 104, 119, 120, 130-134, 136, 140, 143, 145, 151, 154, 158, 168, 173, 174, 176, 177, 180, 185, 186, 188, 191, 193, 198
Bourbeau, André 197
Bourdon, Michel 164
Brassard, Jacques 103, 104, 128
Brault, Romeo 14, 46
Britt, Brian 76
Brownstein, Morton 60, 61, 132
Bush, George 121
Butler, Alan 186
Bye-Bye '89 110

Caisse Desjardins 137
Caisse de Depot et Placement 153, 195
Calder, Bruce 69
Cameron, Neil 13, 36, 37, 39, 54, 57, 58, 68, 76, 82, 86, 89, 92, 95, 97, 101, 108, 134, 135, 147, 158, 174, 181, 189, 195, 196, 201, 205
Campeau, Jean 136
CANADA AM 56
Canada Party 30
Canadian Federation of Independent Business 46
Canadian Jewish Congress 56, 196
Canadian Jewish News, The 39
Canadiens 17
Cannon, Joe 34

Cardinal, Pierrette 102
Carraire, Jacques 71
Catellier, Carmen 89
Cavendish Mall 70, 84, 176, 197, 205
CBC 51, 79, 80, 126, 208
Ceausescu, Nicolae 123
CEGEP 17, 18, 117, 141
CEQ 137
Chagnon, Jacques 198
Chalkoun, Raphael 41, 68
Chambers, Egan 50
Chambers, Gretta 127, 164
Chambers Report 164, 174, 186, 213
Charlottetown accord 174, 176, 179, 180, 184, 193
Chateauguay Valley English Speaking Peoples Association (CVESPA) 36
Cheung, Kenneth 14
Chevrette, Guy 88, 98, 103
Chicago Tribune, The 81
Chretien, Jean 126, 129
Chrysafidis, Philip 46, 61, 67
Ciaccia, John 25, 44, 69, 73
Cinema Law 24, 161
Cipriani, Tony 69
CJAD Radio 25, 34, 39, 42, 51, 53, 54, 76, 116, 185, 206
CKAC 138
Clark, Joe 164
CNTU 137
Coalition of Canadian Quebecers (CCQ) 27-29, 32, 33, 35, 38, 48, 64
Cohen, Herb 196, 202
Commission de la Protection de la Langue Française 188
Communist Party 30
Comtois, Roger 132
Concordia University 13
Conseil de la Langue Française (CLF) 185, 186, 190, 212
Conseil du Patronat 137
Conservative Party of Canada 48, 85, 161, 185, 193
Cooper, Gerald 60, 114
Copps, Sheila 126
Cosgrove, William 49, 50, 51, 199
Côté, Marc-Yvan 96, 122, 126
Côte St. Luc Senior Men's Social Club 200
Cummings, Harold 75
Curran, Jack 13

D'Andrea, Giuliano 169-171
Dawson College 204
Dayan, Simone 84, 89
Decarie, Graeme 13, 59, 67, 71, 186
Decary, Michel 46, 52
DeSantis, David 26-28, 30, 37, 38, 49, 69
DeTony, Lauretta 89
Detroit Free Press, The 81
Devoir, Le 35, 81, 121, 182, 199
Diamond, Chief Billy 135
DiBona, José 69
Different Vision, A 162
Director General of Elections 27, 38, 42
Donderi, Don 137
Donegan, Mike 66
Doucet, Geraldine 13, 38
Doucet, Roger 13, 38
Dougherty, Joan 13, 73, 89
Downtowner, The 50
Doyon, Rejean 103
Drouilly, Pierre 81
Dufour, Ghislain 137, 138
Duplessis, Maurice 89
Dupras, Claude 22
Durivage, Simon 125

École Polytechnique 98
Electoral Act 27
Elkas, Sam 13
Entente Cordiale 13
Equality Party 11, 30, 31, 40-42, 44, 50, 53, 59, 61, 66, 70, 72-74, 76, 78, 80, 85, 87, 88, 92, 93, 98, 101, 109-113, 125, 128, 132, 133, 135, 136, 138, 144, 149, 155, 157, 160, 165, 167, 170-172, 174-177, 180-184, 186, 189-196, 201, 205, 209, 216, 217
Expos 17

Federation des francophones hors Quebec 125
Fillion, Claude 121
Filmon, Premier Gary 85
Finestone, Sheila 209
Ford Decision 31
Fortier, D'Iberville 25, 129, 190
Fraser, Joan 44, 72
Freedman, Gloria 28, 37, 39, 54, 70, 81
Freedom House 29, 36
Freedom of Choice Party 27, 30
Freedom Party 30
French, Richard 33, 71, 190

Friedman, Daniel 191, 192
Fry, Danny 64, 75, 80
FTQ 137

Gagnon, Lysiane 169
Garon, Jean 103
Gaucher, Michel 21, 22
Gauthier, Lew 46
Gazette, The 13, 26, 38, 39, 40, 42-44, 49,
  57, 59, 62, 63, 66, 69, 72-74, 80, 81,
  83, 93, 109, 110, 117, 123, 129, 138,
  141, 149, 159, 160, 162, 164, 165,
  169, 170, 173, 179, 199, 204, 205, 207
Girard, Normand 91
Globe and Mail, The 44, 124
Gobé, Jean Claude 102
Goldbloom, Jonathan 208
Goldbloom, Michael 66, 186
Goldbloom, Sam 28, 56, 64, 75
Goldbloom, Victor 55
Goodman and Associates 146
Goodz, Murray 83
Gordon, Donald 124
Gover, Cliff 29
Greenfield, Howard 178
Grenier, Charles 88
Grey, Julius 116, 131, 137, 150, 162,
  173, 186, 187

Hartt, Joel 13, 186
Helfield, Eric 29, 48
Henderson, Keith 141, 142, 169, 170,
  171, 174, 178-180, 182, 183, 189, 194,
  195
Herzliah High School 15
High Point Day Camp 18
Hogue, Jean Pierre 142
Holden, Arthur 114
Holden, Richard 48-51, 60, 64, 72-74,
  76, 82, 85, 86, 88-90, 92, 93, 95, 97,
  98, 109, 112-115, 119-122, 126, 127,
  133, 135-138, 141, 142, 144, 147, 148,
  150, 157-162, 164, 165, 171, 172
Houde, Albert 102
Humphrey, John 132
Hydro Quebec 134, 135, 145-155, 195,
  198, 200, 204

Iacono, Joanne 69
Individual Rights Party 30
Isoré, Jean Pierre 43, 62, 68, 69, 112,
  114, 115

Jaeger, Richard 20

Jedwab, Jack 196, 202
John Abbott College 14, 36, 82
Johnson, Daniel 96, 191, 193, 194, 196-
  199, 207, 217
Johnson, William 13, 26, 173
Johnston, Donald 13, 116, 162
Jones, Roger 195
Journal de Montréal 204
Journal de Québec 91, 121

Karygiannis, John 61
Keaton, Robert 116, 140, 199
Keith-Ryan, Heather 44
King, Maurice 28, 29, 36, 186, 187
Klein, Gerald 26-28, 30-32, 37-40, 46,
  67, 68, 112, 114, 115
Kohos, John 56
Kondaks, Tony 29, 30, 36, 37, 40, 41,
  47, 64, 72, 75, 83, 90, 134, 174-176,
  179
Krupp, Howard 60

Laberge, Louis 137
Lafreniere, Rejean 102
Lakeshore School Board, The 13
Laliberté, Gerald 87, 108
Lamontagne, Gilles 96
Lang, Mayor Bernard 14, 199
Laporte, Pierre Etienne 212
Larose, Gerald 137
Laurin, Camille 212
Le Cassé 36
Lee, Jeannie 38
Leonard Ostroff Design 20, 21
Lesage, Premier Jean 48, 91
Lesage, Robert 102
Levesque, Gerard D. 45, 96
Levesque, René 75, 77, 109, 154
Levine, Terrence 179
Liberal Party of Canada 13, 61, 126,
  129, 137, 162, 195, 197
Liberal Party of Quebec 11-13, 22, 24,
  26, 28, 31-35, 39, 42-44, 46, 51, 52,
  55, 56, 59-63, 66, 67, 70-74, 76, 82,
  85, 90-92, 99, 102, 104, 109-111, 113,
  115, 128, 129, 136, 139, 140, 142,
  143, 150, 153, 154, 159-161, 164, 168,
  172, 174, 176, 180, 181, 183, 184,
  189-203, 208, 209, 212, 216-218
Libman, Chaimkeh 15
Libman, Dave 60
Libman, Glenn 15
Libman, Goldie 16
Libman, Jamie 15

Libman, Kevin Elliot 130, 158
Libman, Warren 15, 91, 179
Lincoln, Clifford 33, 71, 109, 190
Lord, Richard 68
Lortie, Denis 95

Macdonald, Len 186
Macdonald, Pierre 30
Maciocia, Cosmo 102
MacPherson, Don 26, 40, 41, 44, 63, 88,
    110, 123, 129, 141, 149, 165, 173,
    204, 205
Magnan, Roch 66
Maldoff, Eric 66, 116, 186
Maltais, Ghislain 103
Marx, Eva 83
Marx, Herbert 33, 41, 55, 71, 82-84, 190
Matte, Guy 125
McCall, Storrs 116
McConnell Engineering Building 19
McGill University 15, 18, 20, 22, 102,
    116, 120, 122, 131, 137, 156, 164, 175
McGill University School of Architec-
    ture 18-20
McGill University School of Den-
    tistry 91
McIntyre, Gordon 187
McKenty Live 73
Meech Lake Constitutional Accord
    14, 24, 30, 50, 68, 72, 85, 86, 97, 98,
    104, 114, 115, 119, 122, 123, 126-128,
    130-133, 139, 173, 184, 198
Mercure, Roger 69
Mintzberg, Barbara 193
Montreal Business 54
Montreal Catholic School Commis-
    sion (MCSC) 129, 208
Montreal Daily News, The 12, 40, 62, 90
Morin, Michel 148
Mostovac, Chris 89, 98, 134, 146
Mota, Chris 42
Mulroney, Prime Minister Brian 85,
    86, 109, 126, 133, 137, 142-144, 160,
    171
Munsinger, Gerda 50
Murray, Senator Lowell 85, 86

Nashen, Glenn 179
National Association of Women and
    the Law 122, 123
Nazi Germany 118, 121, 127, 137
Neremberg, Albert 155
Neumayer, Rudolph 69
NEWSWATCH 42, 66, 76

New Yorker 50
Normand, Gilles 158
Norris, Alexander 72, 73
Norsk Hydro 146, 148, 150-153
Noseworthy, Ralph 192
Notwithstanding Clause 30-32, 35,
    109, 128, 181, 184, 185, 188
Nowell, Stephen 35, 37
Nunziata, John 129

O'Connell, Betty 160
Office de la langue française (OLF)
    21, 188
Official Languages Commissioner of
    Canada 24
Oka Crisis 132, 133
Olnyk, Steve 14
O'Neill, Pierre 182
Order of Architects of Quebec (OAQ)
    22
Orr, Royal 34, 37-39, 48, 66
Ouellette, André 137, 143, 144

Pagé, Lorraine 137
Pagé, Michel 92, 93, 97, 98, 154, 161
Pallascio, Michel 129
Paquette-Vernham, June 69
Parent, Marcel 197
Parisella, John 176, 181, 182
Parizeau, Jacques 32, 44, 62, 66, 85, 88,
    89, 92, 96-99, 104, 122, 123, 130, 163,
    171, 172, 176, 194
Parsons, David 29
Parti Indépendantiste 68
Parti Pris movement 36
Parti Québecois, The 12, 17, 22, 24, 25,
    28, 32-35, 39, 44, 60-62, 66, 69, 72,
    73, 88, 89, 92, 98, 99, 102, 103, 107,
    109, 121, 127-129, 132, 135, 136, 143,
    149, 150, 153, 154, 159, 160, 163,
    164, 168-172, 175, 184, 188, 191,
    193-195, 200, 203, 208, 209, 213, 215,
    217, 218
Partition 36, 57
Pascau, Pierre 121
Paterson, Alex 66, 127, 186
Pepin, Gilles 178-180, 194
Perron, Denis 121
Phillip, Dan 29
Picotte, Yvon 103
Pointe, Le 125
Positive Action Committee 33, 116
Press Council of Quebec 127

Presse, La 65, 121, 127, 138, 146, 158, 159, 169
Pringle, T. and Son 20
Progressive Party 30
Protestant School Board of Greater Montreal (PSBGM) 186
Proulx, Gilles 121
PULSE News 38, 42, 49, 66, 76, 179, 191, 192

Quebec Association of Protestant School Boards 186
Quebec Inc. 21, 195
Queen Elizabeth 53, 85, 92

Rabinovitch, Joe 186, 196, 197, 199, 202, 208
Radio Canada 66, 86, 110, 125, 148, 149
Rand, Aaron 155
Reform Party 66
Reich, Erik 169
Remillard, Gil 104
Renaud, Jacques 36, 37, 39-42, 46, 52, 62, 64, 65, 99, 117, 125
Rheaume, Gilles 68
Richard-Robert Lounge 20, 102
Richler, Mordecai 50, 136
Riordon, Peter 186
Ritz Carleton 52, 53, 171, 172
Robillard, Lucienne 188, 191
Robinson, Doug 11, 12, 49, 50, 57, 60, 64-66, 72, 75, 86, 159, 160
Robinson, Jennifer 44, 73
Rousseau, Henri-Paul 142
Ryan, Claude 35, 69, 96, 103, 110, 121-123, 140, 184-190

St. Laurent, Bernie 40, 69, 90, 122
Saintonge, Jean Pierre 93, 96, 100
Sault Ste. Marie 118-123, 131
Savoie, Raymond 128
Schachter, Raphaël 207
Schouella, Lorissa 28
Scott, Stephen 131, 175, 186
Scotti, Ciro Paul 46, 67, 76
Scowen, Reed 116, 162
Seal, Barbara 14
Segal, Martin 60, 160
Seltzer, Ron 50
Sevigny, Colonel Pierre 50
Shaw, Bill 57, 58
Sierra Club 148

Silverman, Ron 37
Sinclair, Gord 39, 116, 185
Sioui, Konrad 137
Sirros, Christos 46
Sivack, Bernard 28,
Sochaczevski, Amos 54
Sochaczevski, Avi 54
Société de Développement Industriel (SDI) 151
Société St. Jean Baptiste 68
Sofati 21
Soleil, Le 87, 121, 126, 138
Sorecom 69
Springate, George 12
Staunton, Senator John Lynch 50, 142
Steinberg, Irwin 50, 193, 196, 199
Stevens, Sid 207
Suburban, The 54, 118, 121, 179
Sun Life 48
Sun Youth 207
Surkis, Bill 14
Taffert, Mort 60, 64,
Task Force on Canadian Federalism 131, 137
Thibault, Hubert 88
Thompson, Elizabeth 159
Todd, Jack 129, 149
Tolchinsky and Goodz Architects 11, 22, 47, 79, 83
Tolchinsky, Hy 43, 83
Toronto Sun, The 81
Townshippers Association 44
Travis, Dermod 146, 148, 149, 199
Tremblay, Gerald 61, 191
Trudeau, Justin 175
Trudeau, Pierre Elliott 24, 175, 195
Turner, John 14, 61, 126
TVA 48

UN International Covenant on Civil and Political Rights 187
Union Nationale 28
United Nations Human Rights Committee 187
United Services Club 53
Unity Party 36, 78, 81, 91, 92, 128, 159, 160
Université de Montréal 117, 132
Université du Québec 81
Université de Laval 89, 152
University of Washington 91
Urban Anglo 155

Valaskakis, Kimon 132
Vanier College 18, 141
Vernham, Peter 69
Voisine, Roch 64

Wagar High School 123
Walesa, Lech 69, 76, 77
Walker, Robert 171
Waller, Adrian 56, 57, 68, 76
Waxman, Gary 56, 71, 176
Weinstein, Gerry 193, 209
Weintraub, William 52
Weiss, June 41, 116
Wertheimer, Earl 37
Williams, Russell 109
Wilson, Barry 49, 192
Winnie's 49
Woody's pub 50, 51
World Bank 49

Zimmerman, Carol 28